PACIFIC FLAVORS

PACIFIC FLAVORS

ORIENTAL RECIPES FOR A CONTEMPORARY KITCHEN

Food Stylists: Jean E. Carey
and Norman Stewart

STEWART, TABORI & CHANG
NEW YORK

HUGH CARPENTER PHOTOGRAPHS BY **TERI SANDISON**

Text copyright © 1988 Hugh Carpenter
Photographs copyright © 1988 Teri Sandison
Published by Stewart, Tabori & Chang, Inc.
740 Broadway, New York, New York 10003

Library of Congress Cataloging-in-Publication Data

Carpenter, Hugh.
　Pacific flavors.

　Includes index.
　1. Cookery, Oriental.　I. Title.
TX724.5.A1C37　1987　641.595　87-26775
ISBN 1-55670-020-2
Distributed in the U.S. by Workman Publishing,
708 Broadway, New York, New York 10003
Distributed in Canada by Canadian Manda Group,
P.O. Box 920 Station U, Toronto, Ontario M8Z 5P9
Distributed in all other territories by Little,
Brown and Company, International Division, 34 Beacon Street,
Boston, Massachusetts 02108

Printed in Italy

10 9 8 7 6 5 4 3
First Edition

This book is dedicated to
Andrew Hammond Burnett
(1909-1987)—scholar,
patron of the arts, friend

ACKNOWLEDGMENTS

So many people contributed their special gifts to *Pacific Flavors*. This book glows because of the efforts of our two food stylists. Our friend Jean E. Carey unstintingly contributed her style, intelligence, and creativity to this book from the day of its inception. Norman Stewart came into the project at the perfect moment and added his joy in food, enthusiasm for the book, and unlimited imagination to photo after photo. We are all deeply grateful to Andy Stewart for the opportunity to publish such a beautiful book.

Many friends helped bring this book into print. Our literary agent, Helene Siegel, was invaluable. Leslie Stoker, Editor-in-Chief at Stewart, Tabori & Chang, made working on this book a pleasure. Many thanks also to food writer Elizabeth Brafford, who did the initial editing of the material, copyeditor Carole Berglie, book designer Rita Marshall and to Roy Finamore and Margaret Orto.

The look of many photographs in the book would not have been possible without the generosity of Nancy Epstein. Nancy allowed us to photograph in her beautiful home, where fine food, good friends, and art mingle harmoniously. At the Nancy Epstein Gallery in Beverly Hills, her partners, Jane Wyler and Carla Tulchin, constantly matched us with the work of the finest ceramic and glass artists.

Carol Sauvion, at Freehand Gallery in Los Angeles, Bullock's Beverly Center, By Design, Country Floors, and Lynne Deutch Ltd., all of Beverly Hills, were rich sources of props and accessories for the photographs. Illustrator Jefferson Stillwell, in Los Angeles, provided his witty set designs on pages 94–95, 139, and 179. Thank you for all your help.

We are grateful to the following food authorities who lent their ideas and techniques to some of the recipes: Ken Hom, Anne Otterson, Jacques Pépin and his book *La Méthode*, Grant and Sharon Showley, Osa Sommermeyer, Barbara Tropp, and Diana and Paul Von Welanetz. This book has gained much from the special insights of the recipe testers. Thank you Florence Antico, Mary Jo Bacino, Binnie Beaumont, Peggy and David Black, Pamela Blair, Nancy and Lou Bon, Jo Bowen, Yvonne Caan, Lynda and Bill Casper, Elizabeth Brafford Cella, Karen and Don Cerwin, Rena Copperman, Claire Dishman, Jonna Dziubala, Suzy Eisenman, Alice Englander, Cary Feibleman, Peter Feit, Diane Ganzell-Brown, Sharie and Ron Goldfarb, Robert Gordon, Blanche Gottlieb, Edie Greenberg, Donna Hodgens, Nancy Huntsinger, Mary Hurst, Fran Jenkins, Joyce Jespersen, Lisa Katzer, Diana Kleinman, Joy and John Knox, Jeannie Komsky, Susan Krueger, Robin Leonhard, Larry Lipstone, Betty Mandrow, Helen Marshank, Dianne Martin, Ruth Matthias, Bernard Menard, Rosalyn Moon, Denis Moore, Michele Nipper, Roy Pingo, Pat Pondella, Diane Ransom, Jeannie Riley, Kathleen Sands, Michele Sciortino, Jerry Sexton, Paul Shane, Ellie Shulman, Elaine Stein, Sari Stern, Jerrie Strom, Anita Tetrault, Suzanne Vadnais, Susan Vollmer, Ruth Walker, Sharon Whelan, Robert Wills, and Marge Yeager.

Other friends who played a part in this book are Julia Child, Mark and Jil Kreher, Pat and Dal Dall'Armi, Rachel Dourec, Lisa Ekus, Nina Gaddis, Jerry Goldstein, Susan Grode, Lena Head, Warren and Mary Ellen Hilgren, Sally and Robert Hunt, Candy and Tim Johnson, Barbara McDonald, Linda, Erin, and Danà O'Connor, Marcea Reynolds, Don Skipworth, David Wheeler, Harvey and Norene Wheeler, and Madame S. T. Ting Wong.

Finally, a special word of thanks to our parents, Warwick and Peggy Carpenter, Robert and Barbara Sandison, and to godparents Andrew Burnett and Louise Squibb for contributions extending far beyond the scope of this book.

FOREWORD

Join us in an exciting sensory adventure. The delicious aroma of Barbecued Spareribs, the soft textures of Peking Pancakes stuffed with shredded Mu Shu Chicken, and the surprise of Chocolate Chip Almond Cookies are just a few of the wonderful sensations that are within everyone's ability to create at home. The recipes in this book use basic equipment, a short list of essential supplies, and simple preparation steps. The beautiful foods available in our country, such as veal, lamb, salmon, and soft-shell crabs are combined with Oriental seasonings to achieve fresh, innovative flavors and colors. Tastes ranging from coconut and mint to fresh ginger and lime juice will bring you the unique flavors of the Pacific. We hope these recipes, prepared with love and presented with enthusiasm, delight the senses and are savored with the same joy we have felt when creating this food for friends old and new.

Hugh Carpenter and Teri Sandison
Los Angeles 1988

INTRODUCTION

We believe easy cooking techniques and sensible menu planning make entertaining a pleasure. We most frequently enjoy this book's delicious dishes, whether as part of a romantic dinner for two or for a large gathering of friends, by *serving only one Oriental dish as part of a meal.* Shredded Chicken Salad, accompanied by crusty bread, a dry white wine, and a concluding fruit tart makes an elegant summer lunch or dinner. Pan-fried Santa Barbara Pot Stickers with steamed buttered peas, or Jade Salad with grilled veal chops, or broiled salmon filets arranged alongside Asparagus in Black Bean Butter Sauce are just a few possible combinations.

Of course there are times when passion strikes for a complete Oriental dinner. On these occasions my wife, Teri, and I use a few simple techniques. We limit the guest list to no more than ten appreciative friends who love to eat. Occasionally they contribute a Chinese or Thai dish or join in the preparation with us. The menu often includes two appetizers, an Oriental salad, perhaps a stir-fried dish wrapped in Peking pancakes, and a dessert. As the evening proceeds, to avoid a big kitchen clean-up, we ask a neighborhood student to act as an assistant, washing dishes as they collect. Meanwhile, we enjoy a succession of Oriental dishes, corks pop off Champagne bottles, and conversation turns to great food and the glorious memories associated with those times. Already the next dinner is being planned.

To aid you with your own menu planning, almost every recipe in this book offers a suggested menu. Skimming through the book to review menu ideas should provide you with many new occasions for serving Oriental food.

What to Drink with Oriental Food

We always serve wine or beer with Oriental dinners, and coffee or perhaps a fine Chinese tea to accompany dessert. Because of the wide variety of flavors from dish to dish, good white wine choices are Sauvignon Blanc, dry Gewürztraminer, and dry Riesling. A red wine such as Pinot Noir or Beaujolais often also complements Oriental meat dishes. For a festive occasion, Champagne goes beautifully with the entire range of Oriental flavors. As for hot tea, the brewing, serving, and replenishing of tea during meals creates an unnecessary extra burden. Serve unsweetened iced tea as a nonalcoholic choice during the meal, and a fine tea or coffee with dessert.

About the Recipes

Before beginning a dish, read the entire recipe, including the introduction and the notes at the end. These may provide you with important menu advice or technical information about successfully completing the recipe.

Review the ingredients list for special supplies. The essential Oriental supplies needed to prepare the recipes in this book are few. These are listed in the Appendices. Purchase the best brands, not those sold at supermarkets. Although the list of ingredients in some recipes may appear lengthy, many of the items are condiments and common staples that can be combined quickly.

When the word *minced* appears, chop the item so finely that it resembles a purée. If you do not wish to mince by hand, use a small electric mini-chopper. This is the most time-saving piece of equipment introduced since the food processor. Of the many brands sold by cookware shops and department stores, four excellent ones are Mouli's Varco, the Electric Mincer, Seb's Minichop, and Cuisinart's Mini-Mate Chopper/Grinder.

When grated or minced orange peel is called for, this means you should use just the outside colored skin. Grating the peel can be an awful chore. Fortunately, the colored skin can be removed quickly with a little tool called a zester, available at all cookware shops and department stores. Once the peel has been zested, it takes little time to complete the mincing.

Unless specifically stated, "Advance Preparation" means that all the preparation steps can be completed in the morning, with the "Cooking" done hours later. When preparation steps are to be done more than six hours in advance, such as when meat has to be marinated for twenty-four hours, the additional time has been noted at the outset. When foods can be assembled far in advance of serving — say, up to twenty-four hours ahead — that has been mentioned, too. In contrast, dishes requiring

assembly just prior to serving have the heading "Last-Minute Assembling."

Some recipes have sauces that are thickened with a cornstarch and water mixture. Though the recipe calls for a generous amount of this thickener, add only a *small* amount of the mixture and bring the sauce to a low boil. Add a little more if the sauce does not lightly glaze your spoon. You will never need to add all the cornstarch mixture.

At the end of the cooking stage, the words "taste and adjust seasonings" mean this is the time to make any adjustments in flavor rather than having your guests do it at the dining room table.

The serving information indicates the number of people the dish should serve. For entrées in this book, we assume you will accompany the dish with rice or noodles and a salad. Unless otherwise stated, all recipes can be doubled or tripled. One exception is stir-fried dishes. When doubling a stir-fry, have a friend or "assistant" simultaneously stir-fry the second portion in another wok, following your every move.

Easy Recipes

If you have never cooked Oriental food or want to find a quick recipe for dinner, the chapter introductions list the easy-to-prepare recipes.

Appetizers set the tone for the evening, tease the palate, mellow the effects of predinner drinks, and generate excitement about the delicacies to follow. Possibilities range from a single appetizer preceding a substantial dinner to an array of little tastes before a meal of homemade soup, salad, and dessert. Surprise your guests with dishes not usually associated with predinner festivities, such as an Oriental salad, a chilled soup, or a diced stir-fried dish served in lettuce cups. Or avoid dinner preparation entirely by serving appetizers to friends who gather at your home before moving on to a restaurant.

Many Oriental appetizers make beautiful

Stuffed Mushrooms with Shrimp.

picnic dishes. You might begin a picnic with three small introductory dishes: crispy, garlic-accented Onion Bread; thin-slices of Smoked Tea Squab; and pungent, spicy Chinese Pickles. Next from the picnic hamper you might pull out juicy Spareribs with Secret Chinese Barbecue Sauce, New Wave Shrimp, and a noodle salad glazed with ginger dressing. Accompany the feast with chilled white wine and conclude with fresh fruit and crisp Chinese Ginger Snaps. This is a perfect way to spend a leisurely afternoon.

Such a picnic is always enhanced by a little attention to details, especially how you serve the food. A variety of Chinese and other Oriental baskets and boxes are available in this country, including many wicker and woven bamboo ones from different regions of the Pacific. Tea fixings can be carried in handsome cloth-lined bamboo tea-set boxes sold by some Chinatown specialty grocers and souvenir shops. Other possible accompaniments are Oriental paper-and-bamboo parasols for shade, or the oversized Chinese thermos bottles for transporting hot or cold beverages.

Easy-to-prepare recipes in this chapter are Spareribs with Secret Chinese Barbecue Sauce, Grilled Quail with Five-Spice Marinade, Mahogany Chicken Wings, Glazed Chicken Livers, Ginger Mint Ceviche, New Wave Shrimp, Chinese Salsa, and Chinese Pickles.

Oriental Dips
These Oriental dips are excellent served with many appetizers and picnic foods such as deep-fried won tons, spring rolls, chilled cooked shrimp, and strips of barbecued meat: Satay Sauce, Chinese Plum Sauce Dip, Piquant Thai Dipping Sauce, Sweet and Pungent Apricot Sauce, Chinese Salsa, Oriental Cucumber Relish, and Lime Dipping Sauce.

STUFFED MUSHROOMS WITH SHRIMP

- 24 small to medium button mushrooms
- ½ pound raw shrimp
- 4 minced water chestnuts, preferably fresh
- 1 green onion, minced
- 2 teaspoons finely minced fresh ginger
- 2 teaspoons dry sherry
- 2 teaspoons light soy sauce
- ¼ teaspoon salt
- ¼ teaspoon ground pepper
- ½ cup chicken stock or water
- 2 tablespoons oyster sauce
- ½ teaspoon sugar
- 1 tablespoon peanut oil

Fresh button mushroom caps, plump with a shrimp filling, absorb this rich oyster-sauce glaze, then release their juicy sweetness at the first bite.

Advance Preparation
Twist stems off mushrooms and discard. Set caps aside.

Shell, devein, and finely mince the shrimp. Combine shrimp, water chestnuts, green onion, ginger, sherry, soy sauce, salt, and pepper. Mix thoroughly. Fill a pastry bag with no tip inserted with the mixture, then pipe the filling into the mushroom caps. Alternatively, fill the mushrooms caps using a spatula or small spoon. Refrigerate mushroom caps until you are ready to cook them. This can be done in the morning, for example (any discoloration of the mushroom caps will disappear during cooking).

In a small bowl, combine stock, oyster sauce, and sugar.

Last-Minute Cooking
Place a 12-inch skillet over medium-high heat. Pour in oil, then add mushrooms, button side down. Fry until oil sizzles and mushroom bottoms begin to brown, about 2 minutes.

Pour in stock mixture, cover skillet, and cook until filling turns white, about 2 minutes.

Remove lid, turn heat to high, and cook mushrooms until all the sauce disappears and glazes mushrooms, about 2 minutes. During the final minute of cooking, toss mushrooms gently so that the sauce glazes the top of the filling. Tip out and serve at once.

Serves: 4 to 8 as a hot appetizer.

Notes: A nice substitute for the chicken stock is the water in which dried black Chinese mushrooms have been soaked. Soak 4 mushrooms in 1 cup very hot water for 30 minutes. Strain the water through a fine sieve or cheesecloth to remove any grit. Combine ½ cup mushroom water with 2 tablespoons oyster sauce. Remove and discard the stems from the mushrooms; finely mince the mushroom caps and add to the filling.

For spicier mushrooms, substitute the sauce from Santa Barbara Pot Stickers or Chicken Curry Dumplings.

To broil these stuffed mushrooms, brush caps generously with melted butter, then stuff them. Lightly brush the tops of the fillings and the sides of the caps with mixture of 1 tablespoon oyster sauce, 3 tablespoons white wine, and ½ teaspoon sugar. Place mushrooms on a greased baking sheet and broil until shrimp filling is cooked, about 4 minutes. Serve at once.

SMOKED TEA SQUABS

2   squabs (see Notes)

1   tablespoon Sichuan peppercorns

1   tablespoon black peppercorns

1½ cups dry sherry

2   tablespoons light soy sauce

1   tablespoon salt

2   green onions, finely minced

2   tablespoons grated or minced tangerine or orange peel

2   tablespoons finely minced fresh ginger

1   cup black tea leaves

½   cup raw white rice

¼   cup hickory or mesquite wood chips

¼   cup packed dark brown sugar

1   tangerine, peeled and separated into segments, for garnish (optional)

     sprigs of fresh coriander (cilantro), for garnish (optional)

Though the multiple cooking stages of steaming, smoking, and roasting make this a time-consuming dish, its magnificent taste is your reward.

Advance Preparation (24 Hours before Serving)

Remove pads of fat from squab cavities. Place squabs in a 1-gallon plastic food bag.

In a dry skillet over high heat, sauté the peppercorns until they smoke lightly, about 3 minutes. Grind coarsely in a spice grinder or crush with a mortar and pestle.

Combine crushed pepper, sherry, soy sauce, salt, green onions, tangerine peel, and ginger. Stir well, then add to the squabs in the plastic bag. Seal bag and refrigerate for 24 hours. Occasionally turn bag over to redistribute marinade.

Cooking

Drain liquid from squabs. Bring water to a boil in the bottom of a Chinese steamer, then place squabs directly on steamer tray. Cover and steam for 10 minutes. Remove squabs, pour accumulated liquid from cavities, and let squabs cool to room temperature.

Line bottom of a wok with a double thickness of heavy-duty aluminum foil. Spread tea leaves, rice, wood chips, and brown sugar evenly in bottom of wok. Spray a small wire rack with cooking spray and place in wok.

Heat wok over medium-high heat until the mixture begins to smoke, about 10 minutes. Place squabs on rack, cover wok, and smoke for 10 minutes for a subtle smokey flavor and 15 minutes for a medium smokey flavor.

Prolonged smoking gives the squabs an overwhelmingly smokey taste, so it is better to err on the side of caution.

Meanwhile, preheat oven to 450°F. When squabs are smoked, remove from wok, place on a small baking sheet lined with foil, and roast in oven until golden, about 10 minutes.

Last-Minute Assembling

If squabs are an appetizer or picnic dish, serve them hot or at room temperature, chopped into bite-size pieces or thinly sliced and placed on the serving dish ringed with tangerine segments and sprigs of fresh coriander. If served as an entrée, present squabs whole or split in half.

Serves: 6 to 8 as an appetizer; 2 as an entrée.

Notes: This is an excellent dish made with duck or game hens. If using duck, steam the bird for 45 minutes, smoke for 20 minutes, and roast for 10 minutes. If using game hens, steam 2 hens for 15 minutes, smoke for 15 minutes, and roast for 10 minutes.

SPARERIBS WITH SECRET CHINESE BARBECUE SAUCE

3 pounds spareribs
Secret Chinese Barbecue Sauce
5 tablespoons hoisin sauce
3 tablespoons plum sauce
2 tablespoons oyster sauce
2 tablespoons dark soy sauce
2 tablespoons honey
1 tablespoon dry sherry
1 tablespoon peanut oil
1 teaspoon Chinese chili sauce (optional)
½ teaspoon five-spice powder
1 tablespoon finely minced garlic
1 tablespoon finely minced fresh ginger

This barbecue sauce creates a wonderful, welcoming aroma as guests arrive for dinner. Spread it across any meat or seafood you plan to barbecue, broil, or roast; it adds a unique flavor. Secret Chinese Barbecue Sauce can be made in large quantities and stored indefinitely in the refrigerator.

Advance Preparation
Have butcher trim cartilage and bone from the top of spareribs.

Cut off the flap of meat on underside of ribs. Also on the underside is a tough white membrane; using your fingernail or a sharp pointed knife, loosen membrane along the bone at one edge, then, gripping membrane with a paper towel, pull it away.

Combine ingredients for barbecue sauce.

Makes approximately 1¼ cups.

Roasting Spareribs
Preheat oven to 350°F. Line a large baking pan with foil. Coat a wire rack with cooking spray, then place rack in baking pan.

Rub spareribs on both sides with barbecue sauce and place on the rack, meat side up. Bake until meat begins to shrink away from the ends of the bones, about 1 hour.

Cut into individual ribs. Serve hot or at room temperature.

Serves: 6 to 8 as an appetizer or picnic dish; 2 as an entrée with a salad.

Notes: Pork baby back ribs and lamb ribs are also terrific cooked this way.

BEEF SATAY

12 bamboo skewers (10 inches long)

1 pound beef filet or top sirloin

¼ cup crushed roasted unsalted peanuts

Satay Sauce

2 tablespoons crushed roasted unsalted peanuts

2 teaspoons lime juice

1 small shallot, minced

1 clove garlic, minced

6 tablespoons unsweetened coconut milk

1 teaspoon best-quality peanut butter

1 teaspoon sugar

½ teaspoon dark soy sauce

¼ teaspoon ground cumin

¼ teaspoon ground coriander

¼ teaspoon Chinese chili sauce

⅛ teaspoon turmeric

Marinade

¼ cup hoisin sauce

3 tablespoons plum sauce

2 tablespoons distilled white vinegar

1 tablespoon honey

1 tablespoon dry sherry

½ teaspoon Chinese chili sauce (optional)

1 green onion, minced

1 tablespoon minced fresh coriander (cilantro)

3 cloves garlic, minced

One of my favorite ways to spend an evening is to sit outdoors on a stool, eating ribbons of tender meat at the famous Satay Club in Singapore. You're under a sultry sky, amidst the shouts of satay cooks and the racket of cicadas. The fiery peanut sauces contribute their own heat, matched by the quantities of cold beer that are washed down as animated conversations about future adventures continue late into the evening — that's the good life!

Advance Preparation (24 Hours before Serving)

Soak skewers in water for 24 hours. This prevents them from burning during cooking.

For the satay sauce, crush peanuts in food processor. Place in saucepan with half the lime juice and all the remaining ingredients. Bring to a low boil and cook for 1 minute, stirring. Pour into a small bowl and let cool to room temperature. When room temperature, stir in remaining lime juice. Taste and adjust seasonings, such as the amount of chili sauce, the intensity of peanut flavor, and the sharpness of lime. Sauce can be made a day ahead and refrigerated.

Preparation

Trim meat of all fat. Cut meat against the grain into 24 ribbon-shaped pieces, about 4 inches long, ½ inch wide, and ⅛ inch thick.

Combine marinade in-gredients, then mix with meat. Thread 2 pieces of meat on each skewer, leaving at least 1 inch of the skewer showing at each end. Pour remaining marinade over meat. Marinate 1 hour or longer in the refrigerator, turning skewers once.

Last-Minute Cooking

If broiling the meat, place broiling rack at highest setting, then preheat broiler to 550°F. When oven is preheated, turn setting to Broil and broil meat until just cooked, about 2 to 4 minutes. (If using an electric oven, leave the oven door slightly ajar during cooking.)

If grilling meat, light coals about 1 hour ahead, so they develop a white ash. Place skewers over medium heat and grill for about 3 minutes, rotating skewers several times.

Bring sauce to room temperature. If sauce is too thick, stir in a little water or coconut milk to thin. Serve meat hot with sauce on the side.

Serves: 6 to 8 people as an appetizer; 3 people as an entrée.

Notes: Substitutes for the beef in this recipe include boned and skinned chicken breasts, slices from a leg of lamb, or shelled and deveined butterflied shrimp.

Curried Lamb Won Tons;
Volcano Scallops; Spicy Thai Noodles.

CURRIED LAMB WON TONS

cornstarch, for dusting
40 won ton skins
peanut oil for shallow frying

Filling

½ yellow onion
2 carrots
½ pound ground lamb
1 tablespoon finely minced fresh ginger
1 tablespoon light soy sauce
1 tablespoon curry powder
1 teaspoon sugar
½ teaspoon Chinese chili sauce (optional)
¼ teaspoon salt
1 egg

Chinese Plum Sauce Dip

½ cup plum sauce
2 tablespoon dry sherry
1 tablespoon lemon juice
¼ to ½ teaspoon ground cinnamon

I always make won tons with fillings of unusual ingredients such as minced swordfish or finely chopped duck breast. These won tons, filled with a curried lamb mixture, can be folded hours in advance, shallow-fried just prior to serving, or — as a last resort — kept warm in a 200°F oven for up to 30 minutes. To vary the flavor, try one of the dumpling fillings in Chapter 7.

Advance Preparation
Prepare filling. In a food processor fitted with the metal chopping blade, separately mince the onion half and the carrots. Place in a small mixing bowl and add lamb, ginger, soy sauce, curry powder, sugar, chili sauce, salt, and egg. Mix thoroughly.

Fold dumplings. Line a cookie sheet with waxed paper and lightly dust with cornstarch. With one point of a won ton skin facing you, place 1 teaspoon of filling in the center of the skin. Fold skin in half by bringing the opposite tip forward over the filling; the won ton tips should not quite meet each other. Roll the won ton once into a cylinder with the side tips still open. Turn the cylinder 180 degrees and lightly moisten each end of the cylinder with water. Touch the moistened tips together, forming a "cap." Place won ton on waxed paper and repeat with remaining skins. (These won tons can be refrigerated, uncovered, for up to 6 hours prior to cooking.)

Combine ingredients for dip, and stir well.

Last-Minute Cooking
In a 12-inch skillet, pour in enough oil to come up ½ inch, then heat to 365°F. To test heat, drop in a little piece of won ton skin; if oil is hot enough, skin will bounce across the surface.

Add about 10 dumplings to oil and fry until golden on one side, then turn and fry on the other side — about 1½ minutes total cooking time. Drain won tons on paper towels, and fry remaining won tons in batches of about 10 at a time. Serve hot with dip.

Serves: 6 to 12 as an appetizer.

STUFFED CHICKEN WINGS

16 chicken wings, tips on

Secret Chinese Barbecue Sauce (page 20)

Stuffing

⅓ cup pine nuts (pignoli)

4 dried black Chinese mushrooms

4 water chestnuts, or ½ cup minced carrots

2 green onions

1 12-ounce bunch spinach, stemmed

½ pound raw shrimp

Sauce

1 tablespoon finely minced fresh ginger

1 clove garlic, finely minced

2 teaspoons light soy sauce

2 teaspoons Oriental sesame oil

2 teaspoons curry powder

1 teaspoon dry sherry

pinch of salt

I prepare the chicken wings for stuffing weeks in advance and freeze the wings. When I want to serve them, I pipe the filling into the cavities using a pastry bag and then, hours later, roast the wings until they are a beautiful caramel color. Guests use the wing tip as a handle to eat the stuffed section. While this is a dish that astounds friends, the recipe is time-consuming and should be accompanied by very easy appetizers such as Chinese Pickles and Onion Bread.

Advance Preparation

Cut off wing drumsticks and reserve for Mahogany Chicken Wings or for making stock. At the drumstick joint, separate the 2 small bones with a small sharp knife. Now cut around the end of the larger bone. With your fingers, push the meat down each bone. Twist to remove each bone, or carefully cut it away. A pocket will appear, which is where the filling will go. Repeat with the remaining wings, and set aside or freeze for future use.

Prepare stuffing. Roast pine nuts in a 325°F oven until golden, about 15 minutes. Soak mushrooms in hot water until softened, about 30 minutes. Discard stems, then mince mushrooms, water chestnuts, and green onions by hand or in a food processor. Drop spinach into boiling water; as soon as spinach wilts (about 15 seconds), pour it into a colander and rinse with cold water. Press out all moisture and mince spinach finely. Shell and devein shrimp, then mince. Combine all stuffing ingredients and mix thoroughly.

Put stuffing in a pastry bag with no tip inserted. Pipe about 2 tablespoons of stuffing into each wing pocket. Refrigerate until ready to cook.

Combine ingredients for sauce.

Roasting Wings

Preheat oven to 375°F. Line a baking pan with foil. Coat a wire rack with cooking spray and place rack in baking pan.

Gently rub stuffed wings with sauce. Place wings on rack and roast for 30 minutes. Brush with sauce, rotate wings, and brush again with sauce. Cook another 30 minutes, until the wings are mahogany color. Serve immediately.

Serves: 6 to 10 people as an appetizer.

Notes: The dumpling fillings in Chapter 7 can be substituted for the shrimp stuffing in this recipe.

GLAZED CHICKEN LIVERS

½ pound chicken livers
1 clove garlic, finely minced
1 tablespoon peanut oil
1 tablespoon dark soy sauce
1 tablespoon sugar
1 tablespoon dry sherry
2 teaspoons Oriental sesame oil
¼ teaspoon Chinese chili sauce (optional)
1½ cups shredded carrots, red bell peppers, or lettuce
1 tablespoon red wine vinegar
Sprigs of fresh coriander, for garnish (optional)

I love chicken livers with Chinese seasonings, briefly stir-fried in a blazing hot wok and served still pink in the center. Sometimes for variation I add a little grated orange peel and a dash of oyster sauce. As for the livers, buy them where they haven't been pre-packaged, and ask the butcher to pick out the firm ones for you.

Advance Preparation
Trim fat pieces from livers, then cut livers into pieces the size of the end of your little finger.

Mix garlic with oil. Combine soy sauce, sugar, sherry, sesame oil, and chili sauce.

Last-Minute Cooking
Spread shredded carrots on a round serving plate.

Place wok over highest heat. When hot, add oil and garlic. Cook until garlic turns white, a few seconds, then add the livers. Stir-fry over highest heat until livers lose all their raw color on the outside, about 1 minute. Pour in the soy sauce mixture and stir-fry until the sauce thickens and glazes the livers, about 1 minute more. The livers should still be pink in the center.

Sprinkle in the vinegar. Taste and adjust seasonings as desired for sweet, hot, and sour effects. Mound the livers on the carrots. Top with a few coriander sprigs and serve at once.

Serves: 6 to 8 as an appetizer.

Notes: Rabbit, duck, and turkey livers make excellent substitutes.

VIETNAMESE SPRING ROLLS

20 6-inch round or triangular rice papers

2 12-ounce bottles of beer

2 eggs, lightly beaten
dipping sauces (see recipes in this chapter)

4 cups peanut oil

20 small bibb lettuce leaves

40 sprigs fresh coriander (cilantro) (optional)

40 fresh mint leaves

Filling

1 ounce bean threads (cellophane noodles)

5 dried black Chinese mushrooms

½ pound raw shrimp

3 green onions, minced

½ cup shredded or minced carrots

½ pound ground pork

3 shallots, minced

3 cloves garlic, finely minced

2 tablespoons dry sherry

1 tablespoon light soy sauce

1 tablespoon oyster sauce

½ teaspoon freshly ground black pepper

½ teaspoon sugar

You can make the spring rolls in the morning, refrigerate them all day, and cook them that evening. And, unlike the Chinese version, they can be reheated simply by frying them in shallow oil until hot or held over in a warm oven for one hour.

Advance Preparation
Prepare filling. Soak bean threads in hot water until softened, about 30 minutes.

Drain, then cut into 1-inch pieces.

Soak mushrooms in hot water until softened, about 20 minutes. Discard stems and mince caps. Shell and devein the shrimp, then chop finely.

Place bean threads, mushrooms, and shrimp in a bowl. Add remaining filling ingredients and mix thoroughly.

Dip a sheet of rice paper in beer to moisten, then shake off excess beer. Place on a flat surface and wait a few moments until paper becomes very pliable. If parts of rice paper don't soften, sprinkle with a little more beer, using your fingers. Shape about 2 tablespoons of filling into a cylinder and place along the bottom third of the round paper. (If using the triangular shape, point the tip of the triangle away from you.) Moisten edges with a little beaten egg. Fold sides over filling, then roll into a cylinder. Continue to form rolls with remaining papers and filling. Place rolls in a single layer on a tray, cover with plastic wrap, and refrigerate until ready to cook.

Prepare the dipping

sauces and set aside.

Last-Minute Cooking
In a 12-inch skillet set over medium-high heat, heat the oil to 325°F. Add all the spring rolls at once, even if they touch or are stacked. The oil temperature will gradually rise to 360°F. Cook rolls until the skins are golden, about 8 minutes, rotating frequently to ensure even cooking. Drain rolls on paper towels.

Serve hot with dipping sauces, lettuce leaves, coriander, and mint leaves. Holding a lettuce leaf in the hand, each person places a little coriander and mint on the leaf, adds the spring roll, and wraps the lettuce around the roll before dipping the package in the sauce.

Serves: 6 to 10 as a hot appetizer.

Notes: Rice papers are very fragile. Examine them carefully before buying and don't purchase them if there are cracks or breaks.

If the spring rolls are added to oil that is hotter than 325°F, the skins cook before the filling. In fact, many Vietnamese cooks place the spring rolls in cold oil and bring the oil to frying temperature.

Instead of using beer, you can dip the rice papers in warm water or lay the rice paper on a counter and brush with beaten egg.

GRILLED QUAIL WITH FIVE-SPICE MARINADE

4 quail

Marinade

3 tablespoons dry sherry

2 tablespoons oyster sauce

1 tablespoon light soy sauce

1 teaspoon Oriental sesame oil

½ teaspoon five-spice powder

½ teaspoon sugar

¼ teaspoon freshly ground black pepper or Chinese chili sauce

2 green onions, minced

3 cloves garlic, minced

2 teaspoons finely minced fresh ginger

2 teaspoons grated or minced orange peel

Tiny quail, marinated with wine, oyster sauce, ginger, and five-spice powder, cook quickly whether grilled or roasted in the oven. They are an excellent appetizer served with Onion Bread, Chinese Pickles, and Shredded Chicken Salad.

Advance Preparation

Split quail in half, or butterfly them by cutting along the breastbones and then gently bending back breasts so birds lie flat.

Combine ingredients for the marinade. Pour over the quail, coating well, and marinate for 2 hours in refrigerator.

If grilling the quail, prepare an open or covered barbecue. About 1 hour before grilling, light coals. If roasting the quail, preheat the oven to 325°F a few minutes ahead.

Cooking

When coals are ready, grill quail, meat side up, over moderate heat for about 5 minutes. Baste quail with remaining marinade. Turn quail over if using an open grill (do not turn quail if barbecue is covered) and cook approximately 10 minutes more.

If using an oven, roast quail, meat side up, for 25 minutes, basting midway through the cooking.

If quail were butterflied, split each piece in half when serving as an appetizer or picnic dish.

Serves: 6 to 8 as an appetizer or picnic dish; 2 as an entrée with a salad.

CHINESE PICKLES

8 **Japanese cucumbers, or 2 hothouse cucumbers**

2 **teaspoons salt**

Pickling Mix

1 **small bottle (12.7 ounces) rice vinegar (1⅔ cups)**

1 **cup sugar**

½ **teaspoon Chinese chili sauce**

½ **teaspoon Sichuan peppercorns**

6 **very thin slices fresh ginger**

5 **cloves garlic, peeled and smashed**

1 **large shallot, thinly sliced**

At her China Moon Restaurant, Barbara Tropp serves Red Onion Pickles, which are the inspiration for this recipe. Serve these Chinese Pickles at parties, but also thinly slice them for hamburgers or chop them in the food processor for hot dog relish.

Advance Preparation (12 Hours before Serving)

Cut ends off cucumbers. Cut Japanese cucumbers in half lengthwise, then place halves together and cut crosswise into ½-inch pieces. For hothouse cucumbers, cut into long, ¼-inch-wide strips, then cut strips into ½-inch lengths.

Toss cucumbers with salt. Set aside for 4 hours, stirring occasionally.

In a stainless-steel saucepan, combine ingredients for pickling mix. Bring to a low boil to dissolve the sugar, about 5 minutes, then let cool completely.

Advance Preparation (8 Hours before Serving)

Place cucumbers in a colander and rinse thoroughly. Press cucumbers lightly with toweling to expel moisture, then add to pickling liquid. Refrigerate at least 8 hours. The flavor will improve for several days, and the cucumbers will keep, refrigerated, for up to 10 days.

Remove cucumbers with a slotted spoon and serve in small dishes, with some of the pickling seasonings, if desired.

Serves: 10 to 14 as an accompaniment for appetizers.

Notes: For added color, include a red bell pepper, seeded and cut into 1-inch strips, when you combine the cucumbers with the pickling solution.

The pickling mixture can be used again to pickle an additional batch of cucumbers.

NEW WAVE SHRIMP

1 **pound medium to large raw shrimp**

Piquant Thai Dipping Sauce

¼ **cup tomato sauce**

3 **tablespoons lime juice**

2 **tablespoons light brown sugar**

¼ **teaspoon Chinese chili sauce**

1 **clove garlic, minced**

2 **teaspoons coarsely chopped fresh mint leaves**

1 **teaspoon grated or minced lime peel**

1 **tablespoon cornstarch**

Served chilled with various Oriental dipping sauces, large butterflied shrimp are one of the easiest and most appreciated appetizers. While we usually serve these shrimp with this Piquant Thai Dipping Sauce, other possibilities are Sweet and Pungent Apricot Dip (see Notes), Satay Sauce, and Chinese Plum Sauce Dip.

Advance Preparation
Prepare shrimp. Remove shells except on the tails. Cut along the top of the curve, starting at the tail and making a progressively deeper cut so the knife nearly cuts through the shrimp at the head end. Rinse out the vein, and continue for remaining shrimp. Bring a large amount of lightly salted water to a rapid boil and drop in shrimp. Cook until shrimp are done, between 1 and 2 minutes. To test, cut a shrimp in half; it should be white in the center. Transfer shrimp immediately to a bowl of ice water to cool. When chilled, drain and refrigerate until ready to use.

Prepare sauce. In a small saucepan, combine tomato sauce, lime juice, brown sugar, chili sauce, garlic, mint, and lime peel. Set aside.

Last-Minute Assembling (up to 1 Hour before Serving)
Combine cornstarch with an equal amount of cold water. Over medium heat, bring sauce ingredients to a low boil, reduce heat to a simmer, and cook for 2 minutes. Return sauce to a low boil and stir in enough of the cornstarch mixture to lightly thicken sauce. Strain sauce through a sieve placed over a small serving bowl. Let sauce cool at least 10 minutes (sauce is best at room temperature). Place bowl of sauce on flat serving plate and ring with chilled shrimp.

Serves: 6 to 8 as an appetizer.

Notes: Sweet and Pungent Apricot Dip. This is a good alternative dip for the shrimp. In a small saucepan combine 12 dried apricot pieces, 12 ounces apricot nectar, ½ cup guava nectar, ¾ cup sugar, ½ cup distilled white vinegar, 1 tablespoon chopped fresh ginger, and ½ teaspoon Chinese chili sauce. Bring to low boil, reduce heat to simmer, cover and cook 20 minutes. Cool and transfer to food processor and purée. If sauce is too thin, return to saucepan and bring to low boil. Stir in a little cornstarch dissolved with equal amount cold water until thickened. Serve at room temperature.

GINGER MINT CEVICHE

¼ pound salmon filet, skinned

¼ pound bay scallops

½ cup lime juice

1 tablespoon finely minced fresh ginger

1 clove garlic, finely minced

4 small hot chilies, seeded, stemmed, and minced

2 tablespoons chopped fresh coriander (cilantro)

2 tablespoons chopped mint leaves

1 green onion, chopped

half a red bell pepper, chopped

1 teaspoon grated or minced lime peel

3 tablespoons safflower oil

1 teaspoon freshly grated nutmeg

½ teaspoon Chinese chili sauce

½ teaspoon salt

16 small bibb lettuce leaves

Cubes of salmon and fresh little bay scallops are "cooked" in lime juice before being tossed with mint, fresh chilies, coriander, and ginger. Served in small lettuce cups, this is a good way to begin a summer dinner.

Advance Preparation: (6 Hours before Serving)
Cut salmon into ¼-inch pieces. Cut scallops in half. Mix with lime juice and refrigerate for 5 hours.

Discard lime juice. Combine salmon and scallops with remaining ingredients except lettuce. Refrigerate for at least 1 hour before serving.

Serve in small lettuce cups.

Serves: 6 to 8 as an appetizer.

SHRIMP TOAST CYLINDERS

½ pound raw shrimp

1 egg white

¾ cup finely minced green onions

½ cup finely minced water chestnuts, preferably fresh

2 teaspoons very finely minced fresh ginger

¾ teaspoon salt

½ teaspoon sugar

½ teaspoon grated orange peel

½ teaspoon white pepper or Chinese chili sauce

¼ cup white sesame seeds

16 slices very thin white sandwich bread

dipping sauces (see recipes in this chapter)

peanut oil for shallow frying

The head dim sum chef at a restaurant in Los Angeles showed me a great technique for shrimp toast. Instead of spreading minced shrimp on small pieces of bread and frying them in oil, the mixture is spread on whole slices of bread, which are then rolled into cylinders. The shrimp has a much more intense flavor, further enhanced when the cylinders are dipped into various sauces. Since this dish requires last-minute cooking, I serve it with appetizers such as Oriental Pâte and Chinese Pickles, which require no additional preparation at serving time.

Advance Preparation
Shell and devein shrimp. In a food processor fitted with the metal chopping blade, mince the shrimp and egg white into a paste. Turn out into a mixing bowl and add green onions, water chestnuts, ginger, salt, sugar, orange peel, and white pepper. Mix thoroughly.

In a small, ungreased skillet set over high heat, toast sesame seeds until light golden, about 2 minutes. Remove from heat immediately and set aside.

Bring water to a boil in the bottom of a Chinese steamer. Trim the crusts off the bread, then place bread slices on steamer tray, cover, and steam until bread is soft and pliable, about 2 minutes. Immediately remove from steamer.

Using a rubber spatula, spread the filling over the surface of each slice in a very thin layer. Scatter on some sesame seeds and carefully roll each slice into a cylinder. Store cylinders, uncovered, on a tray in the refrigerator until ready to cook.

Prepare one or more of the dipping sauces.

Last-Minute Cooking
In a 12-inch skillet, pour enough oil to come up ⅓ inch and set skillet over medium-high heat. Heat oil until a cube of bread can hop across the surface. Gently add 8 cylinders and fry until they turn light golden, about 2 minutes. Watch oil temperature; if the oil is too hot, the cylinders will darken on the outside before their centers are cooked. Drain cooked cylinders on wire rack, then keep warm in the oven for the few minutes it takes to fry the remaining cylinders. Serve at once.

Serves: 6 to 8 as an appetizer.
Notes: These cylinders can be frozen, and then thawed before frying. But they will not be as delicious as they are when cooked fresh.

MAHOGANY CHICKEN WINGS

- **4 pounds chicken wings**
  Marinade
- **1 cup plus 2 tablespoons hoisin sauce**
- **¾ cup plum sauce**
- **½ cup light soy sauce**
- **⅓ cup cider vinegar**
- **¼ cup dry sherry**
- **¼ cup honey**
- **6 green onions, minced**
- **6 large cloves garlic, minced**

These chicken wings are marinated for 24 hours, then roasted until the marinade caramelizes to a beautiful "mahogany" color. But watch that your friends don't snatch the chicken wings as they emerge hot from the roasting pan.

Advance Preparation
Cut off wing tips and save them for making stock. If serving wings in small pieces, cut each in half at the joint.

Combine ingredients for marinade, then mix with the wings to coat well. Cover and refrigerate for 24 hours.

Roasting Wings
Preheat oven to 375°F. Line a baking pan with foil. Coat a wire rack with cooking spray and place rack in baking pan.

Drain the chicken and reserve marinade. Arrange wings on the rack and roast for 30 minutes. Drain accumulated liquid from pan. Baste wings with reserved marinade, turn them, and baste again. Roast until the wings turn mahogany color, another 30 minutes.

Serve hot or at room temperature.

Serves: 10 people as an appetizer or picnic dish.

Notes: The marinade is an all-purpose barbecue sauce for chicken, game hens, and large butterflied shrimp.

PAPER-WRAPPED SALMON

½ pound salmon filet

¼ pound flavorful ham, thinly sliced

32 medium snow peas

4 green onions

16 6-inch squares cooking paper

32 sprigs of fresh coriander (cilantro) (optional)

peanut oil for shallow-frying

Marinade

4 tablespoons dry sherry

2 tablespoons oyster sauce

1 teaspoon Oriental sesame oil

¼ teaspoon sugar

⅛ teaspoon white pepper

1 clove garlic, finely minced

1 tablespoon finely minced fresh ginger

Hidden in these paper envelopes are slices of marinated salmon, crunchy snow peas, and paper-thin rectangles of ham. I fold the packages well in advance or solicit help from early dinner guests. Paper-Wrapped Salmon is a little messy to unfold and eat, so serve this appetizer in the kitchen, as friends have a glass of wine and watch the cooking.

Advance Preparation
Holding your knife on a bias, cut the salmon filet into 16 thin slices about 1½ inches wide and 3 inches long.

Combine ingredients for marinade and mix with salmon slices; set aside for at least 15 minutes.

Cut ham into rectangles the same size as salmon. Snap stems off snow peas and remove strings along top (straight) edge. Cut green onions into very thin shreds.

Lay a paper square on the counter with one corner pointing toward you. In the following order, place in the center of the paper horizontally: a slice of salmon, a piece of ham, 1 snow pea, a few shreds of green onion, and 2 coriander sprigs. Fold the bottom corner (the one pointing toward you) over the ingredients, bringing the tip to within 1 inch of the opposite tip. Crease sharply. Bring one side over a third of the way and crease again. Fold the opposite side over a third of the way and crease. Next fold the bottom over so just the triangle tip is visible. Tuck the tip between the folds to create an envelope. Firmly crease all folds. Repeat with remaining paper and fillings. Place paper package on a tray, salmon side up, and refrigerate until ready to cook. This can be done up to 3 hours in advance of cooking.

Last-Minute Cooking
In a 12-inch skillet set over medium-high heat, pour in enough oil to reach ½ inch. Heat oil until a piece of bread or slice of ginger will skip across the surface. Gently add in 8 packages at a time, salmon side down, and fry for 1 minute. Do not turn. Drain packages on paper towels, pressing them lightly to blot excess oil. Fry remaining packages. Serve at once. Each person opens his or her paper package and eats the ingredients.

Serves: 4 to 8 as a hot appetizer.

Notes: Other types of fish, shellfish, beef filet, or chicken breasts are good in these packages. Choose from a wide variety of vegetables, add fresh herbs from the garden, and arrive at a completely new and delicious variation. When filling the packages, put the longest-cooking ingredient in first and the shortest-cooking ingredient last.

When using ham, choose a mildly smoked type, not a country ham or European ham, which would overwhelm the other flavors.

CHINESE SALSA

- **6 to 8 dried black Chinese mushrooms**
- **4 medium tomatoes (about 1½ pounds)**
- **½ cup chopped green onions**
- **½ cup chopped fresh coriander (cilantro)**
- **2 cloves garlic, finely minced**
- **1 tablespoon finely minced fresh ginger**
- **3 tablespoons red wine vinegar**
- **2 tablespoons Oriental sesame oil**
- **1 tablespoon safflower oil**
- **1½ teaspoons sugar**
- **1 teaspoon Chinese chili sauce**
- **½ teaspoon salt**

This is a recipe just for summer, when vine-ripened home-grown tomatoes or the best supermarket type are plentiful. Perfumed by Chinese seasonings and with the natural flavor of tomato, this salsa is delicious spooned on a grilled swordfish entrée, tossed with chilled shrimp for a simple cocktail dish, or mixed with barbecued meat and packed into warm Peking pancakes for a Chinese burrito.

Advance Preparation

Soak mushrooms in hot water until softened, about 30 minutes. Discard stems and chop caps coarsely.

Cut tomatoes in half and squeeze out seeds. Coarsely chop; you should have about 2 cups.

Combine mushrooms, tomatoes, green onions, and coriander.

Add remaining ingredients judiciously. A good method is to add slightly less of each seasoning called for, then taste the salsa as you add a little bit more of each item until you achieve the desired flavor. Do not refrigerate salsa if serving that day; if prepared a day in advance, bring salsa to room temperature before serving.

Serves: 4 to 8 as a dip for appetizers and picnics.

Notes: A delicious addition to this salsa is 1 coarsely chopped grilled Japanese eggplant (see Grilled Oriental Eggplant).

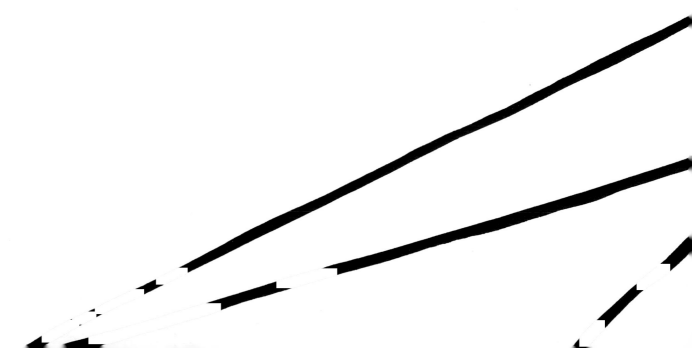

CHINESE BUNS STUFFED WITH BARBECUED MEAT

Filling

1   **pound boned country-style spareribs (fat left on)**

Secret Chinese Barbecue Sauce (page 20)

1   **tablespoon cornstarch**

1   **tablespoon peanut oil**

½   **cup minced green onions**

2   **cloves garlic, finely minced**

Bread Dough

2   **tablespoons sugar**

2   **teaspoons active dry yeast**

2½   **cups warm water (105–115°F)**

2   **teaspoons salt**

2   **tablespoons Oriental sesame oil**

7   **cups all-purpose white flour, plus a little extra**

½   **cup white sesame seeds**

½   **cup finely minced fresh coriander (cilantro)**

These rolls are served for lunch at Chinese dim sum restaurants, but we have also served them as an appetizer, an entrée accompaniment with a tossed green salad, and as one of several picnic dishes.

Advance Preparation

Prepare filling. Preheat oven to 350°F. Rub meat with barbecue sauce, reserving extra sauce. Place meat on baking sheet lined with aluminum foil. Roast in oven until meat is no longer pink in center and internal temperature registers 170°F, about 30 minutes. Save pan drippings.

Combine cornstarch with an equal amount of cold water. Chop meat, including fatty pieces, into ⅛-inch cubes. Heat wok to hot and add peanut oil. Add green onions and garlic, then sauté a few seconds and add meat. Add pan drippings and ¼ cup of the reserved barbecue sauce. Add a little cornstarch mixture to thicken sauce, then turn out into bowl and partially freeze (for 1 hour).

Prepare the bread dough. Stir sugar and yeast into warm water. When bubbles form on top, about 5 minutes, the yeast has been activated. (Do not proceed if this does not occur.) Stir in salt and sesame oil and set aside.

Place flour in a large bowl. In a small, ungreased skillet over high heat, stir sesame seeds until light golden. Add sesame seeds to flour, along with coriander. Slowly pour in yeast mixture and mix well.

Turn out dough onto a well-floured board. Knead dough using your palms until the dough is smooth and no longer sticky, about 8 minutes. Work in more flour, if necessary.

Lightly oil a large bowl, place dough in bowl, and turn a few times to cover surface of dough with oil. Cover bowl with towel, place bowl in warm area of kitchen, and let rise until dough doubles its size, about 2 hours.

Cut dough into 24 pieces. Flatten each piece with your palm, making sure dough is thicker at the center than around the edge (otherwise filling will push through center when bread is steamed). Stir meat mixture. Place 1½ tablespoons of filling in center of each piece of dough. Carefully draw sides up over filling and pinch dough together at top to seal. Turn sealed side down.

Line several Chinese steamer trays with foil, leaving a few holes uncovered on the edges. Lightly oil the foil, then place the buns 1½ inches apart on the foil. Let buns rest 30 minutes, then prepare to steam now or refrigerate filled steamer trays until ready to steam.

Steaming

Bring water to a boil in

the bottom of a Chinese steamer. Place trays over boiling water. If using a metal steamer, cover the top steamer tray with a large dish towel to prevent condensing water from dripping on buns. Cover and steam 12 minutes.

Serves: 24 as an appetizer or picnic dish; 10 as an entrée.

Notes: Any well-seasoned stew meat with a little gravy is delicious as a filling. Chop the meat, combine with a few tablespoons gravy, add 1 or 2 chopped green onions, and then partially freeze the filling. Make bread dough, stuff with filling, and steam. Always be sure to partially freeze the stuffing because if your fingers pick up moisture from the filling, the bread dough will be impossible to seal.

To freeze the buns for later, place uncooked stuffed buns on a cookie sheet lined with waxed paper and lightly dust with cornstarch. Let rise 30 minutes, then place the cookie sheet in freezer. When buns freeze, transfer to a plastic bag and seal. To cook, remove buns from bag and place on oiled foil inside steamer tray. Let defrost 30 minutes, then steam for 18 minutes.

Chinese Buns Stuffed
with Barbecued Meat.

ORIENTAL PATE

½ pound chicken or turkey livers
¼ cup (½ stick) butter
2 shallots, chopped
1 tablespoon finely minced fresh ginger
2 large cloves garlic, minced
1 tablespoon oyster sauce
2 teaspoons dry mustard
1 teaspoon grated or finely minced orange peel
¼ teaspoon salt
½ teaspoon sugar
¼ teaspoon five-spice powder
¼ teaspoon Chinese chili sauce (optional)
3 ounces cream cheese
2 tablespoons Cognac
Sprigs of fresh coriander (cilantro), for garnish (optional)

One of the most beautiful spots to take friends for lunch is Alan Hooker's Ranch House Restaurant in the Ojai Valley outside Los Angeles. Sitting on the terrace among the flowers and herbs, with mountains ringing the small valley, one quickly forgets the fast pace of the city. This pâté is based on one by Alan Hooker, with the addition of Oriental seasonings. It takes only minutes to make in a food processor, and continues to improve in flavor if made a day or two in advance.

Advance Preparation (24 Hours before Serving)

Trim fat from livers and discard. Cut livers in half.

In a 10-inch sauté pan set over medium heat, melt 2 tablespoons butter and sauté shallots, ginger, and garlic for about 30 seconds.

Add livers, cover pan, and cook until livers are no longer pink in center, about 5 minutes.

Transfer livers to a food processor fitted with the metal chopping blade. Scrape all the pan juices into processor, too, then add oyster sauce, mustard, orange peel, salt, sugar, five-spice powder, and chili sauce. Process until completely smooth.

Add cream cheese to food processor and blend briefly. Add remaining butter and blend until very smooth. Add Cognac and blend again briefly.

Transfer purée to a 2-cup mold. Smooth surface and cover with plastic wrap so top of pâté does not discolor. Refrigerate for up to 1 week. Garnish with sprigs of coriander.

Serves: 8 to 10 as an appetizer or picnic dish.

Notes: While it is always quick to serve the pâté with store-bought crackers or bread, we like to spread it in thick layers on Onion Bread.

For a more elegant presentation, when ready to serve, scoop out pâté and mold with a spatula into a round, 1-inch high flat-topped disk. Garnish the sides of the pâté with sprigs of coriander or watercress and little triangles of sweet red pepper.

As an alternate method, bring pâté to room temperature 30 minutes before serving. Pipe through pastry bag onto crackers. Garnish with cilantro and minced red sweet ginger.

ONION BREAD

3 tablespoons white sesame seeds

2 cups unbleached all-purpose flour

¾ cup boiling water

1 tablespoon Oriental sesame oil

salt (see Notes)

2 tablespoons finely minced green onions

2 tablespoons finely minced fresh coriander (cilantro) (optional)

¼ cup peanut oil

Sold by street vendors all across northern China, Onion Bread consists of layers of unleavened dough alternated with sesame oil, green onions, and toasted sesame seeds. Pan-fried and cut into wedges, it makes an excellent appetizer or picnic dish, or is a superb way to sop up gravy from pot roasts, curries, and stews. Easy to make in advance, the bread can be rolled out in the morning and refrigerated for hours before being cooked.

Advance Preparation

In a small, ungreased skillet set over high heat, stir sesame seeds until light golden. Tip out immediately and set aside.

Place flour in a mixing bowl and add boiling water. Stir well, then turn out onto a lightly floured surface. Knead, pressing with the palms of your hands until the dough is smooth and no longer sticky, about 8 minutes. Let dough rest 15 minutes, covered with a towel.

With the surface lightly floured, roll the dough into a circle ½ inch thick. Rub the top with sesame oil. Sprinkle on about 2 teaspoons salt, then evenly spread on the green onions, coriander, and some sesame seeds.

Roll dough circle into a tight cylinder. Pinch the edges closed, then twist cylinder several times. Taking one end, wind the cylinder into a coil, tucking the end into the center of the coil. With your palm, flatten the coil. Sprinkle remaining sesame seeds on both sides.

With a rolling pin, roll the flattened dough coil into a 10- to 11-inch circle about ¼ inch thick. Place dough between waxed paper lightly dusted with flour, then cover with plastic wrap and refrigerate until ready to cook.

Last-Minute Cooking

Place a heavy 12-inch skillet over medium heat. When very evenly heated, add oil. When oil is hot (bubbles form around the tip of a wooden spoon), add dough and fry on both sides, turning frequently, until golden, about 8 to 10 minutes.

Cut bread into wedges and serve as an appetizer, with soups and stews, or at room temperature for picnics. It can also be reheated in a warm oven (but not in a microwave oven, which toughens the bread).

Serves: 6 to 8 people as an appetizer.

Notes: Always add more salt than you think is necessary; without a generous amount of salt the bread will be tasteless.

There are many other ingredients you could place inside the bread, such as olive oil, garlic paste, chopped fresh parsley, grated Parmesan cheese, and finely chopped Chinese sausage.

The garden salads in this chapter are edible works of art. Their dramatic contrasts in color, texture, and flavor stimulate the palate for later triumphs, or complement the main entrée, or contribute the perfect lightness at the end of dinner. Appearing in the middle of a multicourse meal, an Oriental salad offers a break between dishes that require last-minute finishing touches. As another possibility, replace the ubiquitous green dinner salad with an Oriental salad to accompany entrées ranging from grilled veal chops to bouillabaisse. But perhaps the best way to appreciate these salads is to serve them as the main course for elegant luncheons and easy dinners. Match the salad with crusty bread, sweet butter, plenty of Champagne, and a decadent dessert for a simple meal that allows conversations to proceed without a disturbing succession of courses.

Oriental salads provide endless possibilities for creating variations from whatever ingredients the refrigerator yields. Combining leftover cooked meats or seafood, shreds of vegetables, and greens tossed with toasted nuts and perhaps puffs of crispy rice sticks is an exciting way to improvise new salads. The following

Wild Chinese Salad.

quantities, when combined, make a generous serving for six people: 1 cup slivered cooked meat or seafood, 2 cups slivered vegetables (such as bell peppers, fresh mushrooms, summer squash, cucumber, bean sprouts, jicama, green onions, or parboiled broccoli, carrots, and asparagus), 3 cups torn or slivered lettuce, 3 cups slivered toasted won tons or 4 cups deep-fried rice sticks, and ½ cup toasted nuts. Just before serving, toss the salad with a dressing from one of the salads on pages 54, 60, 64, or 68. Make enough salad for second helpings!

Easy-to-prepare recipes in this chapter are Garden Greens with Oriental Dressing, Chinese Duck Salad, Oriental Avocado Salad, Chinese Eggplant Salad, Marinated Mushroom Salad, Jade Salad, Thai Papaya Shrimp Salad, and Ginger Noodle Salad.

WILD CHINESE SALAD

¾ cup best-quality wild rice
1 teaspoon salt
10 snow peas
1 package (3.5 ounces) enoki mushrooms
½ large yellow bell pepper
½ large red bell pepper
2 ounces smoked turkey
½ cup fresh coriander (cilantro) sprigs
   Dressing
¼ cup safflower oil
2 tablespoons rice vinegar
¼ to ½ teaspoon salt
1 tablespoon finely minced fresh ginger

All the main ingredients (wild rice, enoki mushrooms, smoked turkey, and fresh coriander) have wild, nutty, smokey flavors that harmonize perfectly with the delicate dressing. But, if you want a more assertive taste, the salad is also delicious tossed with the dressing from Spicy Swordfish Salad or Jade Salad. Wild Chinese Salad also makes an elegant luncheon dish or a first course preceding grilled salmon or extra-thick veal chops.

Advance Preparation
Rinse rice thoroughly in a sieve, then drain. Bring 3 cups water to a boil, then stir in rice and salt. Cover and simmer until liquid disappears, about 45 minutes. Fluff with a fork or chopsticks. Let cool, then refrigerate.

Snap stems off snow peas, pulling strings off top ridge. Drop snow peas into rapidly boiling water. When they turn bright green (about 5 seconds), transfer immediately with a slotted spoon to a bowl of ice water. Pat dry and cut into slivers to measure ¾ cup. Set aside.

Cut off and discard dirty ends of mushrooms. Separate mushroom threads and set aside. Stem and seed pepper halves, then sliver each. Set aside. Sliver turkey to measure 1 cup. Set aside.

Combine dressing ingredients in a jar and shake vigorously.

Last-Minute Assembling
In a large bowl, toss turkey with wild rice. Add vegetables, including coriander, in small amounts, tossing each until you achieve the proportion of vegetables to rice that you wish.

Shake dressing and toss with salad. Divide salad evenly among 4 plates and serve at once.

Serves: 4 to 6 as a dinner salad.

Menu Ideas: Dinner for 6 — Chicken Curry Dumplings, Salmon in Chinese Pesto Sauce, Asparagus in Black Bean Butter Sauce, Wild Chinese Salad, and Coconut Ice Cream.

Notes: As an alternative to cooking the rice in plain water, soak 5 Chinese dried black mushrooms in 1½ cups water. Strain the soaking liquid into a saucepan and add 1½ cups water for cooking wild rice. Discard stems from mushrooms and sliver caps, then add mushrooms to the salad.

Pan-fried trout; Garden Greens with Oriental Dressing.

GARDEN GREENS WITH ORIENTAL DRESSING

4 cups washed, dried, and torn assorted greens

½ cup slivered red bell pepper

½ cup slivered yellow bell pepper

½ cup thinly sliced red radish

¼ cup chopped fresh parsley

¼ cup slivered green onions

edible flowers such as rose petals, nasturtiums, violas, oregano flowers, rosemary buds (optional)

Dressing

2 tablespoons rice vinegar

1 tablespoon safflower oil

1 tablespoon Oriental sesame oil

1 tablespoon light soy sauce

1 teaspoon hoisin sauce

½ teaspoon dry mustard

½ teaspoon sugar

2 teaspoons finely minced fresh ginger

½ teaspoon finely minced garlic

1 tablespoon minced green onion

A mixture of garden greens tossed with an Oriental dressing provides a change from standard dinner salads. The optional edible flowers in this recipe add a whimsical spring-time look to the salad. Other Oriental dress-ings that work well on tossed green salads are those from Thai Papaya Shrimp Salad, Shred-ded Chicken Salad, and Lemon Shrimp Salad.

Advance Preparation
Place prepared greens in a plastic bag. Put prepared vegetables and edible flowers in individual plastic bags. Refrigerate until ready to use.

Combine dressing in-gredients in a jar and shake vigorously.

Last-Minute Assembling
Combine greens, vege-tables, and flowers in a large bowl. Shake dressing again, then sprinkle on enough dressing to lightly moisten ingredients. Toss salad with your hands or salad spoons.

Taste a salad green. If necessary, add more dressing or adjust flavor for salt, pepper, vin-egar, or oil. Serve at once.

Serves: 4 as a dinner salad.

Menu Ideas: This is excel-lent served with grilled veal chops or broiled fish.

Notes: We first tried this dressing with sliced avo-cados and vine-ripened tomatoes — delicious!

CHINESE DUCK SALAD

½ barbecued duck
½ papaya
1 pear
1 small avocado
 juice of 1 lemon
 arugula leaves (optional)
 Dressing
2 teaspoons grated or
 finely minced lime peel
5 tablespoons lime juice
¼ cup safflower oil
2 teaspoons honey
½ teaspoon Chinese
 pepper mix (see
 Appendix)
½ teaspoon salt
¼ teaspoon Chinese chili
 sauce
2 tablespoons minced
 chives
1 small garlic clove, finely
 minced

Chinese barbecued
duck — mounded in
the center of a pin-
wheel of papaya, pear,
and avocado slices —
goes beautifully with
the lime-honey-chive
dressing. Be sure to
freeze leftover scraps of
duck meat for Chinese
Duck Pizza. As a sub-
stitute for Chinese bar-
becued duck, barbe-
cued chicken or very
fresh crab chunks make
beautiful variations of
this salad.

Advance Preparation
Pull meat and skin away
from bones of duck.
Freeze bones for mak-
ing stock. Trim away
and discard all fat from
the skin and meat. Cut
meat and crisp skin into
matchstick pieces. Set
aside.

Peel and seed papaya;
cut papaya into thin
slices. Core pear but do
not peel; cut pear into
thin slices. Squeeze
juice from half the
lemon over pear.

Seed and remove skin
from avocado; thinly
slice, then squeeze re-
maining lemon juice
over avocado.

Combine ingredients
for dressing in a jar and
shake well. Taste, and
adjust for sweetness.

On a few leaves of
arugula, fan out slices
of papaya, pear, and
avocado on 4 salad
plates. Mound duck in
center of each plate.
Refrigerate.

Last-Minute Assembling
Shake dressing well be-
fore drizzling over fruit
and duck.

**Serves: 4 as a small dinner
salad or light first course.**
**Menu Ideas: Accompany
this with California Won Ton
Soup and Oriental Fruit
Tarts as a light dinner for 4.**

ORIENTAL AVOCADO SALAD

2 ripe avocados

arugula leaves or mixed greens

Dressing

1 tablespoon white sesame seeds

2 tablespoons safflower oil

2 tablespoons balsamic vinegar

1 teaspoon honey

½ teaspoon Chinese pepper mix (see Appendix)

¼ teaspoon salt

1 tablespoon finely minced fresh ginger

The dressing of ginger-flavored balsamic vinegar and toasted sesame seeds adds the perfect contrast to nutty-tasting tree-ripened avocados.

Preparation and Serving

For dressing, toast sesame seeds in a small ungreased skillet set over high heat until they are light golden. Combine sesame seeds with remaining dressing ingredients in a jar and shake well.

Cut avocados in half, seed, and thinly slice. Place arugula leaves or a thin bed of mixed greens on 4 salad plates. Fan half an avocado across each bed of greens. Shake dressing and then drizzle over avocado. Serve at once.

Serves 4.

OVERLEAF: Summer Squid Stir-Fry;
Scallop Thread Soup;
Jade Salad;
Seafood Pot Stickers in Lemon Sauce.

JADE SALAD

½ pound small bay scallops

1 12-ounce bunch spinach, stemmed

1 large red bell pepper

12 very large cultivated mushrooms, caps tightly closed

2 teaspoons lemon juice

2 green onions

½ cup pine nuts (pignoli)

½ cup slivered red sweet ginger

Dressing

2 tablespoons juice from jar of red sweet ginger

2 tablespoons safflower oil

3 tablespoons red wine vinegar

1 tablespoon finely minced fresh ginger

1 teaspoon grated or finely minced orange peel

½ teaspoon Chinese chili sauce

½ teaspoon salt

Slivers of spinach, red bell pepper, bay scallops, and toasted pine nuts provide a perfect foil for this sweet-and-sour, slightly spicy dressing. As a substitute for scallops, good choices either alone or in combination include fresh crab meat, cooked medium shrimp, or poached squid. Another variation is to substitute raspberry vinegar for the red wine vinegar.

Advance Preparation
Drop scallops into 2 quarts rapidly boiling water, then reduce to a simmer. Every 15 seconds, cut a scallop in half; when scallops are white in center (about 1½ minutes), transfer quickly to a container of ice water. Chill, drain, and pat dry.

Wash and thoroughly dry spinach. Bunch spinach together and cut into very thin slivers. Stem and seed pepper, then cut into slivers. Refrigerate spinach and pepper.

Stand mushrooms on their edge (not flat on the cap or stem) and cut caps into very thin, round disks. Stack disks and shred. Sprinkle with a little lemon juice and refrigerate.

Cut green onions into slivers and set aside.

Toast pine nuts in a 325°F oven until light golden, about 15 minutes.

Combine ingredients for dressing in a jar and shake vigorously.

Last-Minute Assembling
Place salad ingredients in a large bowl. Shake dressing, then add and toss immediately. Serve at once.

Serves: 6 as a dinner salad.

Menu Ideas: This is a stunning salad to serve before or after an elegant main course. If you wish, delete the seafood and increase the other ingredients slightly.

Notes: A good alternative method for cooking the scallops is to sauté them in a small skillet, with 1 tablespoon peanut oil and 1 teaspoon finely minced fresh ginger.

CHINESE EGGPLANT SALAD

- 4 to 5 small Oriental eggplants
- 1 large red bell pepper
- ½ pound jicama
- 2 tablespoons safflower oil

Dressing

- ¼ cup safflower oil
- 2 tablespoons Oriental sesame oil
- 2 tablespoons rice vinegar
- 2 tablespoons light soy sauce
- 1 tablespoon lemon juice
- ½ teaspoon Chinese pepper mix (see Appendix)
- 2 small cloves garlic, finely minced
- 2 tablespoons finely minced mint leaves
- 2 tablespoons finely minced fresh coriander (cilantro)
- 2 tablespoons finely minced green onion
- 2 tablespoons white sesame seeds

Oriental eggplant, jicama, and red bell pepper, tossed in a dressing of rice vinegar, mint, and sesame seeds creates an exciting contrast in texture and color. Served with Rack of Lamb in Hunan Barbecue Sauce, baked potatoes, and a good Cabernet Sauvignon, this makes a wonderful quick dinner for four.

Advance Preparation

Cut enough eggplant into ¼-inch-thin circles to fill 2 cups. Stem and seed pepper, then cut pepper into ½-inch cubes or triangles. Peel jicama, then cut into ¼-inch slices. Stack slices and cut into ¼-inch strips; cut strips into 2-inch lengths, making 1½ cups.

In a medium bowl, combine all ingredients for dressing except sesame seeds. Toast sesame seeds in a small, ungreased skillet set over high heat until they are light golden. Add sesame seeds to dressing.

Preheat broiler for 5 minutes. Place eggplant in a small mixing bowl. Add 2 tablespoons of the dressing plus safflower oil. Mix well. Lay eggplant circles on a sheet of aluminum foil. Place in broiler 6 inches from heat and broil until eggplants are light golden on top, about 5 minutes.

Add cooked eggplant, pepper, and jicama to bowl with dressing. Mix thoroughly. This may be done a day in advance of serving. Stir well before serving.

Serves: 4 with barbecued meat.

THAI PAPAYA SHRIMP SALAD

1 pound medium raw shrimp

1½ ripe papayas

1 red bell pepper

½ hothouse cucumber

1 12-ounce bunch spinach, stemmed

¾ cup pine nuts (pignoli)

Dressing

3 tablespoons lime juice

2 tablespoons light brown sugar

2 tablespoons Thai fish sauce

½ teaspoon Chinese chili sauce

2 teaspoons very finely minced fresh ginger

2 small green onions, minced

1 tablespoon minced fresh coriander (cilantro)

Cool papaya chunks, tender whole shrimp, red bell pepper triangles, and crisp cucumber pieces mingle with buttery pine nuts in a Thai sweet-and-sour lime dressing.

Advance Preparation
Shell and devein shrimp. Bring 3 quarts water to a rapid boil and add shrimp. Cook until a shrimp, when cut in half, is white in the center, about 2 minutes. Immediately transfer shrimp to ice water to chill. Drain and pat dry, then refrigerate.

Peel and seed papayas. Cut flesh into ½-inch cubes, then set aside. Stem and seed pepper, then cut into ½-inch cubes or into triangles. Refrigerate.

Split cucumber in half lengthwise and scrape out seeds. Cut cucumber into long ¼-inch strips, then place strips together and cut into ½-inch cubes. Refrigerate.

Wash and dry spinach. Bunch spinach together and cut into shreds. Refrigerate.

Toast pine nuts in a 325°F oven until light golden, about 15 minutes.

Combine ingredients for dressing in a jar and shake vigorously.

Last-Minute Assembling
Spread spinach evenly on 4 salad plates. Place papaya chunks, shrimp, pepper pieces, cucumber cubes, and pine nuts in bowl. Shake dressing, then add and toss. Place on top of spinach and serve at once.

Serves: 4 as a dinner salad; 6 as part of an Oriental meal.

Menu Ideas: Serve this salad as an entrée for 3, with toasted onion bagels and sweet butter.

Notes: As a variation, substitute bay scallops or thinly sliced swordfish for the shrimp. And, during melon season, cantaloupe is great in place of papaya. The salad is also delicious served on a bed of wild rice rather than spinach.

Thai Papaya Shrimp Salad; Beef Satay.

MARINATED MUSHROOM SALAD

4 **cups (about 1 pound) cubed button mushrooms**

3 **cups fresh bean sprouts**

1 **large red bell pepper**

1 **bag (3 ounces) sliced almonds**

6 **tablespoons minced fresh parsley**

Dressing

5 **tablespoons red wine vinegar**

¼ **cup safflower oil**

3 **tablespoons Oriental sesame oil**

2 **tablespoons oyster sauce**

2 **teaspoons sugar**

½ **teaspoon freshly ground black pepper**

¼ **cup minced green onions**

2 **tablespoons finely minced fresh ginger**

I developed this recipe as one of several Oriental salads for a Chinese café in Los Angeles. While the salad is at its peak of texture after marinating for thirty minutes, it can be tossed hours in advance for picnics.

Advance Preparation
Trim ends off mushroom stems, then cut mushrooms into quarters and set aside along with sprouts. Stem and seed red pepper, then cut it into slivers. Set aside.

Toast almonds in a 325°F oven until light golden, about 12 minutes. Set aside.

Combine ingredients for salad dressing and mix thoroughly.

Assembling
Approximately 30 minutes prior to serving, combine the mushrooms, sprouts, pepper, almonds, and parsley in a large mixing bowl. Shake dressing vigorously, then toss with salad. Let salad rest 30 minutes, then serve. If salad is prepared for a picnic, let marinate in refrigerator.

Serves: 6 to 8 as a picnic dish or dinner salad.

Menu Ideas: We have served this as a picnic dish along with cold barbecued chicken, deviled eggs, and Onion Bread.

56

GINGER NOODLE SALAD

¼ pound dried spaghetti-style noodles, preferably Chinese

2 tablespoons safflower oil

¼ pound snow peas

1 large carrot

½ hothouse cucumber

¼ pound good-quality ham, cut into 4 slices

1 cup fresh bean sprouts

Dressing

¼ cup red wine vinegar

2 tablespoons dark soy sauce

2 tablespoons Oriental sesame oil

1½ tablespoons sugar

1 teaspoon Chinese chili sauce (optional)

½ teaspoon crushed Sichuan peppercorns

¼ cup minced green onions

2 tablespoons minced fresh coriander (cilantro) (optional)

2 tablespoons finely minced fresh ginger

1 teaspoon grated or minced orange peel

1 clove garlic, finely minced

Ginger Noodle Salad makes a great appetizer — spicy, sweet, and gingery, the noodles stimulate the palate and soften the edges of hunger.

Advance Preparation

Cook noodles according to instructions on page 61. Stir oil into noodles to prevent sticking, then set aside 4 cups.

Snap stems off snow peas, pulling strings off top ridge. Drop snow peas into rapidly boiling water. When they turn bright green (about 5 seconds), transfer with a slotted spoon immediately to a bowl of ice water, reserving cooking water. Pat snow peas dry and cut into shreds.

Peel carrot, then cut on a sharp diagonal into very thin slices. Overlap slices and shred enough to measure 1 cup. Bring reserved cooking water back to a boil. Place carrot pieces in a colander and pour boiling water over. Rinse under cold water, pat dry, and set aside.

Split cucumber in half and scoop out seeds. Cut into long, very thin strips, then cut strips crosswise into 1-inch pieces. Set aside.

Roll ham slices into cylinders. Cut across cylinders, making slivers. Set aside.

Combine dressing ingredients in a jar and shake thoroughly.

Assembling

This salad can be combined hours in advance. Combine noodles, vegetables, and ham so ingredients are evenly mixed. Add dressing and mix again.

Serves: 10 as an appetizer; 6 as a noodle salad.

Menu Ideas: Serve this salad as one of several Oriental appetizers serving 10 — Ginger Noodle Salad, Smoked Tea Squab, and Seafood Pot Stickers in Lemon Sauce.

OVERLEAF: Lemon Shrimp Salad.

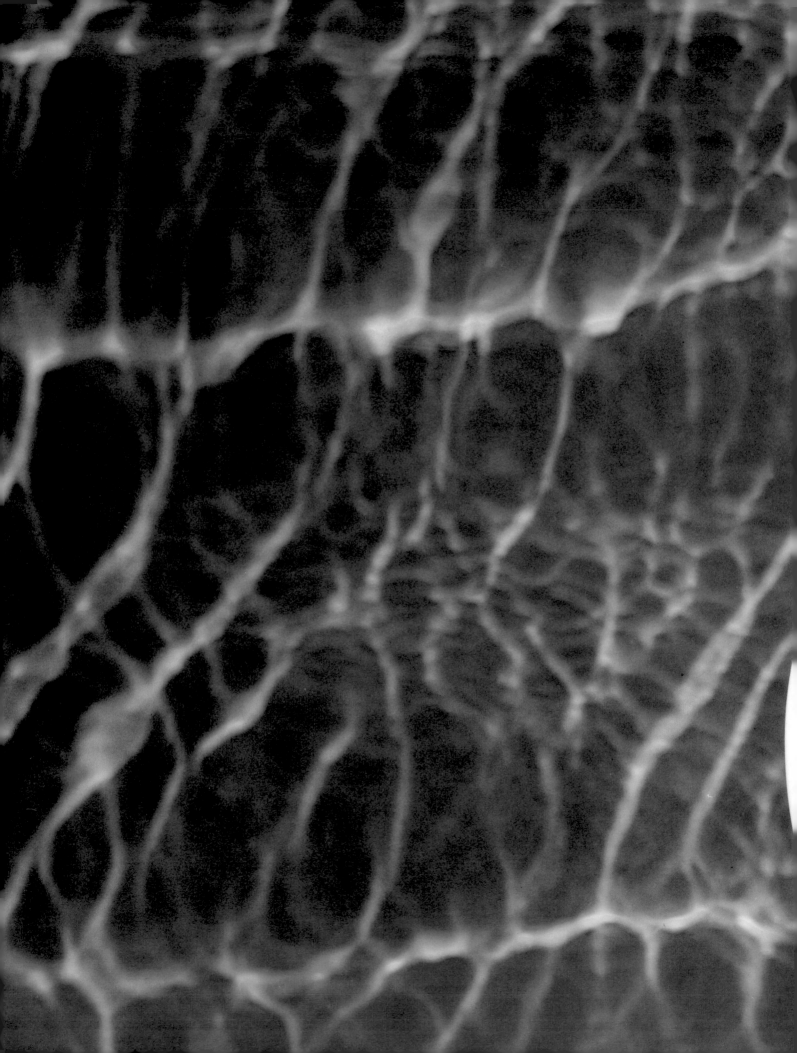

LEMON SHRIMP SALAD

1 pound raw medium shrimp
8 large romaine leaves
1 large carrot
1 pound pencil-thin asparagus
2 green onions
2 ounces rice sticks
peanut oil for shallow-frying (about 3 cups)

Dressing

2 tablespoons grated or minced lemon peel
¼ tablespoons lemon juice
2 tablespoons syrup from preserved stem ginger
2 tablespoons safflower oil
1 tablespoon light soy sauce
½ teaspoon Chinese chili sauce
½ teaspoon salt
1 tablespoon finely minced fresh ginger
1 clove garlic, minced

Lemon Shrimp Salad is a nice alternative to the chicken salad on page 68. With the light citrus taste, it is wonderful to serve on a hot summer night or as a luncheon entrée.

Advance Preparation

Combine dressing ingredients in a jar and shake well.

Shell and devein shrimp. Add shrimp to 3 quarts of rapidly boiling water and cook until white in the center when cut in half, about 2 minutes. Immediately transfer shrimp to ice water and chill, then drain and pat dry. Split shrimp in half, cutting along the back, and set aside.

Stack romaine leaves, then roll into a tight cylinder. Shred the romaine by cutting the cylinder into very thin slices. Refrigerate in a plastic bag.

Peel carrot. Cut on a sharp diagonal into very thin slices, then overlap the slices and shred enough to measure 1 cup. Place carrot slices in colander and pour 1 quart boiling water over them, then rinse under cold water. Pat dry and set aside.

Snap tough ends off asparagus. Cut tender stalks on a sharp diagonal into 1-inch lengths. Bring 2 quarts of water to a vigorous boil and add asparagus. As soon as asparagus turns bright green, scoop out and transfer to ice water. When chilled, drain asparagus and pat dry, then set aside.

Shred green onions and set aside.

Cooking (within 5 Hours of Serving)

In a paper bag, separate the rice sticks into very small bundles. Cook rice sticks as described on page 69.

Last-Minute Assembling

Place all salad ingredients except rice sticks in a very large bowl. Shake dressing, then add and toss immediately. Gently fold in rice sticks, being careful not to crush them. Serve at once.

Serves: 12 as an appetizer; 6 as a dinner salad.

Menu Ideas: This salad makes an excellent luncheon for 6, accompanied by crusty warm bread, sweet butter, white wine, and an Oriental dessert.

▼

SPICY NOODLE SALAD WITH PEANUT DRESSING

¼ **pound dried spaghetti-style noodles, preferably Chinese**

2 **tablespoons safflower oil**

1 **cup shredded iceberg lettuce**

1 **cup fresh bean sprouts**

1 **cup thinly sliced mushrooms (button, enoki, or Japanese shiitake)**

1 **pound pencil-thin asparagus**

1 **large red bell pepper**

Dressing

¼ **cup white sesame seeds**

½ **cup chicken stock, heated to boiling**

½ **cup best-quality peanut butter**

¼ **cup red wine vinegar**

2 **tablespoons dark soy sauce**

2 **tablespoons Oriental sesame oil**

1 **tablespoon dry sherry**

1 **tablespoon sugar**

1½ **teaspoons Chinese chili sauce (optional)**

½ **teaspoon salt**

½ **cup minced green onions**

2 **tablespoons finely minced fresh ginger**

1 **large garlic clove, minced**

One of the pleasures of walking along the streets of ancient Xi'an in the early morning is to sample the rich, spicy noodles available from almost every street vendor. A bowl of these noodles, crisp pan-fried dumplings, and skewers of barbecued lamb are the perfect beginning to an exciting day of China travel.

Advance Preparation

Drop noodles into 6 quarts of lightly salted, rapidly boiling water. Cook over highest heat until noodles are just done, about 4 minutes. Noodles should be firm but no longer raw tasting. Pour cooked noodles into a colander and rinse under cold water, then drain thoroughly. Stir oil into noodles to prevent sticking. Set aside 4 cups of cooked noodles.

Set aside lettuce, sprouts, and mushrooms.

Snap tough ends off asparagus. Cut tender stalks on a sharp diagonal into 1-inch lengths. Bring 2 quarts of water to a vigorous boil and add the asparagus. As soon as asparagus turns bright green, scoop out and transfer to ice water. When chilled, drain asparagus and pat dry. Set aside.

Stem and seed pepper, then cut into slivers. Set aside.

Make the dressing. In a small ungreased skillet set over high heat, stir sesame seeds until light golden. Tip out immediately into a small bowl. Add remaining dressing ingredients to bowl and stir well to blend thoroughly.

Assembling

Combine noodles and vegetables so they are evenly mixed, add dressing, and mix again. The salad can be combined hours in advance but, because the dressing thickens in the refrigerator, bring the salad back to room temperature before serving.

Serves: 10 as an appetizer; 6 as a noodle salad.

Menu Ideas: Include this salad for a picnic along with Mahogany Chicken Wings, Chinese Pickles, Onion Bread, and New Wave Shrimp.

Notes: It is important to always use dried noodles instead of fresh, since the latter quickly become soggy in the salad.

Cooking friends Grant and Sharon Showley substitute hazelnut butter for the peanut butter and get delicious results.

Spicy Noodle Salad with Peanut Dressing;
Coconut Curry Chicken.

62

Spicy Swordfish Salad.

SPICY SWORDFISH SALAD

- 1 **pound grilled or poached swordfish**
- ½ **pound spinach, stemmed**
- 1 **small head radicchio**
- 1 **large yellow bell pepper**
- 2 **ounces fresh Japanese shiitake mushrooms or button mushrooms**
- ½ **cup slivered almonds**
- 14 **won ton skins**
- **peanut oil for shallow-frying (about 2 cups)**

Dressing

- 4 **tablespoons red wine vinegar**
- 2 **tablespoons Oriental sesame oil**
- 2 **tablespoons safflower oil**
- 2 **teaspoons sugar**
- ½ **teaspoon Chinese chili sauce**
- ½ **teaspoon salt**
- 2 **tablespoons finely minced fresh coriander (cilantro)**
- 2 **tablespoons minced green onions**
- 1 **tablespoon finely minced fresh ginger**
- 1 **clove garlic, minced**

Tossing ingredients unknown in classic Chinese cooking, such as swordfish and radicchio, with a Chinese-inspired dressing results in a new-wave Chinese dish. Alternatively, choose more conventional greens and other types of cooked seafood for an equally tasty salad.

Advance Preparation

Cut swordfish into bite-size rectangular pieces.

Wash and thoroughly dry spinach. Bunch spinach together and cut into very thin slivers, about 2½ cups. Refrigerate until ready to assemble.

Sliver enough radicchio to fill 1½ cups. Set aside. Stem and seed pepper, then cut into slivers. Set aside. Cut off and discard mushroom stems. Cut mushrooms into slivers or, if using button mushrooms, into thin slices. Set aside.

Toast almonds on a cookie sheet in a 325°F oven until light golden, about 15 minutes. Set aside.

Cut won tons into ¼-inch strips. Cook as described on page 69. Store in a paper bag at room temperature.

Combine dressing ingredients in a jar and shake vigorously.

Last-Minute Assembling

Place all salad ingredients except won tons in a large bowl. Shake dressing, then add and toss immediately. Gently fold in won tons, being careful not to crush them. Serve at once.

Serves: 4 to 6 as a dinner salad.

Menu Ideas: As a light dinner, serve this salad with a homemade cream of tomato soup, crusty bread, sweet butter, and an Oriental dessert.

SALMON WATERCRESS SALAD

1 pound grilled or poached salmon filet
2 bunches (4 cups) watercress leafy ends
1 large red or yellow bell pepper, seeded and slivered
1 cup slivered jicama
2 green onions, slivered
¼ pound snow peas
½ cup pine nuts (pignoli) or cashews
   Dressing
2 tablespoons safflower oil
1 tablespoon grated or minced lemon peel
4 tablespoons lemon juice
½ teaspoon salt
½ teaspoon Chinese chili sauce
¼ cup preserved stem ginger, minced, plus 2 tablespoons syrup
1 tablespoon finely minced fresh ginger

I first served this salad for friends at their beach house in Santa Barbara. Stuffed tomatoes, warm fresh bread, and homemade ice cream contributed to that balmy evening as we relaxed, watching the sun drop below the distant Channel Islands.

Advance Preparation

Cut salmon into bite-size rectangular pieces. Set aside watercress ends, slivered red pepper, jicama, and green onions.

Snap stems off snow peas, pulling strings off top ridge. Drop snow peas into rapidly boiling water; when they turn bright green (about 5 seconds), transfer immediately to a bowl of ice water. Pat dry and cut each in half on the diagonal. Set aside.

Toast pine nuts or cashews in a 325°F oven until light golden, about 15 minutes. Set aside.

Combine dressing ingredients in a jar and shake well.

Last-Minute Assembling

Place salad ingredients in a large bowl. Shake dressing, then add and toss immediately. Serve at once.

Serves: 6 as a dinner salad.

Menu Ideas: An Oriental dinner for 6 — Spareribs with Secret Chinese Barbecue Sauce, Salmon Watercress Salad, Game Hens in Black-Bean Tomato Sauce, and Mango Sorbet.

OVERLEAF: Shredded Chicken Salad.

65

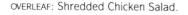

SHREDDED CHICKEN SALAD

- 3 pounds roasted or barbecued chicken
- 1 12-ounce bunch spinach, stemmed
- 1 cup fresh bean sprouts
- 1 large yellow bell pepper, seeded and slivered
- 1 package (3.5 ounces) enoki mushrooms (optional)
- ½ cup slivered almonds
- 10 won ton skins
- 2 ounces rice sticks
- peanut oil for shallow-frying (about 3 cups)
- ¾ cup thinly sliced red sweet ginger

Dressing

- 3 tablespoons red wine vinegar
- 1 tablespoon light soy sauce
- 2 tablespoons Oriental sesame oil
- 1 tablespoon juice from jar of red sweet ginger
- 2 teaspoons hoisin sauce
- ½ teaspoon Chinese chili sauce (optional)
- ½ teaspoon salt
- 3 tablespoons minced green onions
- 1 tablespoon finely minced fresh ginger

No Chinese dish matches this one in popularity. A good Shredded Chicken Salad starts with plenty of barbecued chicken, adds a wide range of shredded vegetables and greens, and tosses in crunchy rice sticks, golden won ton strips, and toasted nuts. With the interplay of colors, textures, and flavors, heightened by the mildly spicy sweet-and-sour dressing, there is always the satisfying murmur of "delicious, delicious. . . ." Serve this salad as the entrée for a light luncheon, as an appetizer, or as a break for the busy cook during an Oriental dinner extravaganza.

Advance Preparation

Pull meat off chicken bones; discard skin. Cut meat into bite-size pieces and set aside.

Wash and thoroughly dry spinach. Bunch spinach together and and cut into very thin slivers. Refrigerate with bean sprouts and pepper until ready to assemble.

Cut off and discard dirty ends of mushrooms. Separate mushroom threads and set aside.

Toast almonds in a 325°F oven until light golden, about 15 minutes. Set aside.

Cut won ton skins into ¼-inch strips. Place rice sticks in a paper grocery bag and, using both hands, pull sticks apart into very small bundles.

Cooking (within 5 Hours of Serving)

In a 10-inch skillet set over medium-high heat, pour in ½ inch of oil and heat until a thread of won ton bounces across the surface. Cook about one third of the won tons at a time, scattering them across the surface. As soon as they turn a very light golden, in about 1 minute, remove to paper towels and drain.

Test oil temperature for cooking rice sticks: When placed in oil, the end of a rice stick should puff up immediately. When ready, add a small number of rice sticks and push apart with chopsticks. As soon as they expand, in about 5 seconds, turn the rice sticks over with chopsticks or tongs and push back into the hot oil to cook 5 more seconds. Drain on paper towels. Repeat with remaining rice sticks, being sure to regulate the heat so oil never smokes. Place won ton strips and rice sticks together in paper bag and store at room temperature.

Combine dressing ingredients in a jar and shake vigorously.

Last-Minute Assembling

Place all salad ingredients except won ton strips and rice sticks in a very large bowl. Shake dressing and add, tossing immediately. Gently fold in won ton strips and rice sticks, being careful not to crush them. Serve at once.

Serves: 12 as an appetizer; 6 to 8 as a dinner salad.

Menu Ideas: A Chinese dinner for 8 — Oriental Pâté, California Won Ton Soup, Shredded Chicken Salad, Scallops in Jade Sauce, and Ginger Crème Brûlée.

Notes: This salad offers so many possible variations. Other cooked meats and seafood can be substituted for chicken; romaine or other greens can be used for the spinach; and you can include whichever vegetables are handy. But be careful when increasing the volume of salad ingredients to also increase the amount of dressing.

Cook the won ton strips and rice sticks within 5 hours of serving, or they will become stale.

■ C H A P T E R   3

Hot-and-sour soup from northern China, lime-scented coconut clam soup from Thailand, and sliced fish in clear chicken stock, all illustrate the diverse flavors of Oriental soups. Spicy Oriental Gazpacho, surrounded by bowls of shredded vegetables, shrimp, and fresh herbs, can become a table centerpiece as an unusual appetizer or as an entrée for a light dinner. Dumplings stuffed with shrimp, ginger, and goat cheese floating in California Won Ton Soup produce an ethereal light taste as a first course. And hearty Velvet Corn Soup, hiding shreds of fresh crab and accompanied by homemade cornbread and a spinach salad, is an utterly delicious dinner. On a spring night, gather friends around the dining table and serve them a big tureen of Scallop Thread Soup, a platter of fresh asparagus glazed with a lemon-butter sauce, and biscuits straight from the oven.

Easy-to-prepare recipes in this chapter are Scallop Thread Soup, Chicken Velvet Soup with Mushrooms, Coconut Clam Soup, and Hot and Sour Seafood Soup.

California Won Ton Soup.

CALIFORNIA WON TON SOUP

40 won ton skins

cornstarch, for dusting

sprigs of fresh coriander (cilantro) or slivered green onions, for garnish

enoki mushrooms, for garnish (optional)

Filling

¾ pound medium raw shrimp

1 12-ounce bunch fresh spinach, stemmed

6 fresh water chestnuts, minced, or ½ cup minced carrots

1 bunch chives, minced

2 green onions, minced

1 tablespoon minced fresh coriander (cilantro)

1 tablespoon finely minced fresh ginger

1 tablespoon curry powder

½ teaspoon salt

¼ teaspoon freshly ground black pepper

4 ounces goat cheese

Clear Soup

8 cups chicken stock

2 tablespoons dry sherry

1 tablespoon Oriental sesame oil

¼ teaspoon white pepper

salt

2 tablespoons cornstarch

California Won Ton Soup typifies the mingling of Pacific cuisines, popularized by California restaurants. The goat cheese in this otherwise authentic Chinese filling gives the dumplings a creaminess and wonderful lightness not always associated with more traditional fillings. This soup, accompanied by a spinach salad and warm individual fruit tarts, is the perfect choice for a romantic dinner.

Advance Preparation

Prepare filling. Shell and devein shrimp, then cut crosswise into the thinnest possible pieces. Drop spinach into 4 inches of boiling water; as soon as spinach wilts (about 15 seconds), pour into a colander and rinse under cold water. Press out all moisture and mince spinach finely. Combine shrimp and spinach with rest of ingredients for filling. Mix well.

Fill and fold dumplings as described on page 23. Set aside.

Last-Minute Assembling

In a large saucepan bring stock to a low boil, then add sherry, oil, white pepper, and salt to taste (about 2 teaspoons). Mix cornstarch with an equal amount of cold water and stir into stock. Keep warm. Bring 6 quarts of water to a rapid boil and add won tons. Stir briefly. When won tons float to surface (about 2 minutes), very gently lift them out of water with a ladle and transfer to hot soup.

Ladle soup into individual bowls or a soup tureen. Garnish with coriander or green onions and mushrooms. Serve at once.

Serves: 3 as an entrée; 6 to 8 as a light first course.

Notes: As a filling variation substitute one of the dumpling fillings in Chapter 7.

CRAB AND ASPARAGUS SOUP

- 1 **small cooked Dungeness crab, cracked and cleaned**
- 6 **cups chicken stock**
- 3 **green onions**
- 4 **dime-size slices fresh ginger**
- 10 **asparagus stalks**
- 1 **egg**
- 1 **tablespoon cornstarch**
- 1 **tablespoon dry sherry**
- 1 **teaspoon Oriental sesame oil**
- ¼ **teaspoon white pepper**
  salt

The flavor of most seafood soups can be enhanced easily by simmering crab, shrimp, or lobster shells in the stock. In this recipe I simmer crab shells in stock for thirty minutes to draw out their flavor. Everything is done hours in advance, with the soup reheated prior to serving.

Advance Preparation
Remove meat from crab shells in large pieces and set aside.

Bring stock to a simmer, then add the crab shells, 1 green onion, and ginger. Simmer, uncovered, for 30 minutes, then strain stock through a dampened cheesecloth or kitchen towel. Let stock cool to room temperature, then refrigerate. Discard shells.

Sliver remaining 2 green onions and set aside.

Snap tough ends off asparagus. Cut tender stalks on a sharp diagonal, rotating each stalk half a turn toward you after each cut. Set aside.

Last-Minute Assembling
Beat egg well. Combine cornstarch with an equal amount of cold water and set aside.

Bring stock to a simmer, then add asparagus. Simmer until asparagus brightens, about 1 minute. Add the sherry, sesame oil, and white pepper and

bring to a low boil. Add 1 tablespoon of hot stock to the beaten egg and stir well, then pour egg mixture in thin stream into the soup, stirring as egg hits the hot liquid. Stir in the cornstarch mixture and let cook at low boil 30 seconds.

Remove soup from heat and add crab meat. Add salt to taste (about 1 teaspoon), then ladle soup into individual bowls or a soup tureen. Garnish with green onion slivers and serve at once.

Serves: 6 as a light first course.

Menu Ideas: Served with Mahogany Chicken Wings and Ginger Noodle Salad, this would be an easy dinner for 4.

Notes: Any other variety of cooked crab with its shell could be substituted for the Dungeness crab. This soup is also excellent with 1½ cups shelled fresh garden peas substituted for the asparagus.

Other variations include simmering 1 cup cubed bean curd in the soup for 5 minutes before adding the sherry and other seasonings, or stirring ⅓ bunch torn spinach leaves into the soup just before serving.

OVERLEAF: Kung Pao Shrimp; Oriental Gazpacho.

ORIENTAL GAZPACHO

- 4 to 6 vine-ripened tomatoes (about 1½ pounds)
- 2 limes, 1 thinly sliced
- 2 tablespoons chopped fresh coriander (cilantro)
- white ends of 4 green onions
- 4 dime-size slices fresh ginger
- 2 cups chicken stock
- 2 tablespoons dry sherry
- 1 tablespoon light soy sauce
- ¼ teaspoon Chinese chili sauce
- salt
- green onion slivers or coriander (cilantro) sprigs, for garnish
- enoki mushrooms, for garnish (optional)

Oriental Gazpacho is made from pureed vine-ripened tomatoes, fresh coriander, lime, and ginger, served chilled with a simple garnish. As a variation, I sometimes serve the soup with small amounts of slivered green onions, sprigs of fresh coriander, enoki mushrooms, chopped jicama, cooked bay shrimp, or flaked crab meat. These garnishes give the soup a more complex taste and texture. On a hot summer night, Oriental Gazpacho is an excellent dinner along with an Oriental salad from Chapter 2, Barbecued Chicken in Satay Sauce, and Ginger Ice Cream.

Advance Preparation
Cut tomatoes in half and squeeze out seeds. Coarsely chop flesh; you should have about 4 cups.

In a saucepan place tomatoes, lime slices, coriander, green onions, ginger, stock, sherry, and soy sauce. Bring to simmer over low heat and cook for 20 minutes. Purée mixture in a food processor or blender, then chill thoroughly.

Add Chinese chili sauce and salt to taste. Grate or finely mince peel of one lime. Stir in a little grated peel and the juice of one or two limes, to taste. Refrigerate until ready to serve, then ladle into chilled bowls.

Last-Minute Assembling
Taste and adjust seasonings. Garnish with green onion slivers and enoki mushrooms.

Serves: 6 as a light first course.

SCALLOP THREAD SOUP

½ **pound large sea scallops**

6 **cups chicken stock**

4 **dime-size slices fresh ginger**

3 **tablespoons dry sherry**

¼ **teaspoon white pepper, or to taste**

   salt

2 **green onions**

2 **ounces good-quality ham, thinly sliced**

2 **tablespoons cornstarch**

The most remarkable transformation occurs when sea scallops are boiled for one hour. Instead of turning into lead shots, each scallop when gently pressed with the back of a fork separates into hundreds of tiny threads. In this soup, their perfumed sweetness mingle perfectly with the slivers of ham, green onions, and a hint of ginger.

Advance Preparation
Rinse scallops with cold water if they have grit or bits of shell on them. Place in a saucepan along with the stock and ginger. Bring stock to low boil over medium heat and skim off any foam that collects on the surface. Cover pan and reduce heat so liquid is at a very low boil. Cook for 1 hour.

Discard ginger and add enough water to bring soup back to original volume. Let soup cool enough so you can rub each scallop between your fingers, separating it into tiny threads. Or, if the soup is still hot, press the scallops with the back of a fork.

Bring soup back to a simmer and add sherry and pepper. Add salt to taste (usually about 1 teaspoon). If made in advance of serving, cool soup to room temperature, then refrigerate until ready to serve.

Cut green onions into slivers. Sliver the ham. Set both aside.

Last-Minute Assembling
Bring soup to a low boil. Taste and adjust seasonings, then combine cornstarch with an equal amount of cold water. Stir into the soup and simmer, uncovered, for 30 seconds. Ladle soup into individual bowls or a soup tureen and garnish with green onions and ham. Serve at once.

Serves: 6 as a light first course.

Menu Ideas: An Oriental dinner for 6 — Scallop Thread Soup, Tender Thai Pork, Marco Polo Noodles, Chinese Eggplant Salad, and fresh fruit.

Chicken Velvet Soup with
Mushrooms; Shrimp Toast Cylinders.

Velvet Corn Soup; Salmon Watercress Salad.

CHICKEN VELVET SOUP WITH MUSHROOMS

4 cups chicken stock

8 large dried black Chinese mushrooms

1 whole chicken breast, boned and skinned

2 teaspoons Oriental sesame oil

¼ teaspoon white pepper

salt

2 tablespoons cornstarch

sprigs of fresh coriander (cilantro) or slivered green onion, for garnish

Marinade

1 egg white

1 tablespoon light soy sauce

2 teaspoons peanut oil

2 teaspoons cornstarch

The meaty texture and earthy flavor of Chinese mushrooms go especially well with homemade stock and thinly sliced chicken breast. You can complete the easy preparation far in advance of serving, then just give the soup a big stir as you add the mushrooms and chicken to the richly flavored stock.

Advance Preparation
Bring stock to a low boil, then remove from heat. Add mushrooms and soak until completely softened, about 1 hour. Gently lift mushrooms from stock. Cut off and discard stems; cut caps into quarters or smaller wedges. Set aside. Strain soup through dampened cheesecloth or kitchen towel and set aside.

For the marinade, lightly beat the egg white to break its gel, then add soy sauce, oil, and cornstarch. Cut chicken into very thin, spoon-size rectangular pieces and combine chicken with the marinade. Refrigerate at least 30 minutes.

Last-Minute Assembling
Bring stock to a low boil over medium heat, then add sesame oil, white pepper, and salt to taste (about 1 to 2 teaspoons).

Combine cornstarch with an equal amount of cold water, then stir into the soup. Stir chicken and add to soup, stirring vigorously to separate the pieces. Add mushrooms and simmer until chicken turns white, about 45 seconds.

Ladle soup into individual bowls or a soup tureen. Garnish with coriander or green onion slivers. Serve at once.

Serves: 4 to 6 as a light first course.

Menu Ideas: A simple Oriental dinner for 6 — Spareribs with Secret Chinese Barbecue Sauce, Chicken Velvet Soup with Mushrooms, Thai Coconut Shrimp, Curried Pineapple Rice, and Ginger Crème Brûlée.

VELVET CORN SOUP

8 ears young corn
½ chicken breast, boned and skinned
2 teaspoons finely minced fresh ginger
1 egg white
¼ teaspoon salt
1 ounce ham, thinly sliced
1 tablespoon cornstarch
3 cups chicken stock
1 teaspoon Oriental sesame oil
¼ teaspoon white pepper
salt
sprigs of fresh coriander, for garnish (optional)

This is a recipe for the freshest corn, picked at the height of the summer crop and shucked as you sprint across the fields toward the kitchen. Velvet Corn Soup looks beautiful in celadon bowls, accompanied by a big garden salad, whole wheat muffins, and fresh peaches.

Advance Preparation
Using a sharp knife, score the center of each row of kernels on 2 ears of corn. Stand ears on end and, using the top of a chef's knife (dull edge), scrape downward with the knife to force out the corn pulp. Set aside ⅔ cup pulp. From remaining ears, cut off and set aside 1 cup corn kernels.

Cut chicken into small cubes and place in bowl. Add ginger, egg white, and salt. Finely mince chicken with seasonings, then set aside.

Roll ham into a cylinder and cut into slivers. Set aside ham as a garnish.

Last-Minute Assembling
Combine cornstarch with an equal amount of cold water. Bring stock to a low boil over medium heat, then stir in cornstarch mixture. Add chicken mixture, stirring well.

Stir corn pulp and kernels into soup, then remove from heat. Season soup with sesame oil, white pepper, and salt to taste (about 1 to 2 teaspoons). Ladle soup into individual bowls or a soup tureen and garnish with ham slivers and coriander sprigs. Serve at once.

Serves: 2 as a main course; 4 to 6 as a light first course.

Notes: A delicious addition just before serving is to stir in ⅓ pound very fresh crab meat.

82   Salmon Flower Soup.

SALMON FLOWER SOUP

6	won tons
2	cups peanut oil
⅓	pound salmon filet, skin removed
1	small napa cabbage (Chinese celery cabbage)
1	package (3.4 ounces) enoki mushrooms (optional)
2	green onions
1	tablespoon finely minced fresh ginger
1½	tablespoons dry sherry
1	tablespoon white sesame seeds
6	cups chicken stock
2	eggs
2	teaspoons Oriental sesame oil
¼	teaspoon white pepper
	salt

A very popular soup in Taiwan involves placing a small amount of napa cabbage, fresh coriander, ginger, and paper-thin slices of raw beef or seafood in each soup bowl, over which is ladled boiling chicken stock. This cooks the ingredients instantly. There are many combinations of greens, wild mushrooms, fresh herbs, and seafood that, when carefully positioned in individual, wide-lipped soup bowls, make a dramatic presentation. If you want to follow the Chinese banquet custom of serving soup after the main entrées, Salmon Flower Soup would be a good choice.

Advance Preparation
Stack won tons, then cut to make thin rectangular pieces. In a 10-inch skillet set over medium heat, heat oil until a strip of won ton skips across the surface. Cook about one-third of the won tons at a time, scattering them across the surface. As soon as they turn a very light golden, in about 1 minute, remove to paper towels and drain.

Cut salmon into very thin rectangular pieces. Set aside.

Tear enough cabbage into small pieces to fill 2 cups, then set aside. Cut off and discard dirty ends of mushrooms; separate mushroom threads and set aside. Sliver green onions and set aside. Moisten ginger with a splash of dry sherry and set aside.

In a small, ungreased skillet set over high heat, stir sesame seeds until light golden, about 2 minutes. Immediately tip out of skillet and set aside.

In 6 individual soup bowls arrange won tons, salmon, cabbage, mushrooms, and green onions to resemble a blossoming flower. Sprinkle over these ingredients the ginger and sesame seeds. Cover bowls with plastic wrap and refrigerate.

Last-Minute Assembling
Bring soup bowls to room temperature. Bring stock to a low boil over medium heat. Beat eggs well, then beat 3 tablespoons hot soup into the eggs. Pour eggs in a thin stream into soup stock, stirring soup as the eggs hit the hot liquid. Stir in remaining sherry, sesame oil, and pepper. Add salt to taste (about 1 teaspoon).

Pour soup into a decorative tureen and bring to table. Place individual soup bowls containing the salmon mixture in front of each person. Individuals ladle the hot soup into their bowls.

Serves: 6 as a light course.
Menu Ideas: Serve this with Oriental Rice Pilaf and Shredded Chicken Salad as a simple but delicious dinner for 6.

COCONUT CLAM SOUP

24 small steamer clams
2 tablespoons cornmeal
1 tablespoon cornstarch
3½ cups unsweetened coconut milk
2 tablespoons dry sherry
3 small green chilies, seeded and slivered, or ½ teaspoon Chinese chili sauce
2 teaspoons grated or finely minced lime peel
1 tablespoon lime juice
 salt
⅓ cup chopped green onions

Steaming Liquid

1 cup chicken stock
½ cup dry white wine
2 tablespoons unsalted butter
4 dime-size slices fresh ginger
3 garlic cloves, peeled and smashed

Tender little steamer clams, pulled from the icy waters of the Pacific Northwest, spring open in the steampot to release the ocean's essence. This fresh clam flavor is combined here with lime zest, green chilies, and coconut milk to produce a rich hot-and-sour citrus taste. Anyone who has explored the twisting outdoor stalls at Newton Circus in Singapore, feasted on Southeast Asian spiny lobsters the size of bowling pins, pulled meat from giant barbecued prawns, or devoured hot chili crabs late into the sultry night will experience gastronomic memories when tasting this soup.

Advance Preparation

Scrub clams under cold water. Place in bowl, cover with cold water, and sprinkle cornmeal across the surface. (The cornmeal makes the clams spit out sand.) Refrigerate for 1 hour, then discard any clams that are not tightly closed. Rinse clams and set aside.

Prepare steaming liquid. In wide saucepan or large frying pan, combine stock, wine, butter, ginger, and garlic. Set aside.

Last-Minute Assembling

Mix cornstarch with an equal amount of cold water. Set aside.

In a 3-quart saucepan, bring coconut milk to a simmer over medium heat. Add sherry and chilies or chili sauce. Keep warm.

Bring steaming liquid to a boil over high heat and add clams, cover, and cook until shells open, about 2 minutes. With a slotted spoon, transfer clams to a bowl.

Strain steaming liquid through a fine-meshed sieve into the simmering coconut milk. Bring to a low boil, then stir in cornstarch mixture and simmer until slightly thickened, about 30 seconds. Remove from heat and stir in lime peel and juice. Add any liquid from the bowl holding the clams. Taste soup, adding salt to taste, about ½ teaspoon. The hot-and-sour taste can be adjusted by adding more chilies or chili sauce or more lime juice.

Stir in green onions, and clams. Ladle soup into individual bowls or a soup tureen. Serve at once.

Serves: 2 for dinner; 6 as part of an Oriental meal.

Menu Ideas: Coconut Clam Soup makes a good dinner for 2 served with buttered noodles, an avocado and tomato salad, and fresh fruit.

Notes: Mussels are an excellent substitute for clams. The same directions for preparation and cooking apply.

HOT-AND-SOUR SEAFOOD SOUP

¼ **pound small raw shrimp**
¼ **pound sea scallops**
¼ **pound crab meat**
¼ **cup dried cloud ears**
½ **bunch (6 ounces)
   spinach, stemmed**
1 **medium carrot**
2 **green onions**
2 **tablespoon cornstarch**
4 **cups chicken stock**
2 **eggs**
   salt
   Seasoning Mix
4 **tablespoons distilled
   white vinegar**
1 **tablespoon dark soy
   sauce**
1 **tablespoon Oriental
   sesame oil**
½ **teaspoon freshly ground
   black pepper**
1 **teaspoon white pepper**
¼ **teaspoon crushed
   Sichuan peppercorns**

Hot-and-sour soup ranks as one of the world's greatest. Served in every home and restaurant across northern and western China, the soup has no standard ingredients other than vinegar and pepper, which give its characteristic flavor. The most delicious version I've tasted is a hot-and-sour sizzling rice tomato soup at the famous Pine Crane Restaurant in Suzhou. You can easily create your own hot-and-sour soup by adding the seasoning mix to an egg drop or won ton soup. Since the sour flavor dissipates quickly as the soup simmers on the stove, always taste the soup and adjust the vinegar or pepper to achieve the hot-and-sour blend you wish.

Advance Preparation
Shell and devein shrimp, then split in half lengthwise. Very thinly slice the scallops. Pull crab meat into small pieces. Set aside shrimp, scallops, and crab.

In 4 cups hot water, soak cloud ears until soft, about 30 minutes. Rinse thoroughly, then chop into spoonsize pieces and set aside.

Tear spinach leaves in half and set aside. Peel carrot, then cut on a sharp diagonal into very thin slices; overlap slices and shred. Shred green onions and set aside.

Combine ingredients for seasoning mix and set aside.

Last-Minute Assembling
Mix cornstarch with an equal amount of cold water. Bring stock to a low boil, add seafood and cloud ears, and bring to a low boil again. Stir in cornstarch mixture. Beat eggs well, then add 2 tablespoons hot soup to the beaten egg and stir well. Pour the egg mixture into soup in a thin stream, stirring soup as the egg hits the hot liquid.

Stir in seasoning mix, then add vegetables. Taste the soup, adding salt to taste (about 1 teaspoon). If necessary, adjust the hot-and-sour flavor by adding more pepper or vinegar.

Ladle soup into individual bowls or a soup tureen. Serve at once.

**Serves: 4 as an entrée; 8
as part of an Oriental meal.**

**Menu Ideas: As a simple
dinner for 4, Hot-and-Sour
Seafood Soup could be
served with a big dish of
buttered asparagus and
Chinese Primavera.**

**Notes: If you are unsure
how hot-and-sour a taste
your guests will like, add
less pepper and vinegar.
Place a small container of
white vinegar and Chinese
chili sauce on the table so
guests can adjust the flavor
of the soup themselves.**

Subtle lemon-ginger marinades, rich black bean sauces, coconut-basil flavors, and spicy tangerine seasonings highlight these seafood dishes ranging from salmon filets to soft-shell crabs. Recipes vary from a simple marinated and barbecued swordfish steak to an elegant and simply delicious seafood "splashdown" on a mound of crisp rice sticks. You might choose to broil clams stuffed with ricotta and ginger as an appetizer; or present a whole Norwegian salmon filet in an Oriental lemon-coriander sauce; or, as a snack, take chilled shrimp flavored with chili and black beans to an outdoor summer concert.

Nowhere is the versatility of Oriental cooking better demonstrated than with seafood. The ability to use sauces interchangeably, or substitute one type of fish for another, or vary the

Scallops in Jade Sauce; Baby
Carrots in Orange Caramel Sauce.

cooking methods leads to exciting new combinations. One night the choices might be broiled sea bass glazed in the sauce from Thai Coconut Shrimp, or stir-fried scallops topped with the fresh tomato-coriander sauce from Summer Squid Stir-Fry. Reading through the chapter should provide you with many ideas for creating your own variations.

Most of the seafood dishes are particularly well suited to be served as the main course for a large gathering. You can steam, broil, or grill fish filets; if your dish requires a sauce, make this separately and add it at the last moment to the cooked fish. Several pounds of poached or steamed shrimp need only be glazed with a sauce taken from Barbecued Sea Bass in Beijing Meat Sauce, Salmon in Chinese Pesto Sauce, Thai Coconut Shrimp, or Summer Squid Stir-Fry. And with a friend, you can prepare a double portion of Seafood Splashdown.

Easy-to-prepare recipes in this chapter are Grilled Swordfish in Lemon-Ginger Marinade, Oriental Sole, Salmon in Ginger Butter Sauce, Salmon in Chinese Pesto Sauce, Thai Coconut Shrimp, and Scallops in Jade Sauce.

SCALLOPS IN JADE SAUCE

1 ½ **pounds large sea scallops**

2 **tablespoons finely minced fresh ginger**

4 **tablespoons butter, cut into small pieces**

salt

freshly ground black pepper

Sauce

1 **12-ounce bunch spinach, stemmed**

1 **bunch chives**

14 **sprigs fresh coriander (cilantro)**

8 **basil leaves**

¼ **cup chicken stock**

¾ **cup heavy (whipping) cream**

½ **teaspoon salt**

¼ **teaspoon Chinese chili sauce**

1 **tablespoon cornstarch**

The ginger-basil sauce in this recipe is delicious spooned around broiled scallops or fish or tossed with freshly cooked noodles.

Advance Preparation

If scallops have any grit or shell fragments, rinse and thoroughly dry. Rub with half the ginger and refrigerate until ready to use.

Make sauce. Wash and thoroughly dry spinach. In a food processor fitted with a metal chopping blade, place spinach, chives, coriander, basil, and 1 tablespoon ginger. Mince the greens to a fine consistency, then add stock and mince 30 seconds more. Add the cream, salt, and chili sauce. Process for 15 seconds, or until it resembles a puréed cream soup. Place mixture in a small saucepan and refrigerate until ready to cook.

Last-Minute Cooking

Preheat oven to 550°F. Place scallops on a baking sheet and dot each with a little bit of butter. Season with a little salt and pepper. Turn oven to Broil and place baking sheet on the highest rack under broiler. Broil scallops without turning until they turn white and are just firm to the touch, about 4 to 6 minutes. If unsure, remove a scallop and cut in half; it should be white in the center.

Meanwhile, combine cornstarch with an equal amount of cold water. Bring sauce to a low boil and, if necessary, stir in a little of the cornstarch mixture to help thicken sauce. Taste and adjust seasonings, especially for salt and pepper.

Glaze 4 dinner plates with the sauce. Position scallops in center of each plate and serve at once.

Serves: 4 as a dinner entrée with rice or noodles and a salad.

Barbecued Sea Bass in Beijing Meat Sauce; Stir-Fried Pork and Shrimp with Tomato Coconut Sauce.

BARBECUED SEA BASS IN BEIJING MEAT SAUCE

2 pounds sea bass filets
2 tablespoons light soy sauce
3 tablespoons dry sherry
1 tablespoon Oriental sesame oil
2 tablespoons cornstarch
1 pound thin asparagus (optional), ends trimmed
2 green onions, shredded

Sauce

1 tablespoon peanut oil
¼ pound ground or shredded pork
1 tablespoon finely minced fresh ginger
1 tablespoon finely minced garlic
¾ cup chicken stock
¼ cup dry sherry
3 tablespoons hoisin sauce
2 tablespoons oyster sauce
1 tablespoon bean sauce (see Appendix)
1 tablespoon red wine vinegar
½ teaspoon Chinese chili sauce

Around the corner from the Beijing Hotel a long, narrow street called Wang Fu Jing is crowded with department stores, art galleries, showrooms filled with the latest three-speed deluxe bicycles, and a number of workers' restaurants serving simple food for just pennies a dish. It is gastronomic paradise to sit in one of these busy restaurants, far removed from the tour-bus circuit. The clatter of plates and animated conversations fill the large room as people slurp up thick home-made noodles covered in a rich meat sauce. This meat sauce is equally good on all firm fish filets, whether steamed, baked, broiled, or barbecued.

Advance Preparation
Prepare sauce. In a 10-inch frying pan set over medium-high heat, add oil. When hot, add pork and sauté, breaking it into little pieces with the back of a spoon, until pork loses all raw color, about 4 minutes. Tip oil out of pan, then add ginger and garlic and cook with pork for 1 minute. Add remaining sauce ingredients. Bring to a low boil, then reduce heat and simmer for 10 minutes. Set aside. Sauce can be made a day in advance and refrigerated.

Combine soy sauce, sherry, and oil. Rub fish with this marinade and refrigerate at least 15 minutes.

Last-Minute Cooking
Bring 8 cups of water to a rapid boil for cooking the asparagus. Combine cornstarch with an equal amount of cold water.

If the sauce has been prepared earlier and refrigerated, bring it to a low boil. Thicken with a little of the cornstarch mixture, then leave sauce over lowest heat.

Barbecue filets over medium heat until they turn very white, just becoming firm to the touch, and begin to flake when prodded with a fork, about 8 minutes. (You can also steam or broil the filets.)

Drop asparagus into rapidly boiling water and cook until it turns bright green, about 30 seconds. Drain. Place a filet on each plate. Radiate the asparagus tips outward from the fish, then spoon sauce over the fish. Garnish with shredded green onions and serve at once.

Serves: 4 as an entrée; 6 to 8 as part of an Oriental dinner.

Menu Ideas: An Oriental seafood dinner for 8 — Marco Polo Dumplings, Scallop Thread Soup, Shredded Crab Salad (Shredded Chicken Salad, but substituting ½ pound crab meat for chicken), Barbecued Sea Bass in Beijing Meat Sauce, and Coconut Ice Cream.

Notes: The meat sauce is delicious on noodles or with cooked shrimp too.

ORIENTAL SOLE

4 filets of sole, each about 6 ounces
1 tablespoon finely minced fresh ginger
2 tablespoons light soy sauce
1 tablespoon lemon juice
4 tablespoons butter, cut into small pieces
1 tablespoon cornstarch
¼ cup chopped chives

Sauce

1 can (14½ ounces) whole tomatoes
1 tablespoon butter
1 tablespoon olive oil
1 tablespoon chopped fresh ginger
3 cloves garlic, chopped
1 large shallot, chopped
1 tablespoon dry sherry
½ teaspoon sugar
⅛ teaspoon Chinese chili sauce

The texture of an ingredient often dictates its cooking method. Sole is a perfect example, for its thin filets and delicate taste make it perfectly suited for brief cooking in a blazing hot broiler. This method yields a taste far superior to breading and pan-frying (a heavy approach to a fragile fish), steaming (gives watery-tasting filets), or barbecuing (the sole quickly disintegrates). If you feel like improvising, substitute the sauce used in Salmon in Chinese Pesto Sauce, Seafood Mousse in Lemon Sauce, or Scallops in Jade Sauce and accompany the sole with baby carrots, rice pilaf, and a cobb lettuce salad.

Advance Preparation
Make sauce (up to a day in advance). Break tomatoes into small pieces with the back of a fork. In a 10-inch sauté pan set over medium heat, add butter and olive oil. When hot, add ginger, garlic, and shallot, then sauté for 1 minute. Add tomatoes and juice, plus sherry, sugar, and chili sauce. Bring sauce to a low boil, then reduce heat to lowest setting and simmer for 30 minutes. Purée sauce for 1 minute in a food processor or blender, then force sauce through a sieve to remove all seeds. Refrigerate until ready to cook fish.

Last-Minute Cooking
Place fish on a lightly oiled baking sheet and rub with ginger, soy sauce, and lemon juice. Position small dots of butter across surface of fish.

Combine cornstarch with an equal amount of cold water, then set aside.

Preheat oven to 550°F, then turn oven setting to Broil. Broil sole on highest rack until it turns white and just becomes firm to the touch, about 2 minutes. Do not turn fish.

Transfer sole to a heated plate. Bring tomato sauce to a low boil and if necessary, thicken with a little of the cornstarch mixture. Carefully spoon sauce around the sole and sprinkle on chives. Serve at once.

Serves: 4 for lunch or dinner.

Notes: Decorate the tomato sauce by using the fine tip of a pastry tube to squeeze a thin line of sour cream around each filet. Take the point of a skewer and make little swirls along the line of sour cream.

STEAMED SHARK IN SPICY BLACK BEAN SAUCE

4 **dried black Chinese mushrooms**
3 **green onions**
1 **red bell pepper**
2 **pounds shark steaks, about 1 inch thick**
3 **tablespoons dry sherry**
2 **tablespoons light soy sauce**
1 **tablespoon oyster sauce**
1 **tablespoon Oriental sesame oil**
1 **tablespoon peanut oil**
2 **tablespoons unsalted butter**
1 **tablespoon cornstarch**

Sauce

1 **tablespoon salted black beans (Pearl River Bridge brand)**
1 **tablespoon finely minced fresh ginger**
1 **tablespoon finely minced garlic**
½ **cup chicken stock**
2 **tablespoons dry sherry**
2 **tablespoons light soy sauce**
1 **tablespoon Oriental sesame oil**
1 **teaspoon Chinese chili sauce**
½ **teaspoon sugar**

This sauce, which takes only minutes to make, is delicious on any steamed, baked, broiled, or grilled fish; poured over poached or sautéed shrimp; or tossed with a steaming bowl of fresh noodles. The key, however, is to use the same type of salted black beans as do Chinese chefs in this country and in Hong Kong — even if it means getting these through mail order.

Advance Preparation
Prepare vegetables. Soak dried mushrooms in hot water until soft, about 20 minutes. Discard stems and shred mushroom caps. Finely mince 1 green onion and set aside. Cut remaining green onions into 2-inch shreds. Seed, steam, and shred the pepper. Refrigerate vegetables.

Combine sherry, soy sauce, oyster sauce, sesame oil, and minced green onion. Rub fish with this marinade. Marinate at least 20 minutes (can be done hours in advance).

Prepare sauce. Place black beans in a sieve and rinse briefly under cold water, then chop coarsely. Combine ginger and garlic with black beans and set aside. In a small bowl combine remaining sauce ingredients, then set aside.

Last-Minute Cooking
Place a layer of foil in a Chinese steamer tray, covering all but 1 inch around the edges to allow steam to circulate. Rub foil with a little cooking oil. Bring water to a rapid boil in the bottom of the steamer, then lay steaks on foil and place steamer tray over boiling water. Cover and steam until shark turns white, just becomes firm to the touch, and begins to flake when prodded with a fork, about 10 minutes.

Place a 10-inch sauté pan over medium-high heat. Add 1 tablespoon butter. When hot, add the black bean mixture and sauté until garlic turns white, about 20 seconds. Add black mushrooms, red pepper, and green onion shreds. After a few seconds, when pepper brightens, add the sauce mixture and bring to a low boil. Mix cornstarch with an equal amount of cold water, then stir a little of this into the sauce to lightly thicken it. Remove from heat and stir in remaining butter.

When fish is cooked, remove steamer tray from boiling water. Lift out foil and slide fish onto a platter or dinner plates. Spoon sauce over top. Serve at once.

Serves: 4 as an entrée; 6 to 8 as part of an Oriental dinner.

Menu Ideas: A Chinese dinner for 6 — Sichuan Roasted Game Hens, Marinated Mushroom Salad, Steamed Shark in Spicy Black Bean Sauce, Marco Polo Noodles, and fresh fruit.

OVERLEAF: Salmon in Chinese Pesto Sauce.

SALMON IN CHINESE PESTO SAUCE

- 1 **pound salmon filet, in 1 or 2 pieces**
- 1 **tablespoon light soy sauce**
- 1 **tablespoon dry sherry**
- 1 **tablespoon Oriental sesame oil**
- 2 **tablespoons peanut oil**
- 1 **tablespoon cornstarch**

Sauce

- 2 **tablespoons finely minced green onions**
- 1 **tablespoon finely minced fresh coriander (cilantro)**
- 2 **tablespoons finely minced fresh ginger**
- 2 **cloves garlic, finely minced**
- 3 **tablespoons lemon juice**
- 3 **tablespoons rice vinegar**
- 2 **tablespoons light soy sauce**
- 2 **tablespoons sugar**
- ½ **teaspoon salt**
- ½ **teaspoon crushed Sichuan peppercorns**
- ¼ **teaspoon freshly ground black pepper**

Chinese pesto sauce, perfected thousands of years ago, was taken to Italy in small jars by Marco Polo along with carefully wrapped bundles of dried noodles, gunpowder formulas, diagrams for folding dumplings, magnets to guide him home, treatises on the art of eating, and a portable printing press to publicize these great advances to twelfth-century Europeans. Here is his pesto sauce.

Advance Preparation

Prepare sauce. Mince green onions and coriander, then set aside. Finely mince ginger, setting aside half of this to later rub over fish. Combine rest of ginger with garlic and set aside. Combine remaining sauce ingredients.

Combine soy sauce, sherry, sesame oil, and reserved minced ginger. Rub fish with this marinade. Marinate at least 20 minutes. (This can be done several hours in advance.)

Last-Minute Cooking

Place a layer of foil in a Chinese steamer tray, covering tray except for 1 inch around edges to allow steam to circulate. Rub foil with a little peanut oil. Bring water to a rapid boil in bottom of Chinese steamer. Lay salmon on foil, place steamer tray over boiling water, and cover. Steam salmon until it turns a lighter pink, just becomes firm to the touch, and flakes when prodded with a fork. A ½-inch-thick filet should take about 5 minutes.

Combine cornstarch with an equal amount of cold water. Place 10-inch sauté pan over medium-high heat. Add 1 tablespoon peanut oil. When hot, add ginger and garlic mixture. Sauté 15 seconds, then add lemon juice mixture. Bring to a very low boil, stir in green onions and coriander, then stir in a little of the cornstarch mixture to lightly thicken sauce. Remove from heat.

When salmon is cooked, remove steamer tray from boiling water. Lift out foil and slide fish off onto platter or dinner plates. Spoon sauce over fish. Serve at once.

Serves: 2 as a main course; 6 as part of an Oriental dinner.

Menu Ideas: A romantic dinner for 2 — Spareribs with Secret Chinese Barbecue Sauce, a garden salad, Salmon in Chinese Pesto Sauce, Oriental Rice Pilaf, and Oriental Fruit Tart.

Notes: The salmon is excellent served at room temperature or eaten cold while you stand right in front of the refrigerator! The pesto sauce is good on any steamed, baked, broiled, or grilled firm-fleshed fish filet.

SUMMER SQUID STIR-FRY

1½ pounds small squid

8 dried black Chinese mushrooms

6 green onions

3 cloves garlic, finely minced

2 cups seeded and chopped vine-ripened tomatoes

½ cup coarsely chopped fresh coriander (cilantro)

3 tablespoons peanut oil

Sauce

¼ cup dry sherry

1 tablespoon oyster sauce

2 teaspoons curry powder

1 teaspoon Oriental sesame oil

½ teaspoon sugar

2 tablespoons cornstarch

Tiny twists of squid display their diamond pattern among the chopped fresh summer tomatoes, black mushrooms, and fresh coriander — achieving sort of a Tex-Chinese look! Served with Mahogany Chicken Wings, Marinated Mushroom Salad, and individual fruit tarts, this makes a nice dinner.

Advance Preparation
Clean squid. Pull head from squid and cut tentacles off in one piece. If black mouth is in the center of the tentacles, pull this away and discard. Discard rest of head. Under cold running water, rub off squid skin with your fingers. Run a thin knife inside the squid and cut squid open into a flat steak. Clean inside thoroughly. Make light lengthwise cuts ½ inch apart along the inside of squid steak, being careful not to cut all the way through. Make light crosswise cuts ½ inch apart, creating a diamond pattern. Cut each steak into 4 quarters, then refrigerate, along with tentacles, until ready to cook.

Soak mushrooms in hot water until soft, about 20 minutes. Discard stems and cut mushrooms into quarters. Cut green onions on a diagonal into 1-inch lengths and set aside with mushrooms.

For sauce, in a small bowl combine sherry, oyster sauce, curry powder, sesame oil, and sugar. Set aside until ready to cook.

Last-Minute Cooking
Combine cornstarch with an equal amount of cold water and set aside. Thoroughly dry squid.

Place wok over highest heat. When wok becomes very hot, add 2 tablespoons peanut oil to center. Roll oil around sides of wok. When oil just begins to smoke, add squid and stir-fry until it just turns white, about 15 seconds. Transfer squid to work platter.

Immediately return wok to highest heat. Add remaining tablespoon peanut oil to center. Add garlic and sauté a few seconds, then add mushrooms and green onions. Stir-fry until green onions brighten, about 1 minute.

Add tomatoes and coriander and stir-fry until tomatoes are just heated, about 20 seconds. Return squid to wok and add sauce. When sauce comes to a low boil, stir in a little of the cornstarch mixture so sauce glazes the food. Taste and adjust seasonings. Pour out onto a heated platter and serve at once.

Serves: 2 as an entrée; 4 to 6 as part of an Oriental dinner.

FESTIVAL FISH

6 dried black Chinese mushrooms

8 water chestnuts, preferably fresh

3 green onions

3 fresh hot green chilies

1 whole rock cod or snapper (about 3 pounds) scaled and cleaned

2 tablespoons grated or minced tangerine or orange peel

1 tablespoon finely minced fresh ginger

1 tablespoon finely minced garlic

1 teaspoon crushed Sichuan peppercorns

Sauce

¾ cup chicken stock

3 tablespoons dry sherry

1 tablespoon light soy sauce

1 teaspoon dark soy sauce

1 teaspoon red wine vinegar

¼ teaspoon salt

2 tablespoons cornstarch

1 tablespoon peanut oil

Whole fish that are good for steaming include red snapper, rock cod, freshwater bass, sea bass, large lake trout, pike, and catfish. But the real key to this dish is picking fish whose sparkling skin, bulging eyes, and scarlet gills proclaim its freshness.

Advance Preparation
Soak mushrooms in hot water until soft, about 20 minutes. Discard stems and cut caps into quarters or eighths. Thinly slice water chestnuts. Cut green onions on a sharp diagonal into 1-inch lengths. Seed and mince chilies. Set vegetables aside.

With the knife angled toward the head, cut diagonally from the back fin to the belly, making 4 deep cuts to the bone on each side of the fish. Inside the slashes place minced chilies, tangerine peel, ginger, garlic, and peppercorns. Refrigerate fish until ready to steam.

In small bowl combine stock, sherry, soy sauces, vinegar, and salt.

Last-Minute Cooking
Combine cornstarch with an equal amount of cold water.

Bring water to a rapid boil in the bottom of a Chinese steamer. Place a double layer of foil in steamer tray, making sure there is plenty of room around edges to allow steam to circulate. Turn edges of foil up to help trap accumulated juices. Rub foil with a little cooking oil, then lay fish on foil, place steamer tray over boiling water, and cover. Steam fish until flesh becomes white and a chopstick easily sinks into the meat, about 15 minutes.

When fish is cooked, pour liquid that accumulates around fish into the bowl with sauce mixture. Slide fish from foil onto heated platter. Place a 10-inch skillet over high heat. When hot, add oil. When oil is hot, add mushrooms, water chestnuts, and green onions. Sauté until onions brighten, then add sauce mixture. Bring to a low boil, then stir in a little of the cornstarch mixture to lightly thicken sauce. Pour over fish and serve.

Serves: 2 as an entrée; 6 to 8 as part of an Oriental dinner.

Menu Ideas: Chinese dinner for 8 — Vietnamese Spring Rolls (make filling a day ahead; roll spring rolls morning of dinner); Hot-and-Sour Seafood Soup (except for adding seafood at last moment, soup can be made 2 days in advance and simply reheated); Shredded Chicken Salad (make salad dressing a day ahead; buy a roast chicken from the market to shorten preparation time); Festival Fish; Oriental Rice Pilaf; fresh fruit and Chocolate Chip Almond Cookies (make cookie dough ahead and store in the freezer; bake on day of dinner).

Festival Fish; Asparagus in Black Bean Sauce.

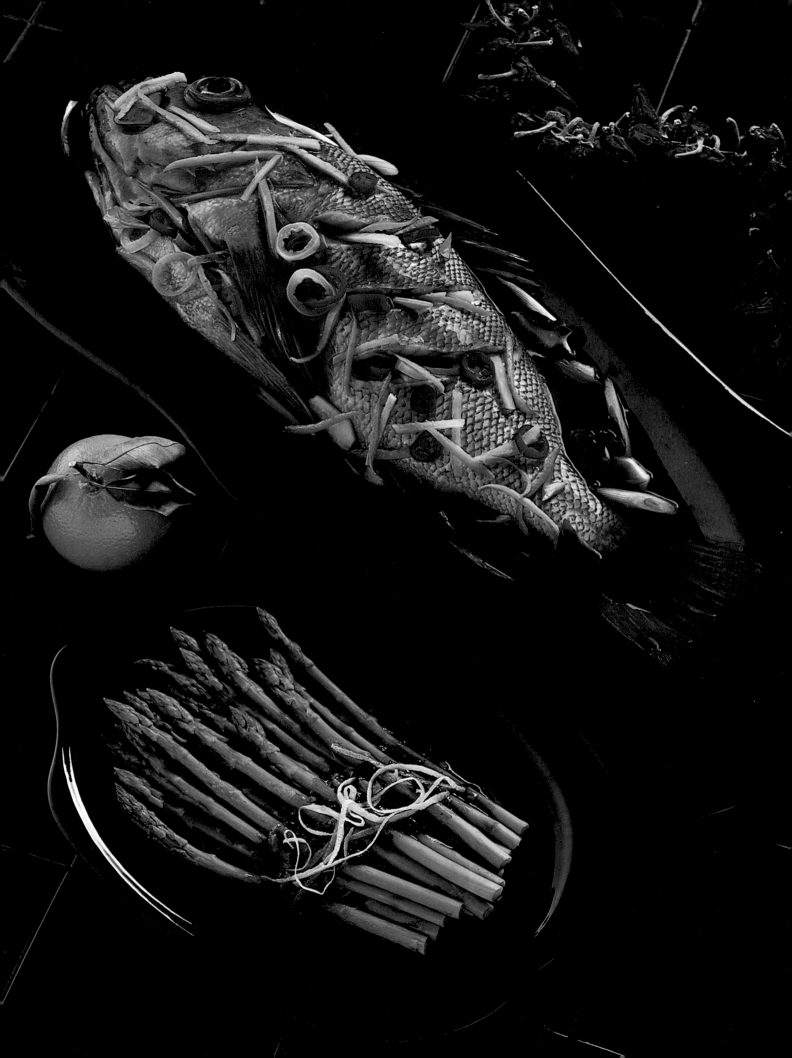

SALMON IN GINGER BUTTER SAUCE

2 salmon filets, ½ pound each

3 tablespoons dry sherry

2 tablespoons light soy sauce

1 tablespoon Oriental sesame oil

1 tablespoon finely minced fresh ginger

2 tablespoons chopped fresh parsley

2 tablespoons butter

freshly ground black pepper

salt

1 lemon

This is a perfect dish for those nights you want to minimize time in the kitchen. After marinating and briefly cooking the filets, the fish is transferred to heated plates and served, accompanied by lemon wedges, sourdough rolls, and a green salad.

Advance Preparation

Combine sherry, soy sauce, and oil. Rub filets with this marinade. Rub ginger across top of filets, then sprinkle on parsley. Dot butter evenly across surface. Add black pepper and a sprinkling of salt to taste. (This can be done several hours in advance.)

Cut lemon into wedges.

Last-Minute Cooking

To broil, preheat oven to 550°F, then turn oven to Broil. Place salmon about 4 inches below heat and cook without turning until fish turns a lighter pink, just becomes firm to the touch, and begins to flake when prodded with a fork, about 5 minutes.

To steam, place a layer of foil in a Chinese steamer tray, covering all but 1 inch around the edges to allow steam to circulate. Rub foil with a little oil. Bring water to a rapid boil in bottom of steamer, then lay salmon on foil. Place steamer tray over boiling water, cover, and steam salmon until it turns a light pink, just becomes firm to the touch, and begins to flake when prodded with a fork, about 10 minutes.

Transfer filets to heated dinner plates. Garnish with lemon wedges.

Serves: 2 as a dinner entrée.

RAINBOW STEAMED FISH

1 whole rock cod or snapper (about 3 pounds) scaled and cleaned
1 cup slivered green onions
½ cup slivered ham
½ cup slivered hot red chilies or red bell peppers
¼ cup very finely slivered or minced fresh ginger
½ cup fresh coriander (cilantro)
6 tablespoons dry sherry
¼ cup Oriental sesame oil
3 tablespoons light soy sauce
3 tablespoons oyster sauce
1 teaspoon sugar
2 tablespoons cornstarch

A fish that only moments ago swam in the ocean depths is scored and decorated with slivers of green onion, coriander, red pepper, and ginger, to be steamed and brought to the table.

Advance Preparation
With the knife angled toward the head, cut diagonally from the back fin to the belly to make 4 deep cuts to the bone on each side of the fish. Inside the slashes place the green onions, ham, chilies, ginger, and coriander.

Combine sherry, sesame oil, soy sauce, oyster sauce, and sugar. Sprinkle mixture evenly over both sides of fish and in the slashes. Marinate fish 3 hours.

Last-Minute Cooking
Drain fish, reserving marinade in a small saucepan.

Combine cornstarch with an equal amount of cold water.

Bring water to a rapid boil in the bottom of a Chinese steamer. Place a double layer of foil in the steamer tray, making sure there is plenty of room around edges to allow steam to circulate. Turn edges of foil up to help trap accumulated juices and rub foil with a little oil. Lay fish on foil, place steamer tray over boiling water, and cover. Steam fish until flesh becomes white and a chopstick easily sinks into the meat, about 15 minutes.

Pour accumulated liquid around fish into saucepan with marinade. Slide fish from foil onto a heated platter. Bring marinade to a low boil and lightly thicken with a little of the cornstarch mixture, then pour over fish.

Using a fork and spoon, each person pulls pieces of fish filet away from the bones.

Serves: 2 as an entrée; 6 to 8 as part of an Oriental dinner.

Menu Ideas: Nearly half the weight of a 3-pound rock cod is the head and bones. While you could serve the fish as an entrée for 2 or 3, accompanied by a rice dish and salad, this dish has more impact as part of several Oriental dishes for a larger party. Choose do-ahead appetizers (New Wave Shrimp or Mahogany Chicken Wings), one of the salads from Chapter 2, Oriental Braised Veal Shanks, and Fireworks Rice — dishes that do not require much last-minute attention in the kitchen.

SEAFOOD MOUSSE IN LEMON SAUCE

- ¼ cup butter
- 4 teaspoons grated or finely minced lemon peel
- 2 teaspoons finely minced fresh ginger
- ½ pound (exactly) very fresh white sea bass, sole, or grouper filets, cut into 1-inch cubes
- 1 egg
- ¾ teaspoon salt
- ¼ teaspoon white pepper
- 1¼ cups heavy (whipping) cream, very cold
- ¼ cup minced water chestnuts, preferably fresh
- 2 ounces fresh crab meat, flaked

  dill sprigs, parsley, or watercress, for garnish

  Sauce
- ½ cup lemon juice
- ¼ cup plus 2 tablespoons sugar
- ¼ cup chicken stock
- 2 tablespoons light soy sauce
- ½ teaspoon salt
- 2 tablespoons cornstarch

Served hot or chilled, this seafood mousse is bathed in a lemon sauce and makes a stunning lunch entrée or a small first course before the dinner entrée.

Advance Preparation
Generously butter twenty-four 1-ounce molds, sixteen 1½-ounce molds, or one 3-cup mold.

In a food processor with a metal cutting blade, place 1½ teaspoons lemon peel, the minced ginger, fish cubes, and egg. Purée until mixture is completely smooth, then place processor bowl in refrigerator for 2 hours. Chill thoroughly.

Return processor bowl to machine and add salt and white pepper. With machine on, slowly pour chilled cream down feed tube in a thin stream. Turn mixture into a bowl and stir in water chestnuts and crab meat. You should have approximately 3 cups.

Spoon mixture into buttered mold(s). If serving chilled, proceed with cooking. If serving mousse hot, mixture can be refrigerated up to 8 hours prior to cooking.

For sauce, in a small saucepan, place lemon juice, sugar, stock, soy sauce, salt, and remaining lemon peel. Set aside.

Last-Minute Cooking
Preheat oven to 325°F. Generously butter one side of parchment paper(s) and then cover mold(s) with paper(s). Place mold(s) in baking pan and put in oven. Carefully pour enough hot water into pan to come halfway up mold(s). Cook as follows: 10 minutes for 1-ounce molds, 12 minutes for 1½-ounce molds, and 24 minutes for 3-cup mold. Mousse is cooked when a knife inserted in the mousse comes out clean.

Carefully remove baking pan from oven, then remove mold(s) from water. Turn upside down onto serving plate or individual plates. Tap lightly on top with spoon, shaking gently to unmold. Combine cornstarch with an equal amount of cold water. Bring lemon mixture to a low boil, then stir in a little of the cornstarch mixture to lightly thicken. Ladle sauce over mousse and serve hot.

If serving mousse chilled, let lemon sauce return to room temperature, then ladle over chilled mousse just before serving.

Garnish with dill sprigs, parsley, or watercress.

Notes: It is very important to use very fresh fish and to chill the fish and cream thoroughly, or the mousse will separate during cooking. Use exactly ½ pound fish, or there will be either too little fish to bind with the cream or too much fish, which results in a heavy mousse.

Seafood Mousse in Lemon Sauce.

TROUT WITH SPICY TANGERINE SAUCE

6 dried black Chinese mushrooms

8 water chestnuts, preferably fresh

3 green onions

¼ cup cornstarch, for dusting

2 trout, ½ pound each (preferably with bones in)

½ cup peanut oil

1 tablespoon finely minced fresh ginger

1 tablespoon grated or minced fresh tangerine or orange peel

1 clove garlic, finely minced

Sauce

¾ cup chicken stock

3 tablespoons dry sherry

1 tablespoon light soy sauce

1 tablespoon Oriental sesame oil

½ teaspoon salt

½ teaspoon Chinese chili sauce

¼ teaspoon sugar

2 tablespoons cornstarch

I like the technique of briefly sautéeing trout, temporarily removing them from the pan while the sauce boils down to pick up the lingering fish flavor, and then turning the trout back and forth in the sauce before serving. Other sauces used in this chapter that work well with trout are those from Barbecued Sea Bass in Beijing Meat Sauce, Steamed Shark in Spicy Black Bean Sauce, Salmon in Chinese Pesto Sauce, and Seafood Mousse in Lemon Sauce.

Advance Preparation
Prepare vegetables. Soak dried mushrooms in hot water until soft, about 20 minutes. Discard stems and cut mushroom caps into quarters. Thinly slice water chestnuts. Cut green onions diagonally into 2-inch lengths. Set vegetables aside.

For sauce, combine stock, sherry, soy sauce, sesame oil, salt, chili sauce, and sugar in a small bowl.

Last-Minute Cooking
Mix 2 tablespoons cornstarch with an equal amount of cold water and set aside.

Place trout on a layer of newspaper. Dust with ¼ cup cornstarch, shaking to remove excess.. Place a heavy 12-inch sauté pan over medium-high heat. When very hot, add oil. When oil becomes very hot (should appear thinner and give off a little haze), add trout. Agitate pan to prevent skin from sticking and pan-fry trout for about 3 minutes on each side, regulating heat so oil always sizzles but does not smoke. Trout are cooked when the end of a chopstick easily sinks into the flesh.

Remove trout to a layer of paper toweling and pour oil from frying pan. Return frying pan to medium-high heat and add ginger, tangerine peel, and garlic. Sauté a few seconds, then add mushrooms, water chestnuts, and green onions. Sauté until onions brighten, then add sauce mixture. Bring sauce to a low boil. Stir in a little of the cornstarch mixture to lightly thicken sauce, then immediately return trout to pan. Turn trout over in sauce, then transfer to a heated platter or plates. Spoon sauce over trout. Serve at once.

Serves: 2 as a dinner entrée.

Menu Ideas: Dinner for 6 — Mahogany Chicken Wings, Trout with Spicy Tangerine Sauce (triple the recipe), Curried Pineapple Rice, and Mango Sorbet.

▼ ▼ ▼

KUNG PAO SHRIMP

- 1 **pound medium raw shrimp**
- 1 **green bell pepper**
- 2 **green onions**
- 1 **cup shelled and skinned raw peanuts**
- 1 **cup peanut oil plus 2 tablespoons for stir-frying**
- 1 **tablespoon finely minced fresh ginger**
- 1 **tablespoon finely minced garlic**
- ½ **cup small dried red chilies**
- Sauce
- ¼ **cup dry sherry**
- 1 **tablespoon dark soy sauce**
- 1 **tablespoon hoisin sauce**
- 1 **tablespoon Oriental sesame oil**
- 2 **teaspoons red wine vinegar**
- 1 **teaspoon Chinese chili sauce**
- ¼ **teaspoon crushed Sichuan peppercorns**
- ¼ **teaspoon salt**
- 1 **tablespoon cornstarch**

The most famous dish from Sichuan, Kung Pao Shrimp is named after a famous nineteenth-century general, whose chef created this dish of shrimp, chilies, and peanuts. In restaurants the fiery taste comes from searing dried chilies until they blacken. Without commercial venting systems this dish is best seasoned at home with Chinese chili sauce and fistfuls of chilies thrown in just to add a colorful garnish.

Advance Preparation

Shell and devein shrimp. Pat dry and cut shrimp into ¼-inch pieces. Refrigerate until ready to cook.

Seed and cut pepper into ¼- to ½-inch cubes. Cut green onions into ¼-inch pieces. Set aside both pepper and green onions.

Place peanuts in a small saucepan. Add 1 cup peanut oil and place saucepan over highest heat. Stir peanuts continually until they turn a very light gold, about 2 minutes. Pour peanuts into a sieve placed over a heatproof bowl, then cool drained peanuts on paper toweling. Set aside.

For sauce, in a small bowl combine sherry, soy sauce, hoisin sauce, sesame oil, vinegar, chili sauce, peppercorns, and salt. Set aside.

Last-Minute cooking

Combine cornstarch with an equal amount of cold water. Set aside.

Place wok over highest heat. When wok becomes very hot, add 1 tablespoon peanut oil to center. Roll oil around sides of wok. When oil just begins to smoke, add shrimp and stir-fry until they just turn white, about 2 minutes. Transfer shrimp to work platter.

Immediately return wok to highest heat and add 1 tablespoon peanut oil to center. Add ginger and garlic and sauté a few seconds. Add vegetables and stir-fry until vegetables brighten, about 2 minutes.

Return shrimp to wok and add peanuts and chilies, then pour in sauce. When sauce comes to a low boil, stir in a little of the cornstarch mixture so the sauce glazes the food. Taste and adjust seasonings, then tip out onto a heated platter or individual plates. Serve at once.

Serves: 2 as the dinner entrée with rice and salad; 6 to 8 as part of an Oriental dinner.

Menu Ideas: A "cook-in" for 3 couples — Kung Pao Shrimp (double recipe; use 2 woks and have one of the guests stir-fry a portion duplicating your every move); Oriental Rice Pilaf; Marinated Mushroom Salad; then Hot-and-sour Seafood Soup; concluded by chilled melon balls and ice cream.

Notes: As a variation, for the shrimp substitute 2 marinated boned and cubed chicken breasts (see Chicken with Pine Nuts). Or, raw cashews are excellent in place of the peanuts.

THAI COCONUT SHRIMP

1 pound medium raw shrimp

¼ pound small button mushrooms

1 tablespoon peanut oil

1 tablespoon butter

4 cloves garlic, finely minced

¼ cup chopped purple basil

¼ cup chopped mint leaves

¼ cup chopped green onions

Sauce

1 cup unsweetened coconut milk

1 tablespoon dry sherry

½ teaspoon Chinese chili sauce

¼ teaspoon salt

1 tablespoon cornstarch

1 tablespoon lime juice

Homemade coconut milk is made by shattering a coconut and prying the white flesh away from the shell. The flesh is then grated and processed with hot water in a food processor to make a purée. As a final step, the coconut purée is placed in a thin cloth and squeezed to extract all the beautiful coconut milk. Luckily, all Oriental markets sell canned Thai coconut milk that will add exactly the same wonderful Pacific flavor to this dish.

Advance Preparation
Shell and devein shrimp, splitting them nearly in half. Pat dry and refrigerate until ready to cook.

Wipe mushrooms clean and trim off ends of stems; set aside.

For sauce, in a small bowl combine coconut milk, sherry, chili sauce, and salt. Set aside.

Last-Minute Cooking
Combine cornstarch with an equal amount of cold water. Set aside.

Place wok or sauté pan over highest heat. When very hot, add oil and butter. When butter melts and begins to bubble, add garlic. Sauté a few seconds, then add shrimp. Stir and toss shrimp over highest heat until shrimp just turn white, about 2 minutes. Add mushrooms, basil, mint, and green onions. Stir-fry 15 seconds, then add coconut-milk. When mixture comes to a low boil, stir in a little of the cornstarch mixture to lightly thicken. Stir in lime juice, then spoon sauce onto a heated platter or dinner plates. Serve at once.

Serves: 2 as a dinner entrée; 6 to 8 as part of an Oriental dinner.

Menu Ideas: Quick dinner for 6 — Barbecue Chicken in Satay Sauce (roast individual pieces and serve as a first course at room temperature), Garden Greens with Oriental Dressing, Thai Coconut Shrimp (double recipe), buttered noodles, and ice cream.

Notes: This sauce is also delicious on spaghetti-type Chinese noodles. Omit shrimp and in a 10-inch sauté pan sauté garlic in a little butter. Add basil, mint, and green onions and cook briefly. Add coconut-milk mixture and bring to a simmer, then cook for 5 minutes. Thicken with a little cornstarch and add lime juice. Pour over noodles and serve at once.

Thai Coconut Shrimp; basmati rice.

VOLCANO SCALLOPS

1 pound sea scallops
1 small green bell pepper
1 small red bell pepper
2 green onions
2 tablespoons cornstarch
3 tablespoons peanut oil
¼ pound ground pork
6 cloves garlic, finely minced
2 teaspoons finely minced fresh ginger
   salt
   Sauce
2 tablespoons dry sherry
1 tablespoon dark soy sauce
1 tablespoon Oriental sesame oil
2 teaspoons red wine vinegar
1 teaspoon Chinese chili sauce
½ teaspoon sugar
¼ teaspoon crushed Sichuan peppercorns

Thick rain clouds clung to the hills, forbidding any escape from the industrial megalopolis of Chongqing, in the heartland of China. A psychic gloom blanketed us as we rode silently that evening to the Small Cave From Heaven Restaurant. Thirty courses later, having consumed quail eggs on velvet chicken, whole flathead fish, sautéed geese tongues with greens, and a terrific chili scallop dish with peppers and ground pork, we staggered back to our hotel rooms convinced that even in adversity a great dinner brings hope.

Advance Preparation
Thinly slice the scallops and refrigerate until ready to use.

Stem and seed the peppers, then cut into ½-inch cubes. Cut green onions on a diagonal into ½-inch pieces. Place vegetables together in a bowl and refrigerate until ready to use.

For sauce, in a small bowl combine sherry, soy sauce, sesame oil, vinegar, chili sauce, sugar, and peppercorns. Set aside.

Last-Minute Cooking
Combine cornstarch with an equal amount of cold water and set aside.

Place wok over highest heat. When wok becomes very hot, add 1 tablespoon oil to center. Roll oil around sides of wok. When oil just begins to smoke, add scallops and stir-fry until they just turn white, about 1 minute. Transfer scallops to work platter.

Immediately return wok to highest heat and add remaining oil. Add pork and stir-fry until it loses all raw color, about 1 minute. Press the meat with the back of your spoon to break it into grounds.

Pour excess oil from wok, then add garlic and ginger and stir-fry with pork for a few seconds. Add vegetables and stir-fry until vegetables brighten, about 2 minutes.

Return scallops to wok and pour in sauce. When sauce comes to a low boil, stir in a little of the cornstarch mixture so sauce glazes the food. Taste and adjust seasonings, especially for chili flavor and salt. Turn out onto a heated platter and serve at once.

Serves: 2 to 3 as a dinner entrée; 6 to 8 as part of an Oriental dinner.

Notes: The pork gives this dish a rich taste, but you can leave it out or substitute ground lamb.

BLACK BEAN SCALLOPS ON JULIENNED VEGETABLES

1 tablespoon salted black beans

3 cloves garlic, finely minced

2 tablespoons butter

2 tablespoons peanut oil

1½ cups finely slivered carrots

1½ cups finely slivered snow peas

1½ cups finely slivered turnips

1 pound bay scallops

Sauce

¼ cup chicken stock

2 tablespoons dry sherry

1 tablespoon sesame oil

1 tablespoon light soy sauce

½ teaspoon Chinese chili sauce

½ teaspoon sugar

salt

1 tablespoon cornstarch

Stir-fried meat or seafood tossed with vegetables can result in a hodgepodge of ingredients. Instead, stir-fry the shredded vegetables and position them on a platter to act as a colorful throne upon which to put the glistening meat or seafood. This recipe is an example of such a presentation.

Advance Preparation
Place black beans in a sieve and rinse briefly under cold water, then coarsely chop. Combine with garlic and set aside.

For sauce, in a small bowl combine stock, sherry, sesame oil, soy sauce, chili sauce, sugar, and salt. Set aside.

Last-Minute Cooking
Combine cornstarch with an equal amount of cold water. Set aside.

Place wok over highest heat. When wok becomes very hot, add 1 tablespoon butter and 1 tablespoon peanut oil to center. Roll around sides of wok. When butter begins to foam, add vegetables and stir-fry until they brighten, about 1 minute. Turn onto a heated serving platter and spread in an even layer.

Immediately return wok to highest heat and add remaining tablespoon peanut oil to center. Add black beans and garlic, then sauté a few seconds. Add scallops and stir-fry until they turn white, about 2 minutes.

Pour in sauce. When sauce comes to a low boil, stir in a little of the cornstarch mixture so sauce glazes the food. Stir in remaining butter. Taste and adjust seasonings, especially for salt. Pour scallops into center of vegetables and serve at once.

Serves: 2 to 3 as a dinner entrée; 6 to 8 as part of an Oriental dinner.

Menu Ideas: An Oriental dinner for 6 — Chinese Pickles, New Wave Shrimp, Shredded Chicken Salad, Black Bean Scallops on Julienned Vegetables, Marco Polo Noodles, and a rich homemade chocolate cake.

SEAFOOD SPLASHDOWN

Midway through a fourteen-course banquet at a friend's home, we turned up the music, went outside, and danced under a starry sky. The joy of eating is often the catalyst for good conversation, unplanned events, and the uncorking of extra champagne. This banquet finale was an elaborate stir-fry in a delicate shrimp sauce, "landed" on a thick bed of crispy white rice sticks. Quite a landing! Quite a splashdown!

Seafood Splashdown.

SEAFOOD SPLASHDOWN

⅓ pound medium raw shrimp

¼ pound small button mushrooms, stems trimmed

¼ pound thin asparagus

10 water chestnuts, preferably fresh

3 green onions

2 ounces rice sticks

3 cups peanut oil, plus 2 tablespoons for stir-frying

⅓ pound bay scallops

⅓ pound lump crab meat or ½ pound king crab claws in the shell

Sauce

1 tablespoon chopped fresh ginger

3 cloves garlic, chopped

1 cup chicken stock

¼ cup dry sherry

1 tablespoon light soy sauce

1 tablespoon Oriental sesame oil

¼ teaspoon white pepper

¼ teaspoon salt

2 tablespoons cornstarch

Advance Preparation

Shell and devein shrimp, splitting in half lengthwise. Save shells. Pat shrimp dry and refrigerate until ready to cook.

Prepare sauce. In a food processor with a metal cutting blade, place shrimp shells, ginger, garlic, stock, sherry, soy sauce, sesame oil, white pepper, and salt. Blend for 1 minute, then transfer to a small saucepan. Bring to a simmer, cover, and cook over low heat for 30 minutes. Return mixture to processor and process once again for 1 minute. Strain mixture through a fine-mesh sieve or cheesecloth, then cool to room temperature. Refrigerate until ready to use.

Thinly slice mushrooms. Snap off and discard tough asparagus ends, then cut asparagus on a very sharp diagonal into 1-inch pieces. Thinly slice water chestnuts. Cut green onions diagonally into 1-inch lengths. Place vegetables together in a bowl and refrigerate until ready to use.

Place rice sticks in a paper bag and separate into very small bundles. Cook rice sticks as described on page 69.

Last-Minute Cooking

Break rice sticks into shorter lengths, then spread evenly across the surface of a platter.

Combine cornstarch with an equal amount of cold water.

Place wok over highest heat. When wok becomes very hot, add 1 tablespoon oil to center. Roll oil around sides of wok. When oil just begins to smoke, add shrimp and scallops and stir-fry until shrimp just turn white, about 2 minutes. Transfer shrimp and scallops to work platter.

Immediately return wok to highest heat and add remaining tablespoon oil. Add vegetables and stir-fry until asparagus brightens, about 2 minutes. Add crab meat or claws and return shrimp and scallops to wok, too. Pour in sauce. When sauce comes to a low boil, stir in a little of the cornstarch mixture so sauce glazes the food. Taste and adjust seasonings, especially for salt, pepper, and sesame oil. Pour out onto rice sticks and serve immediately.

Serves: 2 as a dinner entrée; 6 to 8 as part of an Oriental dinner.

GRILLED SWORDFISH IN LEMON-GINGER MARINADE

2 pounds swordfish steaks, 1 inch thick

Marinade

1 tablespoon grated or minced lemon peel

⅓ cup lemon juice

¼ cup dry white wine

3 tablespoons safflower oil

2 tablespoons light soy sauce

¼ teaspoon black pepper

¼ cup minced green onions

1 tablespoon finely minced fresh ginger

2 cloves garlic, finely minced

A simple ginger-lemon marinade brushed across the top of swordfish steaks during cooking keeps the fish moist and gives a lingering flavor. Serve this swordfish with one of the rice dishes from Chapter 7 and a tomato-avocado salad.

Advance Preparation

Combine marinade ingredients. Place swordfish in a ceramic, glass, or stainless-steel container (not aluminum or iron) and cover with marinade. Let marinate for 1 hour.

Cooking

Remove fish from marinade. Pour marinade into small saucepan over high heat. Bring to a vigorous boil, then remove from heat.

Prepare a charcoal fire and grill swordfish over medium heat, brushing marinade over fish as it cooks. Or preheat oven to 550°F, then turn oven setting to Broil and broil swordfish on highest rack for about 8 minutes. Turn swordfish once, basting with the marinade. Swordfish is done when it just becomes firm to the touch and begins to flake when prodded with a fork.

Place swordfish on heated plates. Spoon a little of the marinade over each piece. Serve at once.

Serves: 6 as part of a light lunch; 4 for dinner.

MUSSELS IN COCONUT SAFFRON SAUCE

- 16 mussels, preferably from New Zealand
- ¼ teaspoon saffron threads
- ½ cup chicken stock
- ½ cup dry white wine
- 2 tablespoons parsley stems
- 1 tablespoon unsalted butter
- ¼ teaspoon Chinese chili sauce
- 2 teaspoons Sichuan peppercorns
- 2 tablespoons cornstarch
- 1 cup unsweetened coconut milk
- 1 bunch chives, chopped

Among the most delicious new foods appearing in our markets are the large, green-lipped New Zealand mussels, whose shells enclose a bright orange interior infinitely more tender and sweeter than their North American cousins. This recipe is one we have served for six guests, along with Oriental Pâté (made two days in advance),

Shredded Chicken Salad (prepared that morning and tossed when we moved to the dining room), Oriental Rice Pilaf, and a fruit tart or homemade ice cream.

Advance Preparation
Within 4 hours of cooking, scrub mussels, pulling away any seaweed from between the shells. Refrigerate mussels until ready to cook.

In a 12-inch frying pan combine saffron and stock. Bring to a low boil, then remove from heat and let cool. Add wine, parsley stems, butter, and chili sauce. Set aside.

Place a 10-inch frying pan over high heat. Add the peppercorns and roast until they begin to smoke, about 3 minutes. Remove from pan. Add half the peppercorns to the stock mixture and reserve the rest.

Last-Minute Cooking
Combine cornstarch with an equal amount of cold water.

Over high heat, bring stock mixture to a rapid boil, then add mussels. Cover and steam until mussels open, about 4 minutes. Put mussels into a colander lined with cheesecloth, reserving liquid. Discard any mussels that have not opened.

Immediately return frying pan to stove and pour steaming liquid back into it. Add coconut milk and bring to a low boil. Stir in a little of the cornstarch mixture to lightly thicken sauce, then add remaining roasted peppercorns and chives.

Return mussels to pan and toss briefly in sauce. Turn out onto a heated platter or plates. Serve at once.

Serves: 2 as a dinner entrée; 4 to 8 as part of an Oriental dinner.

Mussels in Coconut Saffron Sauce.

CHINESE CLAMS CASINO

- **22** littleneck clams, tightly shut
- **2** tablespoons cornmeal
- **1** 12-ounce bunch fresh spinach, stemmed
- **6** tablespoons butter
- **½** cup finely minced red bell pepper
- **½** cup plain bread crumbs
- **2** shallots, minced
- **2** teaspoons finely minced fresh ginger
- **1½** teaspoons grated or finely minced lemon peel
- **¼** teaspoon white pepper
- **½** cup ricotta cheese
  dry white wine (optional)
  rock salt
  lemon wedges

The shells from tender clams such as littleneck and cherrystones are perfect containers for this mixture of chopped clams, spinach, ginger, and ricotta. Served hot on a bed of rock salt, Chinese Clams Casino make a great appetizer or light first course, or a dinner entrée for two with salad.

Advance Preparation
Scrub clams, then cover with cold water. Add cornmeal and soak for 1 hour. Rinse clams and discard any that are not tightly closed. In a 12-inch frying pan, bring ½ inch water to a rapid boil over high heat. Add clams, cover, and steam until they open, about 5 minutes. Discard any clams that do not open. Place clams in a bowl and cool. Strain liquid through a fine sieve and also save liquid that accumulates in bowl. Remove clams from shells and chop finely. Add clams and reserved clam liquid to a mixing bowl. Set aside 16 shell halves.

Wash spinach. Drop into 4 inches of boiling water. As soon as spinach wilts (about 15 seconds), pour into a colander and rinse under cold water. Press out all moisture and mince finely, then add to clams.

Place a 10-inch sauté pan over high heat and add 3 tablespoons butter. When butter begins to foam, add red pepper and sauté 30 seconds. Add bread crumbs and continue stirring for 1 minute. Stir half the bread crumb mixture into the clams and set aside the rest.

Add shallots, ginger, lemon peel, white pepper, and ricotta to the clams. Mix thoroughly. If mixture seems dry, add a little white wine to moisten.

Fill 16 shell halves with mixture, then sprinkle on reserved bread crumbs. Dot each clam with little bits of the remaining butter. Refrigerate until ready to broil.

Last-Minute Cooking
Preheat oven to 550°F. Lay rock salt in bottom of several foil pie plates and position clams on the salt. Turn oven to Broil, then place plates 4 inches from heat and cook until the clams are browned on top, about 3 minutes. Immediately place pie plates on a heatproof dish and serve at once, garnished with lemon wedges.

Serves: 4 as a light first course; 8 as an appetizer.

Menu Ideas: Serve these as an appetizer preceding a dinner of Spicy Soft-Shell Crabs, fresh pasta with olive oil and grated Parmesan, and a tossed green salad.

Notes: This recipe is also very good when mussels are substituted for clams. Another approach is to broil the stuffed clams or mussels on a cookie sheet. When cooked, transfer to a heated platter. Separately in small sauté pan make the sauce from Barbecued Sea Bass in Beijing Meat Sauce or Asparagus in Black Bean Butter Sauce. Lightly thicken sauce with a mixture of cornstarch and water before spooning sauce over clams.

SPICY SOFT-SHELL CRABS

- 4 soft-shell crabs, cleaned
- ½ cup dry white wine
- 1 tablespoon Oriental sesame oil
- ½ teaspoon Chinese chili sauce
- ¼ teaspoon crushed Sichuan peppercorns
- ¼ teaspoon sugar
- 2 tablespoons cornstarch
- 1 tablespoon peanut oil
- 1 tablespoon butter
- 1 tablespoon grated or minced tangerine or orange peel
- 3 cloves garlic, finely minced
- 3 tablespoons chopped fresh coriander (cilantro) or green onions, for garnish

This easy recipe is a high-impact dish, especially for those enjoying the novelty of eating the sweet crab for the first time. The paper-soft shell is highlighted by a mildly spicy tangerine sauce. Served with basmati rice and a tomato-basil salad, this makes an utterly delicious dinner. Soft-shell crabs are extremely perishable and should be cooked within four hours of purchase.

Advance Preparation
Place crabs on a plate. Cover with a damp cloth and refrigerate until ready to cook.

In a small bowl combine wine, sesame oil, chili sauce, peppercorns, and sugar. Set aside.

Last-Minute Cooking
Combine cornstarch with an equal amount of cold water and set aside.

Place a 12-inch frying pan over medium-high heat. Add oil and butter, then add tangerine peel and garlic. Sauté garlic a few seconds. Add crabs and sauté about 1 minute, then pour in wine mixture.

Cover and cook over medium-high heat until crabs turn red, about 3 minutes.

Push crabs to one side. Stir in a little of the cornstarch mixture to lightly thicken sauce, then turn out mixture onto a heated platter or plates. Sprinkle with coriander or green onions and serve at once.

Serves: 2 as a dinner entrée.

Notes: I have found it quite easy to double this recipe, sautéeing crabs in 2 frying pans simultaneously and serving these as an entrée for 4. And this would make a spectacular dish as part of an Oriental dinner for 8, augmented by other, more substantial dishes.

This chapter captures the essence of Pacific-style food: inexpensive ingredients, easy cooking techniques, and innovative tastes achieved with readily available Oriental condiments and European herbs. Whether the dish is barbecued chicken, whose marinade lies trapped between the skin and meat; or stir-fried chicken with tangerine and pine nuts; or roasted game hens glistening in a spicy lemon sauce, the preparation and cooking techniques are elementary and the time required to finish each dish is minimal.

Easy-to-prepare recipes in this chapter are Barbecued Chicken in Satay Sauce, Chicken with Chinese Herbs, Roast Citrus Chicken, Bangkok Chicken, Grilled Chicken with Oriental Cucumber Relish, Pan-Fried Sichuan Chicken, Sichuan Barbecued Game Hens, Roast Game Hens in Spicy Orange Glaze, and Roast Game Hens in Spicy Lemon Sauce.

Chicken with Pine Nuts.

119

CHICKEN WITH PINE NUTS

4 chicken breast halves, boned and skinned
1 tablespoon dry sherry
1 tablespoon light soy sauce
1 tablespoon plus 2 teaspoons cornstarch
2 tablespoons plus 2 teaspoons peanut oil
1 cup pine nuts (pignoli)
2 small zucchini
2 green onions
4 cloves garlic, minced
1 tablespoon grated or minced tangerine or orange peel
Sauce
¼ cup dry sherry
2 tablespoons tomato sauce
1 tablespoon Oriental sesame oil
2 teaspoons hoisin sauce
2 teaspoons distilled white vinegar
1 teaspoon Chinese chili sauce
¼ teaspoon salt

Tender marinated chicken, buttery pine nuts, and cubes of zucchini, stir-fried in a sizzling wok and served with a spicy tomato sauce, make a satisfying dish whether one is eating alone or entertaining.

Advance Preparation
Cut chicken lengthwise into ¼-inch-wide slices. Place slices together and cut crosswise into ¼-inch cubes. Mix chicken cubes with sherry, soy sauce, 2 teaspoons cornstarch, and 2 teaspoons oil. Refrigerate until ready to cook.

Toast pine nuts in a 325°F oven until very light golden, about 10 minutes. Tip into a small bowl and set aside.

Cut zucchini in half lengthwise, then lengthwise again into quarters. Place strips together and cut crosswise into ¼-inch pieces. Cut green onions on the diagonal into ¼-inch pieces. Combine with zucchini and refrigerate until ready to cook.

In a small bowl, combine ingredients for sauce. Set aside.

Last-Minute Cooking
Combine remaining 1 tablespoon cornstarch with an equal amount of cold water; set aside.

Place wok over highest heat. When wok becomes very hot, add 1 tablespoon oil to center of wok. Roll oil around sides of wok. When oil just begins to smoke, add chicken and stir-fry until it just loses raw outside color, about 2 minutes. Transfer chicken to a work platter.

Immediately return wok to highest heat. Add remaining 1 tablespoon oil to center, then add garlic and tangerine peel. Sauté a few seconds, then add vegetables and stir-fry until vegetables brighten, about 2 minutes.

Return chicken to wok and pour in sauce. When sauce comes to a low boil, stir in a little of the cornstarch mixture so sauce glazes the food. Stir in pine nuts, then taste and adjust seasonings. Spoon onto a heated platter or individual plates. Serve at once.

Serves: 4 as an entrée with rice and salad; 6 to 8 as part of an Oriental dinner.
Menu Ideas: A quick Chinese dinner for 6 — 2 pounds of chilled shrimp with 2 dipping sauces, Marinated Mushroom Salad, Chicken with Pine Nuts, Marco Polo Noodles (double recipe), and fresh fruit.

BARBECUED CHICKEN IN SATAY SAUCE

- 1 **3-pound chicken, split in half**
- 4 **cloves garlic, finely minced**
- 1 **tablespoon finely minced fresh ginger**
- 1 **shallot, minced**
- 1 **green onion, minced**
- 1 **tablespoon minced fresh coriander (cilantro)**
- 3 **tablespoons dry sherry**
- 2 **tablespoons hoisin sauce**
- 1 **tablespoon light soy sauce**
- 1 **tablespoon dark soy sauce**
- 1 **tablespoon distilled white vinegar**
- 1 **tablespoon Oriental sesame oil**
- 1 **tablespoon plum sauce**
- 1 **tablespoon smooth peanut butter**
- 1 **tablespoon honey**
- 1 **teaspoon Chinese chili sauce**

One of the most effective techniques for barbecuing or roasting poultry, whether it be a tiny quail or a giant Tom turkey, is to work the marinade between the skin and meat. Trapped in this tight envelope, with the remaining marinade slathered on the outside, the aromatic seasonings permeate the meat during cooking, then provide an intense release of flavor with each bit. This chicken makes an easy dinner entrée accompanied by a salad, or it could be a picnic dish when cut into pieces. You can easily vary the flavor by using one of the other barbecue sauces in this book or by creating your own blend of fresh garden herbs, oil, and Oriental condiments.

Advance Preparation
Taking 1 chicken half, loosen the skin along the top of the breast. Gently push your index finger underneath the skin, moving it along the breast, thigh, and drumstick and being careful not to dislodge the skin attached to the backbone.

Combine remaining ingredients and stir well. Spoon about one-fourth of the marinade under the skin and, with your fingers, massage the outside of the skin to work the marinade over the breast meat, thigh, and drumstick. Rub another one-fourth of the marinade over the entire outside surface of chicken, then set the chicken half aside. Repeat process with other chicken half, then let the chicken marinate in the refrigerator for at least 2 hours.

Cooking
Prepare a charcoal fire. When coals are ash-colored, grill chicken halves until the temperature reaches 165°F on a meat thermometer, about 30 minutes. When pierced with a fork, juices should run clear. Or roast chicken halves meat side up in a 425°F oven for about 30 minutes.

Serve chicken hot, at room temperature, or cold. If you wield a Chinese cleaver with great dexterity, chop chicken into bite-size pieces before serving cold as part of a picnic.

Serves: 2 as an entrée.

ROAST CHICKEN WITH CHINESE HERBS

2 3-pound chickens, cut into pieces

salt

freshly ground black pepper

3 tablespoons butter, cut into pieces

Sauce

2 tablespoons cornstarch

4 cloves garlic, finely minced

1 tablespoon finely minced fresh ginger

1 shallot, minced

2 green onions, minced

¼ cup minced fresh coriander (cilantro)

1 cup chicken stock

¼ cup dry sherry

¼ cup hoisin sauce

2 tablespoons Oriental sesame oil

1 tablespoon dark soy sauce

1 teaspoon sugar

½ teaspoon Chinese chili sauce

Roasted or barbecued chicken pieces tossed in an Oriental sauce make a satisfying dinner when served with a big garden salad and a rice dish from Chapter 7. You might serve an imported dark beer to match the robust taste.

Cooking

Preheat oven to 425°F. Place chicken in a roasting pan and season with salt and pepper. Dot chicken with butter, then roast chicken for about 30 to 40 minutes, basting every 10 minutes with the pan juices. Chicken is done when the juices run clear.

While chicken roasts, combine cornstarch with an equal amount of cold water. Combine garlic, ginger, shallot, green onions, and coriander in a bowl. In a separate container, combine remaining ingredients. Set aside.

When chicken is cooked, temporarily remove it from roasting pan. Discard all but 2 tablespoons fat from the roasting pan, then place roasting pan over high heat and add the garlic-green onion combination. Sauté until the green onions brighten, about 1 minute. Add stock mixture and bring to a low boil, scraping up pan drippings. Stir in a little cornstarch mixture to lightly thicken sauce, then taste and adjust seasonings. Return chicken to pan and coat evenly with sauce. Place chicken on heated dinner plates and serve at once.

Serves: 6 as an entrée.

Notes: This sauce is good served on boiled new potatoes or fresh pasta. Other excellent sauces for these roasted chicken pieces are the Beijing Meat Sauce, Spicy Black Bean Sauce, and Lemon Sauce.

Roast Chicken with Chinese Herbs;
Curried Pineapple Rice.

123

ROAST CITRUS CHICKEN

2 3-pound chickens, cut into pieces

freshly ground black pepper

3 tablespoons butter, cut into pieces

2 tablespoons white sesame seeds

2 tablespoons cornstarch

Sauce

1 tablespoon finely minced fresh ginger

3 green onions, minced

1½ tablespoons grated or minced orange peel

¾ cup chicken stock

1 tablespoon light soy sauce

3 tablespoons dry sherry

1½ tablespoons Oriental sesame oil

1½ tablespoons oyster sauce

1 teaspoon sugar

½ teaspoon Chinese chili sauce

¼ teaspoon crushed Sichuan peppercorns

Orange peel, ginger, and chili flavorings enhance the tender roast chicken and crisp skin. For a quick dinner, this is a good selection.

Cooking

Preheat oven to 425°F. Place chicken in a roasting pan and season with pepper. Dot chicken with butter, then roast for about 30 to 40 minutes, basting chicken every 10 minutes with the pan juices. Chicken is done when the internal temperature reaches 165°F on a meat thermometer and when the juices run clear.

While the chicken roasts, toast sesame seeds in an ungreased skillet until golden and set aside. Combine cornstarch with an equal amount of cold water.

Prepare sauce. Combine ginger, green onions, and orange peel. In a small bowl, combine remaining sauce ingredients.

When chicken is cooked, remove from roasting pan. Discard all but 2 tablespoons fat from pan, then place pan over high heat and add ginger mixture. Sauté until green onions brighten, about 1 minute. Add stock mixture. Bring to a low boil, scraping up pan drippings, and stir in a little cornstarch mixture to lightly thicken sauce. Taste sauce and adjust seasonings. Return chicken to pan and coat evenly with sauce. Sprinkle with sesame seeds. Place chicken on heated dinner plates and serve at once.

Serves: 6 as an entrée.

Menu Ideas: Do-ahead Chinese dinner for 10 — chilled large shrimp (2 pounds) with dipping sauces, Chinese Pickles (double recipe), Spicy Swordfish Salad (double recipe), Roast Citrus Chicken (double recipe), Chinese Primavera (triple recipe), and homemade apple pie.

BANGKOK CHICKEN

- 1 3-pound chicken, cut into pieces
- freshly ground black pepper
- 3 tablespoons butter, cut into pieces
- 1 tablespoon cornstarch

Sauce

- 3 cloves garlic, finely minced
- 1 tablespoon finely minced fresh ginger
- ¼ cup minced green onions
- ¼ cup minced fresh basil
- 2 tablespoons minced fresh mint
- 1 cup unsweetened coconut milk
- 2 tablespoons light soy sauce
- ½ teaspoon turmeric
- ½ teaspoon Chinese chili sauce
- ¼ teaspoon salt
- mint sprigs, for garnish

Bangkok: In this city of golden palaces, houses on stilts lining old canals, modern office structures, and massage parlors, talented chefs create gastronomic magic. One night a few years ago, our taxi inched forward along roads clogged with motor bikes, black-windowed limousines, and diesel trucks and then with a spasmodic thrust sped past somber militia and blurred saffron-colored robes toward a distant restaurant. Here is my version of one of the dishes we ate that night, a barbecued chicken bathed in coconut herb sauce.

Cooking

Preheat oven to 425°F. Place chicken in a roasting pan and season with pepper. Dot chicken with butter, then roast for about 30 to 40 minutes, basting every 10 minutes with pan juices. Chicken is done when internal temperature reaches 165°F on a meat thermometer and when the juices run clear.

While the chicken roasts, combine cornstarch with an equal amount of cold water. Combine garlic, ginger, green onions, basil, and mint. In a separate bowl, combine remaining sauce ingredients. Set aside.

When chicken is cooked, remove it from roasting pan. Discard all but 2 tablespoons fat from pan, then place pan over high heat and add garlic mixture. Sauté until green onions brighten, about 1 minute. Add coconut mixture. Bring to a low boil, scraping up pan drippings, and stir in a little cornstarch mixture to lightly thicken sauce. Taste sauce and adjust seasonings. Return chicken to pan and coat evenly with sauce. Place chicken on heated dinner plates and garnish with mint sprigs. Serve at once.

Serves: 4 as an entrée.
Menu Ideas: Thai dinner for 10 — Beef Satay (double recipe), Thai Papaya Shrimp Salad (double recipe), Bangkok Chicken (quadruple recipe), Spicy Thai Noodles (triple recipe), Coconut Ice Cream.

OVERLEAF: Snow Peas on Turnip Nest; Grilled Chicken with Oriental Cucumber Relish.

GRILLED CHICKEN WITH ORIENTAL CUCUMBER RELISH

4 chicken breast halves, boned and skinned

2 tablespoons light soy sauce

1 tablespoon dry sherry

1 tablespoon safflower oil

1 teaspoon grated or minced lime peel

1 tablespoon lime juice

¼ teaspoon ground cinnamon

1 clove garlic, finely minced

Relish

½ cup seeded and chopped hothouse cucumber

1 plum tomato, seeded and chopped

¼ cup chopped fresh coriander (cilantro)

1 jalapeño chili, seeded and finely minced

1 clove garlic, finely minced

1 teaspoon grated or minced lime peel

2 tablespoons lime juice

2 tablespoons fish sauce

1 tablespoon vegetable oil

2 teaspoons sugar

This is one of the easiest recipes in the book. The boneless chicken breasts can marinate in the refrigerator all day. They are then grilled and served alongside a spicy cucumber relish.

Advance Preparation
Rinse chicken and pat dry. Combine soy sauce, sherry, oil, lime peel and juice, cinnamon, and garlic. Marinate chicken in mixture for at least 1 hour.

Prepare relish. Mix cucumber, tomato, coriander, chili, and garlic. Add remaining ingredients and stir well.

Cooking .
Prepare a charcoal fire. When coals are ash-colored, grill chicken about 2 minutes on each side. Chicken is done when it is firm to the touch.

Serve accompanied with relish to spoon over chicken.

Serves: 2 as an entrée with rice and a salad.

ROAST GAME HENS IN SPICY ORANGE GLAZE

2 game hens, split in half
2 tablespoons unsalted butter
Sauce
2 tablespoons finely minced fresh ginger
1 green onion, minced
1 tablespoon grated or minced orange peel
¼ cup white sesame seeds
3 tablespoons hoisin sauce
2 tablespoons orange marmalade
2 tablespoons dry sherry
2 tablespoons red wine vinegar
1 tablespoon plum sauce
1 teaspoon Chinese chili sauce

This spicy orange and sesame-seed barbecue sauce is also delicious as a marinade for veal chops and then brushed across the top of the meat as it grills. In this recipe the remaining sauce is reduced to a glaze in the roasting pan and then spooned across the top of the game hens.

Advance Preparation
Prepare sauce. In a small bowl, combine ginger, green onion, and orange peel. Toast sesame seeds in an ungreased skillet over high heat until golden, then add to the bowl along with remaining sauce ingredients.

Loosen skin of game hens. Spoon some of the sauce under the skin and work the sauce over the breast meat, thigh, and drumstick. Rub a little more over the outside of the game hens. Marinate for at least 2 hours in the refrigerator.

Cooking
Preheat oven to 425°F. Drain off excess marinade into a small bowl. Place game hens, meat side up, in a roasting pan. Dot with small pieces of butter and roast until golden, basting every 10 minutes. Game hens are done when internal temperature reaches 165°F on a meat thermometer and the juices from the meat run clear, about 30 minutes.

Place game hens on 2 warmed dinner plates. Discard fat from roasting pan. Place roasting pan over highest heat and add reserved marinade. Boil sauce, scraping pan drippings, until sauce begins to thicken. Brush over game hens and serve them at once.

Serves: 2 to 4 as an entrée.
Menu Ideas: Dinner for 2 — Roast Game Hens in Spicy Orange Glaze, steamed asparagus, homemade rolls, fresh fruit.

CLASSIC MU SHU CHICKEN

3 chicken breast halves, boned and skinned

1 tablespoon dry sherry

2 teaspoons dark soy sauce

1 tablespoon plus 2 teaspoons cornstarch

3 tablespoons plus 2 teaspoons peanut oil

6 dried black Chinese mushrooms

⅓ cup dried cloud ears (optional)

2 cups shredded green cabbage

3 green onions, shredded

4 eggs

12 Peking pancakes (see Appendix)

2 cloves garlic, finely minced

2 teaspoons finely minced fresh ginger

¾ cup hoisin sauce

Sauce

3 tablespoons chicken stock

2 tablespoons dry sherry

1 tablespoon dark soy sauce

1 tablespoon Oriental sesame oil

½ teaspoon sugar

½ teaspoon salt

¼ teaspoon freshly ground black pepper

An old Chinese proverb states: "In Heaven paradise; on earth Mu Shu Chicken." Shredded chicken, mushrooms, cabbage, and eggs are rolled in tender, steamed Peking pancakes.

Advance Preparation

Cut chicken lengthwise into thinnest possible slices. Place slices together and cut crosswise into 1-inch lengths. In a bowl, mix chicken shreds with sherry, soy sauce, 2 teaspoons cornstarch, and 2 teaspoons peanut oil. Refrigerate until ready to cook.

Soak dried mushrooms in hot water until soft, about 20 minutes. Discard stems; stack caps and cut into shreds. Soak cloud ears in hot water until soft and expanded, about 20 minutes. Place cloud ears in a colander and rinse with cold water, then squeeze out excess water. Push cloud ears into a mound and cut into slivers. Combine mushrooms, cloud ears, cabbage, and green onions. (If not using cloud ears, add an extra cup slivered cabbage.)

Break eggs into a small bowl. Set aside. Combine ingredients for sauce and set aside.

Last-Minute Cooking

Beat eggs well. Combine remaining 1 tablespoon cornstarch with an equal amount of cold water and then set aside.

Fold pancakes into quarters. Place in a Chinese steamer tray, overlapping them to fit them all in, and cover together and cut crosswise into 1-inch lengths. In a bowl, mix steamer. Steam over rapidly boiling water for 2 minutes. Keep warm.

Place wok over highest heat. When wok becomes very hot, add 1 tablespoon peanut oil to center of wok. Roll oil around sides of wok. When oil just begins to smoke, add eggs. Stir-fry the eggs, scrambling them until they become firm, about 1 minute. Place cooked eggs in a bowl.

Immediately return wok to highest heat. Add 1 tablespoon peanut oil to center of wok and roll around sides. Add chicken and stir-fry until the chicken just loses raw outside color, about 2 minutes. Transfer chicken to bowl with eggs.

Immediately return wok to highest heat. Add remaining 1 tablespoon peanut oil to center, then add garlic and ginger. Sauté a few seconds, then add vegetables, stir-frying until cabbage brightens, about 2 minutes.

Return eggs and chicken to wok, then pour in sauce mixture. When sauce comes to a low boil, stir in a little of the cornstarch mixture so sauce glazes the food. Taste and adjust seasonings, then trans-

fer to a heated platter. Serve chicken mixture with hot pancakes and a dish of hoisin sauce. Each person spreads a little hoisin sauce across the center of a pancake, places about ½ cup filling on top of sauce, then rolls the pancake into a cylinder, folding the bottom end upward to keep the fill-ing from escaping. Filled pancakes are eaten with the fingers.

Serves: 4 as an entrée; 6 to 8 as part of an Oriental dinner.

Menu Ideas: This dish makes a beautiful dinner for 4 accompanied by steamed or poached broc-coli in an herbed butter sauce, a garden salad, and a rich dessert.

Notes: As a substitute for the chicken, use ¾ pound diced or slivered pork loin, top sirloin, lamb (from leg), or medium shrimp (shelled, deveined, and split in half).

Overloading the wok with a double portion usually re-sults in terrible-tasting food, but Mu Shu Chicken is the exception! You can double this recipe and stir-fry it as the entrée for a dinner party for 8.

Classic Mu Shu Chicken.

PAN-FRIED SICHUAN CHICKEN

8 chicken breast halves, boned and skinned

2 oranges, for garnish

3 green onions, for garnish

salt

freshly ground black pepper

½ cup plus 2 tablespoons cornstarch

5 tablespoons butter

¼ cup peanut oil

Sauce

4 cloves garlic, finely minced

1 tablespoon finely minced fresh ginger

1¼ cups chicken stock

¼ cup dry sherry

3 tablespoons hoisin sauce

1½ tablespoons oyster sauce

1 tablespoon bean sauce (see Appendix)

1 tablespoon red wine vinegar

½ teaspoon sugar

½ teaspoon Chinese chili sauce

¼ teaspoon crushed Sichuan peppercorns

Boned chicken breasts are lightly flattened with a meat pounder or rolling pin, then pan-fried and topped with a rich sauce. Serve Pan-Fried Sichuan Chicken as an elegant dish accompanied by steamed carrots in a parsley-butter sauce, Oriental Rice Pilaf, dilled cucumber salad, and melon sorbet.

Advance Preparation

Place a chicken breast on a piece of plastic wrap and cover with another piece of plastic. Using a meat pounder, rolling pin, or bottom of a heavy pot, lightly pound the chicken to increase its surface area by about one-third. Remove chicken from plastic and trim edges to form ovals. Repeat with remaining chicken breast halves. Refrigerate until ready to cook.

Cut oranges into thin slices or curl into twists for garnish. Shred green onions for garnish. Set aside.

In a small bowl combine garlic and ginger. In another small bowl combine remaining sauce ingredients.

Last-Minute Cooking

Preheat oven to 175°F. Place 4 dinner plates in oven.

Sprinkle chicken pieces on both sides with a little salt and pepper. Place ½ cup cornstarch on a plate or layer of waxed paper. Dust chicken pieces on both sides, shaking off excess cornstarch.

Place a 12-inch skillet over high heat. When hot, add 4 tablespoons butter and oil. When the butter begins to bubble and lightly brown, add about 4 pieces of chicken and pan-fry until they turn white but are not quite cooked in the center, about 1 minute on each side. Transfer chicken to heated plates and put back in warm oven. Cook remaining chicken pieces, transferring to oven when nearly cooked.

Pour out all but 2 tablespoons fat from skillet. Add ginger and garlic, and sauté over highest heat for 10 seconds. Add stock mixture, bring to a vigorous boil, and cook sauce until reduced by about one-third, about 5 minutes.

Combine remaining 2 tablespoons cornstarch with an equal amount of cold water. Reduce heat to medium and stir in a little cornstarch mixture to lightly thicken sauce. Remove sauce from heat and stir in remaining tablespoon butter.

Remove plates from oven. Spoon sauce over chicken, then garnish plates with orange rounds or twists and a sprinkling of green onion shreds. Serve at once.

Serves: 4 as an entrée.

COCONUT CURRY CHICKEN

4	chicken breast halves, boned and skinned
1	tablespoon dry sherry
1	tablespoon light soy sauce
1	tablespoon plus 2 teaspoons cornstarch
2	tablespoons plus 2 teaspoons peanut oil
1	red onion
1	large green bell pepper
3	cloves garlic, finely minced
1	tablespoon finely minced fresh ginger

Sauce

½	cup unsweetened coconut milk
2	tablespoons dry sherry
1	tablespoon light soy sauce
1½	tablespoons curry powder
2	teaspoons Oriental sesame oil
½	teaspoon sugar
½	teaspoon Chinese chili sauce
¼	teaspoon salt

Boneless chicken breasts, marinated, then stir-fried in a blazing hot wok are full of flavor and incredibly tender. This easy dish makes a good choice as part of an Oriental dinner accompanied by one of the rice dishes from Chapter 7.

Advance Preparation
Cut chicken into ¼-inch cubes, then mix with sherry, soy sauce, 2 teaspoons cornstarch, and 2 teaspoons peanut oil. Refrigerate until ready to cook.

Peel onion, then cut or chop into ½-inch cubes. Stem and seed pepper, then cut into ½-inch cubes. Combine onion and pepper and refrigerate until ready to cook.

In small bowl combine ingredients for sauce.

Last-Minute Cooking
Combine remaining 1 tablespoon cornstarch with an equal amount of cold water. Set aside.

Place wok over highest heat. When wok becomes very hot, add 1 tablespoon peanut oil to center of wok. Roll oil around sides of wok. When oil just begins to smoke, add chicken and stir-fry until it just loses raw outside color, about 2 minutes. Transfer to a work platter.

Immediately return wok to highest heat. Add re-maining 1 tablespoon peanut oil to center, then add garlic and ginger. Sauté a few seconds, then add onion and pepper. Stir-fry until onion pieces separate and green pepper brightens, about 2 minutes.

Return chicken to wok and pour in sauce. When sauce comes to a low boil, stir in a little cornstarch mixture so sauce glazes the food. Taste and adjust seasonings, then spoon onto a heated platter or individual plates. Serve at once.

Serves: 4 as an entrée; 6 to 8 as part of an Oriental dinner.

Menu Ideas: Chinese dinner for 6 — Onion Bread (roll out in the morning), Oriental Gazpacho (make a day in advance), Coconut Curry Chicken with Fireworks Rice (simmer rice on the stove while you stir-fry the chicken), and Ginger Ice Cream (make a few days in advance).

Roast Game Hens in Spicy Lemon Sauce;
Steamed Shark in Spicy Black Bean Sauce.

Sichuan Barbecued Game
Hens; Ginger Noodle Salad.

135

ROAST GAME HENS IN SPICY LEMON SAUCE

4 game hens
4 lemons
salt
freshly ground black pepper
¼ cup (½ stick) butter, cut into pieces
2 tablespoons cornstarch
2 cloves garlic, finely minced
1 tablespoon finely minced fresh ginger
sprigs of fresh dill, for garnish

Sauce
½ cup chicken stock
2 teaspoons grated or finely minced lemon peel
⅓ cup lemon juice
⅓ cup sugar
¼ cup dry sherry
2 tablespoons light soy sauce
½ teaspoon Chinese chili sauce
¼ teaspoon crushed Sichuan peppercorns
¼ teaspoon salt

Often the simplest approach results in the best taste. In this recipe game hens are rubbed with lemon juice and seasonings, then cooked in the oven; the sauce in the roasting pan is reduced to concentrate the flavor.

Cooking

Preheat oven to 425°F. Remove pads of fat from game hen cavities. Place hens in a roasting pan. Cut lemons in half and squeeze a lemon half over each game hen, then place an unsqueezed lemon half inside each cavity. Season outsides with a little salt and black pepper. Dot game hens with butter. Roast hens for about 30 minutes, basting every 10 minutes with pan drippings. Hens are done when internal temperature reaches 165°F on a meat thermometer and juices run clear.

In a small bowl, combine sauce ingredients; set aside. In a separate bowl, stir cornstarch with an equal amount of cold water; set aside.

When game hens are done, place on heated plates. Pour off all but 1 tablespoon fat from roasting pan, then place pan over medium-high heat. Add garlic and ginger and sauté briefly. Add sauce and bring to a boil, scraping bottom of pan to incorporate drippings into sauce.

Stir in a little of the cornstarch mixture to lightly thicken sauce. Taste and adjust seasonings, then spoon sauce over game hens. Garnish with dill sprigs and serve at once.

Serves: 4 to 6 as an entrée.

Menu Ideas: You can easily double the quantities to serve this as an entrée for 8, along with Asparagus in Black-Bean Butter Sauce (triple recipe), Oriental Rice Pilaf (double recipe), and Jade Salad (increase recipe by half). Begin the festivities in the living room or on the terrace with Spareribs with Secret Chinese Barbecue Sauce and conclude the evening with Mango Sorbet as you enjoy after-dinner drinks.

SICHUAN BARBECUED GAME HENS

2	game hens, split in half, or 1 3-pound chicken, split in half
2	green onions, minced
2	tablespoons minced fresh coriander (cilantro)
1	tablespoon finely minced garlic
1	tablespoon finely minced fresh ginger
3	tablespoons dry sherry
2	tablespoons hoisin sauce
2	tablespoons light soy sauce
1½	tablespoons red wine vinegar
1	tablespoon dark soy sauce
1	tablespoon Oriental sesame oil
2	teaspoons sugar
1	teaspoon Chinese chili sauce

Why not begin a picnic with these game hens, whose spicy marinade hides beneath the crisp skin? Next from the picnic basket might come Chinese Pickles, Onion Bread, Ginger Noodle Salad, New Wave Shrimp, and Chocolate-Chip Almond Cookies.

Advance Preparation

Loosen the skin of the game hens or chicken along the top of the breast. Gently push your index finger underneath the skin, moving down along the breast, thigh, and drumstick. Be careful not to dislodge the skin attached to the backbone.

Combine remaining ingredients. Stir well, then spoon a little of the marinade under the skin. With your fingers, massage the outside of the skin, working the marinade over the breast meat, thigh, and drumstick. Rub a little more marinade over the outside of the game hens or chicken. Marinate for at least 2 hours in the refrigerator.

Cooking

Drain off excess marinade into a small saucepan. Prepare a charcoal fire. When coals are ash-colored, add game hens meat side up. Cover and grill about 20 minutes for game hens and 30 minutes for chicken. The meat is cooked when internal temperature reaches 165°F on a meat thermometer and the juices from the meat run clear.

Meanwhile, simmer marinade for 5 minutes. Serve game hens hot, at room temperature, or cold accompanied with the extra marinade to spoon over the pieces. If desired, chop the game hens or chicken into bite-size pieces, using a heavy knife or cleaver.

Serves: 2 to 4 as an entrée.

LEMON CHICKEN

4   **chicken breast halves, boned and skinned**

1   **cup all-purpose flour**

1¼   **cups carbonated water, approximately**

½   **cup plus 1 tablespoon lemon juice**

¼   **cup plus 2 tablespoons sugar**

¼   **cup chicken stock**

2   **tablespoons light soy sauce**

¾   **teaspoon salt**

2   **teaspoons grated or finely minced lemon peel**

2   **teaspoons finely minced fresh ginger**

2   **tablespoons cornstarch**

2   **lemons, thinly sliced, for garnish**

     parsley sprigs, for garnish

4   **cups peanut oil**

¼   **red bell pepper, stemmed, seeded, and shredded**

Strips of chicken breast, fried until their lacy batter turns golden, are a taste and textural marvel. Since Lemon Chicken requires last-minute attention, serve this as an entrée for only two to four people.

Advance Preparation

Cut chicken breasts lengthwise into 1-inch-wide strips, then refrigerate until ready to cook. Place flour in a heavy 4-cup bowl, then put in freezer. Chill the carbonated water.

In a small saucepan, combine ½ cup lemon juice, sugar, stock, soy sauce, ½ teaspoon salt, lemon peel, and ginger. Set aside.

Last-Minute Cooking

Combine cornstarch with an equal amount of cold water; set aside.

Place lemon slices around outside of serving platter or on individual dinner plates. Put a parsley sprig between each lemon slice. Set aside. Place a wire rack on a baking sheet and put sheet near stove.

Bring lemon sauce to a low boil, dissolving the sugar. Stir in a little cornstarch mixture to lightly thicken sauce; keep warm over low heat.

Meanwhile, mix chicken strips with remaining tablespoon lemon juice. Remove bowl of flour from freezer and slowly pour in chilled carbonated water. Add remaining ¼ teaspoon salt and stir batter with a spoon. Heat a large, heavy frying pan over high heat until very hot. Add oil and heat until oil reaches 375° F; to test, see if a thin slice of ginger will quickly move across the surface. Dip a chicken strip into and out of batter;

the batter should have small lumps and be so thin that hardly any clings to the chicken. If necessary, stir in more carbonated water.

Add all the chicken to batter and mix to coat. Add about one-third of the chicken pieces, one strip at a time, to the hot oil and deep-fry until batter turns golden, about 2 minutes. Turn pieces midway through cooking. If unsure whether chicken is done, remove a strip and cut in half to check that interior is white. Drain chicken strips on wire rack. Let oil return to 375°F before frying next batch of chicken strips.

Glaze the bottom of the serving platter or individual dinner plates with one-third of the sauce.

Cut across chicken strips to make 1-inch cubes, then carefully transfer cubes to platter or plates. Drizzle some of remaining lemon sauce over chicken. You may not need all the sauce; each piece should be partially crispy, partially glazed with sauce. Garnish center of platter or plates with shredded red pepper and serve at once.

Serves: 2 as an entrée; 4 as part of a light dinner.

Menu Ideas: Dinner for 4 accompanied by a dry white wine — cream of asparagus soup, Lemon Chicken, Fireworks Rice, a spinach salad, and Mango Sorbet.

Notes: Use a heavy or non-stick frying pan but never an electric fryer, which does not generate enough heat to keep the oil hot during cooking. The carbonated water makes a crisper coating. The ice-cold batter and lumpy consistency help achieve a golden, crunchy coating.

As a variation, substitute 1¼ pounds large shrimp for the chicken. Remove shells except for tail ends. Butterfly shrimp by cutting deeply along top and rinsing out vein. Pat dry. Holding tail shell, dip each shrimp into batter and then place carefully into hot oil. Cook until batter turns golden and shrimp are white in the center (cut into one to check that shrimp are cooked). Coat with sauce and serve at once.

GAME HENS IN BLACK-BEAN TOMATO SAUCE

2 game hens, split in half
salt
freshly ground black pepper
½ cup all-purpose flour
3 tablespoons olive oil
3 tablespoons butter
1 tablespoon cornstarch

Sauce

½ cup tomato purée
1 cup chicken stock
¼ cup dry sherry
1 tablespoon oyster sauce
1 tablespoon Oriental sesame oil
2 teaspoons black bean hot sauce (see Appendix)
½ teaspoon sugar
3 cloves garlic, finely minced
1 tablespoon finely minced fresh ginger
3 tablespoons chopped fresh coriander (cilantro)

I first cooked this easy dish at a New Year's Eve dinner at a beach-front home in Santa Barbara. It was an evening of great food and good conversation set against the music of distant crashing waves.

Cooking

In a bowl, combine all sauce ingredients. Season game hens with a little salt and pepper. Sprinkle flour onto a piece of waxed paper, then lightly dust game hens, shaking off excess flour.

Place a 12-inch skillet over medium-high heat. Add olive oil and butter. When butter begins to foam, add game hens, meat side up. Brown the hens on both sides until golden, about 8 minutes. Regulate the heat so oil is always sizzling but never smoking. When game hens are browned, pour off all fat. Add the sauce and bring to a low boil. Cover pan, reduce heat to low, and simmer game hens for 15 minutes.

Place hens on large dinner plates. Stir cornstarch with an equal amount of cold water and spoon a little of this into the simmering sauce to lightly thicken. Spoon sauce over game hens and serve at once.

Serves: 2 to 4 as an entrée; 8 if cut into smaller pieces as part of an Oriental meal.

Menu Ideas: New Year's Eve dinner for 10 — Spareribs with Secret Chinese Barbecue Sauce (double recipe), Salmon Dumplings, Ginger Noodle Salad (double recipe), Game Hens in Black-Bean Tomato Sauce (double recipe), Oriental Rice Pilaf (double recipe), Oriental Fruit Tart.

Notes: You can substitute small, 2½-pound chickens, split in half, but they will require a longer cooking time of 20 to 25 minutes. Also, 1½ pounds cubed meat from country-style spareribs or lamb stewing meat is terrific when cooked in this sauce. Brown the meat in 2 tablespoons each of olive oil and butter. When browned, pour off oil, then simmer meat in sauce until tender. At this point it can be set aside and reheated later. Just before serving, stir in 3 cups cubed zucchini, broccoli flowerettes, or bite-size asparagus pieces. Simmer until vegetables brighten, then thicken with cornstarch mixture and serve at once.

RABBIT CHINOIS

1 cup walnut halves

12 dried black Chinese mushrooms

6 green onions

1 rabbit (about 4 pounds), cut into 12 pieces, liver reserved

salt

freshly ground black pepper

½ cup plus 1 tablespoon cornstarch

¼ cup (½ stick) butter

¼ cup olive oil

watercress or fresh coriander (cilantro), for garnish

Sauce

2 cloves garlic, finely minced

1 tablespoon finely minced fresh ginger

1½ cups chicken stock

¼ cup dry sherry

1 tablespoon Oriental sesame oil

1 tablespoon oyster sauce

½ teaspoon sugar

¼ teaspoon ground white pepper

Rabbit is common in Europe, but only recently has it begun to appear with any regularity in our markets. This stew improves in flavor when cooked hours earlier and reheated just before dinner. The liver is essential for this dish, giving the sauce a rich flavor without a liver taste.

Advance Preparation
Preheat oven to 325°F. Place walnuts in a small saucepan and cover with cold water. Place over high heat and bring to boil, then boil nuts for 5 minutes. Drain, rinse with hot water, and drain again. Spread nuts on a cookie sheet and roast in oven for 30 minutes, turning nuts after 15 minutes. Let cool for at least 1 hour. These nuts can be stored indefinitely in an airtight jar.

Soak dried mushrooms in hot water until soft, about 20 minutes. Discard stems and cut caps in half or quarters. Set aside.

Cut green onions on a sharp diagonal into 2-inch lengths; set aside.

Finely mince the rabbit liver, then place in a bowl with sauce ingredients. Set aside.

Cooking
Place rabbit on a layer of waxed paper. Lightly season with salt and black pepper. Dust with cornstarch, shaking each piece well to remove excess cornstarch.

Place a 12-inch skillet over medium-high heat. Add butter and oil. When butter begins to bubble, add rabbit and brown on both sides until golden, about 8 minutes. Regulate heat so fat always sizzles but never smokes.

Remove rabbit from skillet and pour off fat. Return rabbit to skillet and add mushrooms and sauce. Bring sauce to a low boil, cover, and reduce heat to lowest setting. Simmer rabbit until there is no resistance when meat is pierced with a fork, about 40 minutes. Midway through the cooking, rotate pieces. The dish can now be cooled, refrigerated, and reheated a day later.

When ready to serve, reheat rabbit and sauce. Combine remaining 1 tablespoon cornstarch with an equal amount of cold water. Stir green onions into stew. When their color brightens, in about 1 minute, stir in a little of the cornstarch mixture to lightly thicken sauce. Stir in walnuts, then turn out onto a heated platter or dinner plates. Garnish with watercress or coriander and serve at once.

Serves: 4 as light entrée; 6 to 8 as part of an Oriental meal.

Salmon in Ginger Butter
Sauce; Orange Caramel Duck.   142

ORANGE CARAMEL DUCK

I first taught this dish for a class with more than thirty students. There were no problems with the dish when I quadrupled the recipe. Duck pieces are browned, then simmered in a sweet-and-sour orange-anise sauce, which is later reduced to a caramel syrup.

ORANGE CARAMEL DUCK

1   **5-pound duck**
2   **green onions, shredded, for garnish**
2   **oranges, thinly sliced, for garnish**
    Sauce
1   **cup fresh orange juice**
1   **cup chicken stock**
⅓   **cup red wine vinegar**
¼   **cup sugar**
¼   **cup dry sherry**
1   **tablespoon light soy sauce**
¼   **teaspoon crushed Sichuan peppercorns**
½   **teaspoon salt**
¼   **teaspoon ground white pepper**
½   **star anise**
2   **cloves garlic, finely minced**
1   **tablespoon finely minced fresh ginger**

Advance Preparation

Have the butcher cut duck into 6 pieces (breast split in half, 2 thighs, and 2 drumsticks), cutting out the backbone. Freeze the backbone and wings for enriching a future chicken stock. Cut away excess fat from around each duck piece, especially the thighs. Using a sharp knife, score the skin in a tight crisscross pattern. In a bowl, combine sauce ingredients.

Cooking

Place a 12-inch frying pan over medium-high heat. When very hot, add duck pieces, skin side down, and brown the duck, turning the pieces occasionally, until the skin becomes very dark brown and the meat loses its raw outside color, about 12 minutes. Regulate the heat so rendered fat is always sizzling but never smoking. (Do not pour off the fat that accumulates, since this helps render away more of the fat from the skin.)

Remove duck pieces from pan and pour off all the oil. Return frying pan to stove and increase heat to high. Add duck, skin side up, then pour in sauce. Bring to a low boil, cover pan, reduce heat to lowest setting, and simmer duck for 30 minutes. Preheat oven to 150°F.

Remove duck from pan and keep warm in oven Discard anise. With strips of paper toweling, dab up fat on the surface of the sauce.

Turn heat to high and boil sauce vigorously until reduced to ½ cup, about 15 minutes. During last few minutes, stir continually to prevent sauce from scorching.

Add duck to frying pan and rotate pieces so duck is glazed with the sauce. Place on heated dinner plates and garnish with shredded green onions. Place orange slices or twists on each plate and serve at once.

Serves: 2 as an entrée; 6 to 8 as one of several Oriental dishes (chop the duck into smaller pieces while the sauce reduces).

Notes: This is a disappointing dish if made with chicken. A good variation, however, is to use 1½ pounds country-style sparerib meat cut into ½-inch cubes. Heat frying pan to hot, add 2 tablespoons oil, and brown the meat. Pour off oil, add sauce, and simmer meat until tender, about 1 hour. Remove meat, boil down sauce, and return meat to pan to glaze.

CRISPY QUAIL

4 quail
½ cup dry sherry
3 tablespoons light soy sauce
2 tablespoons hoisin sauce
1 tablespoon Oriental sesame oil
½ teaspoon Chinese chili sauce
4 cloves garlic, finely minced
1 tablespoon finely minced fresh ginger
2 green onions, minced
3 cups peanut oil
½ teaspoon salt
½ teaspoon ground Chinese pepper mix (see Appendix)

Marinated quail are steamed, cooled, and quickly fried to re-heat the meat and crisp the skin. Serve these cut into pieces as an appetizer or picnic dish. Or, if you are planning a romantic dinner for two, then accompany them with one of the rice dishes from Chapter 7, a tossed green salad, and Champagne.

Advance Preparation (8 Hours before Cooking)
Remove fat pads from cavities of quail. In a bowl, combine sherry, soy sauce, hoisin sauce, sesame oil, chili sauce, garlic, ginger, and green onions. Place quail in a large plastic food bag, pour in marinade, seal, and refrigerate for 8 hours or overnight.

Cooking
Bring water to a rapid boil in the bottom of a Chinese steamer. Drain quail, then place on steamer tray. Set over boiling water and cover, steaming quail for 8 minutes. Remove quail from steamer and let cool to room temperature, about 30 minutes.

Thoroughly pat quail dry with paper towels, especially inside the cavities.

Place wok over highest heat. When very hot, add peanut oil. When oil is hot enough — when it bubbles around the end of a wooden spoon dipped into the wok (365°F) — add quail. Deep-fry quail until a deep golden, turning them over in the oil with chopsticks or tongs, for between 15 and 30 seconds. Immediately transfer to wire rack and sprinkle with salt and Chinese pepper mix. Place quail on heated dinner plates and serve at once.

Serves: 2 as an entrée.
Notes: Chinese restaurants use this technique to cook squab, however the oil splatters terribly because of their greater size and moister meat. Enjoy these at restaurants instead!
The quail are wonderful topped with Black-Bean Butter Sauce, Lemon Sauce, and Spicy Tangerine Sauce.

Spicy Stir-Fried Duck.

Lettuce-Wrapped Squab and Shrimp.

SPICY STIR-FRIED DUCK

- 1 5-pound duck
- 1 tablespoon light soy sauce
- 1 tablespoon dry sherry
- 2 teaspoons hoisin sauce
- 2 tablespoons plus 2 teaspoons cornstarch
- 2 tablespoons plus 2 teaspoons peanut oil
- 1 bunch broccoli
- 2 medium carrots
- 2 green onions
- 3 cloves garlic, finely minced
- 1 tablespoon grated or finely minced tangerine or orange peel

  Sauce
- 3 tablespoons dry sherry
- 1 tablespoon light soy sauce
- 1 tablespoon Oriental sesame oil
- 1 tablespoon distilled white vinegar
- 2 teaspoons dark soy sauce
- ½ teaspoon Chinese chili sauce
- ½ teaspoon salt
- ¼ teaspoon crushed Sichuan peppercorns

Here's a dish that a band of us had at a famous Suzhou establishment, The Moon in View Restaurant.

Advance Preparation
Cut the meat from the duck in large pieces. Trim off all fat. Cut meat into ¼-inch-thick slices that are 1 inch long and ½ inch wide; although there are many tendons in leg meat, it is not necessary to remove these. Add the soy sauce, sherry, hoisin sauce, 2 teaspoons cornstarch, and 2 teaspoons peanut oil to the duck meat. Refrigerate until ready to cook.

Set aside 1½ cups broccoli flowerettes. Cut carrots crosswise into ¼-inch slices. Bring 8 cups water to a vigorous boil, then add broccoli. When broccoli turns a bright green, about 2 minutes, scoop out with a slotted spoon and transfer to a bowl of ice water. To the same boiling water, add carrots and cook until they turn brighter, about 3 minutes. Transfer immediately to bowl holding broccoli. When chilled, drain and pat vegetables dry. Cut green onions on a diagonal into 1-inch lengths. Add to broccoli and carrots and refrigerate until ready to cook. Combine sauce ingredients; set aside.

Last-Minute Cooking
Combine remaining 2 tablespoons cornstarch with an equal amount of cold water; set aside.

Place wok over highest heat. When wok is very hot, add 1 tablespoon peanut oil to center. Roll oil around sides of wok. When oil just begins to smoke, add duck and stir-fry until it just loses raw outside color, about 2 minutes. Transfer duck to a work platter.

Immediately return wok to highest heat. Add remaining 1 tablespoon oil to center. Add garlic and tangerine peel and sauté a few seconds. Add vegetables and stir-fry until green onions brighten and broccoli is heated through, about 2 minutes.

Return duck to wok and pour in sauce. When sauce comes to a low boil, stir in a little of the cornstarch mixture so sauce glazes the food. Taste and adjust seasonings, then pour onto a heated platter or individual plates. Serve at once.

Serves: 2 to 4 as an entrée; 6 to 8 as part of an Oriental dinner.

Menu Ideas: A delicious dinner for 2 — Spicy Stir-Fried Duck, a spinach salad, hot rolls with sweet butter, and a good red wine.

Notes: You can substitute 4 chicken breast halves for the duck, though the dish will not be as rich tasting.

LETTUCE-WRAPPED SQUAB AND SHRIMP

8   dried black Chinese mushrooms
10 fresh water chestnuts, or one medium carrot, diced
1   red bell pepper, stemmed, seeded, and diced
2   green onions, diced
½   cup pine nuts (pignoli)
1   large squab or 3 chicken thighs
2   teaspoons dry sherry
1   teaspoon dark soy sauce
1   teaspoon finely minced fresh ginger
1   tablespoon plus ½ teaspoon cornstarch
3   cups plus 2 tablespoons and ½ teaspoon peanut oil
½   pound raw shrimp
3   heads iceberg lettuce
2   ounces rice sticks
    Sauce
2   tablespoons dry sherry
1   tablespoon light soy sauce
1   tablespoon oyster sauce
1   tablespoon Oriental sesame oil
½   teaspoon sugar
¼   teaspoon Chinese chili sauce

Diced squab served in lettuce cups is standard fare in the Far East, where labor is plentiful and cheap. In this version the dark meat is augmented with diced shrimp to lessen the preparation time and produce a more complex taste. One of the nicest ways to serve this dish is as an appetizer for six to eight friends before going to a nearby restaurant.

Advance Preparation
Soak dried mushrooms in hot water until soft, about 20 minutes. Discard stems and dice caps. Combine with water chestnuts or carrot, red pepper, and green onions. Refrigerate until ready to cook.

Toast pine nuts in a 325°F oven until they turn a light golden, about 8 minutes. Set aside.

Cut meat from squab or chicken thighs. Chop meat coarsely, then add sherry, soy sauce, ginger, ½ teaspoon cornstarch, and ½ teaspoon peanut oil. Mix well. Shell and devein shrimp. Cut shrimp crosswise into very thin slices. Mix with squab mixture and refrigerate until ready to cook.

Cut top third off each head of lettuce. Carefully separate leaves of tops; you should end up with about 18 round cups, about 3 to 5 inches across. Refrigerate leaves (I reserve the rest of the lettuce for salads).

Cook the rice sticks. In a paper bag, separate rice sticks into very small bundles. Cook rice sticks as described on page 69. Place cooked rice sticks in a paper bag and store at room temperature.

In a small bowl combine ingredients for sauce. Set aside.

Last Minute Cooking
Combine remaining cornstarch with an equal amount of cold water; set aside. With your hands, break rice sticks into small pieces. Spread in an even layer on a round serving platter.

Place wok over highest heat. When wok becomes very hot, add 2 tablespoons peanut oil to center. Roll oil around sides of wok. When oil just begins to smoke, add squab and shrimp mixture. Stir-fry until shrimp turn white, about 2 minutes.

Immediately add vegetables and stir-fry until vegetables brighten in color, about 1 minute.

Add pine nuts and sauce. When sauce comes to a low boil, stir in a little of the cornstarch mixture so sauce glazes the food. Pour out onto rice sticks. Serve at once with lettuce cups. Each person puts some of the filling in a lettuce cup, gently cups the edges up, and eats it quickly!

Serves: 2 as an entrée; 6 to 8 as an appetizer.

■ C H A P T E R 6

This chapter features meats not usually associated with Chinese cooking, which are combined with Oriental seasonings for unexpected and delicious tastes. Slices of raw beef dipped in a spicy lime sauce and lettuce-wrapped meatballs seasoned with freshly grated nutmeg tease the palate; barbecued rib eye thinly sliced and rolled with shredded greens inside Peking pancakes serves as the entrée for a summer party; thick, juicy veal chops glazed with a Sichuan lemon sauce or a rack of lamb permeated with hoisin sauce, curry powder, and orange are perfect entrées for a special dinner; and the several stews in this chapter are hearty main courses, complemented by plenty of crusty bread and a good Cabernet Sauvignon.

Easy-to-prepare recipes in this chapter are Tender Thai Pork, Lettuce-Wrapped Spicy Meatballs, Oriental Braised Veal Shanks, Veal Scaloppine in Shiitake Cream Sauce, Sichuan Lemon Veal Chops, Coconut Lamb Stew, and Rack of Lamb in Hunan Barbecue Sauce.

Barbecued Rib Eye with Peking Pancakes.

BARBECUED RIB EYE WITH PEKING PANCAKES

1 3-pound rib eye (Delmonico) or New York strip (top loin) steak

Secret Chinese Barbecue Sauce (page 20)

8 cups shredded salad greens

2 packages (3.5 ounces each) enoki mushrooms

2 bunches fresh coriander (cilantro)

1 cup hoisin sauce

30 Peking pancakes (see Appendix)

Oriental parties are fun when friends who cook contribute dishes. A summer menu might include thin slices of barbecued rib eye steak glazed with a Chinese sauce. Each person places shredded lettuce, enoki mushrooms, coriander, a beef slice, and hoisin sauce on a steaming Peking pancake and rolls it in a cylinder like a Chinese-style burrito. With guests contributing easy do-ahead dishes such as Spicy Swordfish Salad, Oriental Gazpacho, and chilled Chinese Ratatouille, there is practically no last-minute cooking to divert attention from the party.

Advance Preparation
Trim fat from meat. Marinate meat in barbecue sauce for 1 hour.

Place salad greens in a plastic food bag; refrigerate until ready to serve. Trim dirty ends from enoki mushrooms, then pull mushroom threads apart. Place in another plastic food bag and refrigerate.

Cooking
Prepare a charcoal fire. When coals are ash-colored, grill meat, rotating occasionally and brushing on barbecue sauce as it cooks. Meat is done when temperature on a meat thermometer reaches 140°F.

Place greens, mushrooms, and coriander on a serving platter. Put a small bowl with hoisin sauce nearby.

Fold pancakes in quarters and overlap on a Chinese steamer tray. Place over rapidly boiling water, cover, and steam for 2 minutes. Place pancakes in a

basket lined with a cloth napkin, then fold napkin over top and bring to table. (If you steam pancakes in a bamboo steamer, just bring steamer to the table.)

Remove meat from grill and bring to table. Thinly slice steak. Each person opens a pancake, spreads a little hoisin sauce across the surface, adds a sprinkling of greens, mushrooms, a coriander sprig, and a slice of meat, and rolls the pancake into a cylinder to eat.

Serves: 6 to 8 as an entrée.

Notes: There are many good variations. Skewer shrimp and substitute these for the meat. Avocado slices and other shredded vegetables provide a wider choice of filling ingredients. Along with the hoisin sauce, you might add small dishes of chutney, plum sauce, Dijon mustard, and Oriental Salsa.

TENDER THAI PORK

1 pound boneless pork shoulder, butt, or meat from country-style spareribs
1 cup chicken stock
¼ cup dry sherry
1 tablespoon Oriental sesame oil
1 tablespoon smooth peanut butter
1 tablespoon dark soy sauce
1 tablespoon hoisin sauce
½ teaspoon Chinese chili sauce
3 tablespoons peanut oil
1 tablespoon garlic, finely minced
1 tablespoon finely minced fresh ginger
2 shallots, minced
¼ cup chopped fresh coriander (cilantro)
½ cup chopped green onions
2 Japanese cucumbers, or ½ hothouse cucumber
1 pint cherry tomatoes
1 tablespoon cornstarch
  juice of 1 lime

Crunchy cucumbers and cherry tomatoes simmer with pork cubes in a rich, nutty sauce to create a delicious stew. Other good vegetable combinations for this stew are asparagus and red peppers, zucchini and carrots, or snow peas and yellow peppers. Add the vegetables toward the end of the cooking and simmer just until tender. Tender Thai Pork is best served with mashed potatoes, steamed rice, or buttered noodles.

Advance Preparation

Cut pork into ½-inch cubes, trimming away all fat. Set aside until ready to cook.

In a small bowl, combine stock, sherry, sesame oil, peanut butter, soy sauce, hoisin sauce, and chili sauce. Set aside.

Advance Cooking

Place a wok or heavy 12-inch frying pan over high heat. When very hot, add oil. When oil just begins to smoke, add meat and stir-fry until meat loses its raw outside color, about 5 minutes.

Pour off fat and add garlic, ginger, shallots, coriander, and green onions. Stir-fry with meat for 2 minutes, then add reserved stock mixture. Bring to a low boil, cover, and reduce heat to lowest setting. Simmer until meat is tender, about 1 hour. (Recipe up to this point can be made a day ahead.)

Last-Minute Cooking

If using Japanese cucumbers, cut in half lengthwise. Place halves together and cut crosswise to make ½-inch cubes. For hothouse cucumber, cut in half lengthwise, scoop out seeds with a spoon, then cut cucumber into strips. Place strips together and cut crosswise, producing enough ½-inch cubes to fill 1 cup.

Remove stems from cherry tomatoes. Set aside with cucumbers. Combine cornstarch with an equal amount of cold water.

If reheating stew, simmer for 5 minutes to heat through, then bring to a low boil. Stir in cucumbers and tomatoes. When stew returns to a low boil, stir in a little of the cornstarch mixture to lightly thicken sauce, if necessary. Remove from heat. Add the lime juice and serve at once.

Serves: 2 to 3 as an entrée.

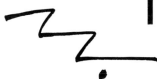

THAI TARTARE

- 1 **pound top-quality beef filet**
- 1 **cup finely shredded daikon radish**
- 1 **cup finely shredded carrots**
- 1 **cup finely shredded raw beets**
- 2 **tablespoons minced roasted (unsalted) peanuts**
- 2 **teaspoons grated or finely minced lime peel**
- ½ **teaspoon freshly grated nutmeg**
- ¼ **cup minced fresh coriander (cilantro)**
  Dipping Sauce
- 2 **tablespoons Thai fish sauce**
- 2 **tablespoons lime juice**
- 2 **teaspoons sugar**
- ½ **teaspoon Chinese chili sauce**
- 1 **clove garlic, finely minced**

While in Bangkok several years ago I tasted a dish of paper-thin raw beef sprinkled with chopped peanuts, fresh coriander, and red chilies. Each person dipped the slices into a spicy lime sauce, then ate the meat with shredded raw vegetables. This very pretty dish is a great conversation starter to begin an evening.

Advance Preparation
Have the butcher trim all fat from beef. Place filet in freezer and chill until nearly frozen. Cut meat into paper-thin slices, then overlap slices on a large platter and cover with plastic wrap. Press wrap onto surface of meat so the seal is airtight; this stops the meat from darkening. Refrigerate until ready to serve.

Place shredded radish, carrots, and beets in separate plastic food bags and refrigerate until ready to serve.

In a small bowl, combine dipping sauce ingredients. Add 2½ tablespoons water and refrigerate.

Last-Minute Assembling
Remove plastic wrap from meat. Leaving space in center of platter for the bowl of sauce, rearrange slices evenly around the center of platter or roll each slice into a cylinder before placing back on platter.

Across the surface of the meat sprinkle the peanuts, lime peel, nutmeg, and coriander. Place bowl with sauce in center of platter, then decorate outside edge of platter with shredded vegetables. Serve within 1 hour. Each person, using chopsticks or a small fork, dips a slice of filet into the sauce and eats the meat along with some of the shredded vegetables.

Serves: 6 to 8 as an appetizer; 3 to 4 as an entrée.

Menu Ideas: As an entrée for 2 to 3 people, this is excellent with a homemade vegetable soup, green salad, and individual fruit tarts.

Notes: There are a number of good variations on this recipe. Substitute another dipping sauce, such as Satay Sauce, or use very thinly sliced raw tuna or yellowtail instead of beef. Artfully arrange the slices of raw fish on a chilled platter and serve several dipping sauces for a spectacular presentation.

LIONS' HEADS

6 dried black Chinese mushrooms

1 pound ground pork

3 green onions, minced

6 water chestnuts, preferably fresh, minced

3 cloves garlic, finely minced

1 tablespoon finely minced fresh ginger

3 tablespoons cornstarch, plus cornstarch for dusting

2 tablespoons dry sherry

1 tablespoon light soy sauce

1 tablespoon oyster sauce

½ teaspoon sugar

¼ teaspoon freshly ground black pepper

6 tablespoons peanut oil

1 small head green cabbage

Sauce

1½ cups chicken stock

¼ cup dry sherry

2 tablespoons oyster sauce

1 tablespoon light soy sauce

1 teaspoon dark soy sauce

1 teaspoon Oriental sesame oil

½ teaspoon sugar

¼ teaspoon freshly ground black pepper

The Chinese have a romantic view of culinary terms and recipe titles. They are aghast at our references to "soy bean cake," "black fungus," and "dumplings," preferring instead "meat without bones," "cloud ears," and "swallowing the clouds." Perhaps it was after one-too-many drinking games that the originator of this dish, a Shanghai chef, imagined these giant meatballs on a bed of shredded cabbage as lions' heads trailing long manes.

Advance Preparation
Prepare meatball mixture. Soak mushrooms in hot water until soft, about 20 minutes. Discard stems and mince caps. Place mushrooms in large bowl and add pork, green onions, water chestnuts, garlic, ginger, 1 tablespoon cornstarch, sherry, soy sauce, oyster sauce, sugar, and pepper.

Mix thoroughly, then rub a little oil on your hands. Form 3 giant meatballs of the mixture. Place on a lightly oiled plate and refrigerate until ready to cook.

Shred enough cabbage to fill 6 cups. Set aside. In a 2-cup bowl, combine ingredients for sauce. Set aside.

Cooking
Lightly dust meatballs with cornstarch. Place a 10-inch skillet over medium-high heat. When hot, add ¼ cup peanut oil. As oil gives off just a wisp of smoke, add meatballs.

Brown on all sides until light golden, about 8 minutes.

Gently transfer meatballs to a saucepan big enough to just hold them. Turn heat to high and pour in sauce. Bring sauce to a low boil, cover, and reduce heat to lowest setting. Simmer meatballs for 20 minutes.

Just before meatballs are cooked, place wok over highest heat. When hot, add remaining 2 tablespoons peanut oil. When oil just begins to smoke, add cabbage and stir and toss until it turns bright green, about 1 minute.

Spread cabbage on a heated serving plate and place meatballs in center. Combine remaining 2 tablespoons cornstarch with an equal amount of cold water and set aside. Bring sauce to a low boil, then add a little cornstarch mixture to lightly thicken. Pour sauce over meatballs and serve at once. Each person scoops up some of the cabbage, cuts a piece from one of the meatballs, and glazes it all with a spoonful (or more) of the sauce.

Serves: 2 to 3 as an entrée; 6 to 8 as part of an Oriental meal.

STIR-FRIED PORK WITH PINE NUTS AND ONIONS

1 pound boneless pork tenderloin or boned and trimmed loin chops
1 tablespoon dark soy sauce
1 tablespoon dry sherry
1 tablespoon plus 2 teaspoons cornstarch
2 tablespoons plus 2 teaspoons peanut oil
1 cup pine nuts (pignoli)
1 large red onion
4 cloves garlic, finely minced
2 teaspoons finely minced fresh ginger
2 teaspoons grated or minced tangerine or orange peel

Sauce

2 tablespoons dry sherry
2 tablespoons light soy sauce
2 teaspoons hoisin sauce
2 teaspoons Oriental sesame oil
2 teaspoons red wine vinegar
1 teaspoon Chinese chili sauce
½ teaspoon sugar
½ teaspoon crushed Sichuan peppercorns
¼ teaspoon salt

When served with steamed rice and slices of melon, this simple stir-fry makes a satisfying dinner for two to four people. For a variation, I often finely dice all the ingredients and serve the stir-fry in lettuce cups (see page 149).

Advance Preparation

Trim fat from meat and cut into very thin slices. Cut slices into pieces about 1 inch long and ½ inch across, then place in a bowl. Add soy sauce, sherry, 2 teaspoons cornstarch, and 2 teaspoons peanut oil. Mix thoroughly and set aside until ready to cook.

Toast pine nuts in a 325°F oven until very light golden, about 10 minutes. Tip into a small bowl and set aside.

Peel onion, then chop into ½-inch cubes; set aside.

In a small bowl combine ingredients for sauce and set aside.

Last-Minute Cooking

Combine remaining tablespoon cornstarch with an equal amount of cold water and set aside.

Place wok over highest heat. When wok becomes very hot, add 1 tablespoon peanut oil to center, then roll oil around sides of wok. When oil just begins to smoke, add pork and stir-fry until it loses its raw outside color, about 2 minutes. Transfer pork to a work platter.

Immediately return wok to highest heat. Add remaining tablespoon peanut oil to wok, then put in garlic, ginger, and tangerine. Sauté a few seconds, then add onion and stir-fry until onion separates into individual pieces, about 2 minutes.

Return pork to wok and pour in sauce. When sauce comes to a low boil, stir in a little of the cornstarch mixture so sauce glazes the food. Add the pine nuts, then taste and adjust seasonings. Pour out onto a heated platter or individual plates. Serve at once.

Serves: 2 as an entrée; 6 to 8 as part of an Oriental dinner.

STIR-FRIED BEEF WITH WILD MUSHROOMS

¾ pound beef tenderloin

1 tablespoon dark soy sauce

2 teaspoons dry sherry

1 tablespoon plus 2 teaspoons cornstarch

2 tablespoons plus 2 teaspoons peanut oil

¼ pound wild mushrooms (see Notes)

3 green onions

3 medium stalks bok choy

3 tablespoons unsalted butter

3 cloves garlic, finely minced

2 teaspoons finely minced fresh ginger

Sauce

¼ cup rich chicken stock

2 tablespoons dry sherry

1 tablespoon light soy sauce

1 tablespoon oyster sauce

1 tablespoon Oriental sesame oil

½ teaspoon sugar

¼ teaspoon freshly ground black pepper

Sunny days following a rainstorm mean early-morning hikes through damp grass toward distant oaks and firs harboring large clumps of honey mushrooms, fairy rings of blewits, and rippled golden chanterelles. When such mushrooms are sautéed in butter and garlic, their meaty flavors are a perfect match with thin slices of filet mignon and a rich oyster sauce.

Advance Preparation
Trim any fat from meat, then cut into very thin slices. Cut each slice into strips 1 inch long and ½ inch wide, then place in a bowl. Add dark soy sauce, sherry, 2 teaspoons cornstarch, and 2 teaspoons peanut oil. Mix well, then refrigerate until ready to cook.

Trim tough stems from mushrooms, then cut caps into bite-size pieces; set aside. Cut green onions on the diagonal into 1-inch lengths; set aside.

Cut bok choy on a sharp diagonal, twisting stalk half a turn after each cut to produce diamond-shaped pieces. Set aside.

In a small bowl, combine ingredients for sauce. Set aside.

Last-Minute Cooking
Combine remaining tablespoon cornstarch with an equal amount of cold water and set aside.

Place wok over highest heat. When wok becomes very hot, add 1 tablespoon peanut oil to center, then roll oil around sides of wok.

When oil just begins to smoke, add beef and stir-fry until it loses its raw outside color, about 2 minutes. Transfer to a work platter.

Immediately return wok to highest heat and add remaining tablespoon peanut oil along with 2 tablespoons butter. Add garlic and ginger and sauté a few seconds. Add vegetables and stir-fry until bok choy brightens and mushrooms are cooked, about 1 minute.

Return beef to wok and add sauce. When sauce comes to a low boil, stir in a little of the cornstarch mixture so that sauce glazes the food. Stir in remaining tablespoon butter, then pour beef mixture onto a heated platter or individual plates.

**Serves: 2 as an entrée; 8 as part of an Oriental dinner.
Menu Ideas: Party for 10 — Mahogany Chicken Wings (marinate a day in advance); Marco Polo Dumplings; Spicy Noodle Salad with Peanut Dressing (toss ingredients with dressing just before dinner; do not refrigerate); Hot and Sour Seafood Soup (double recipe; complete soup in afternoon and just reheat to serve); Stir-Fried Beef with Wild Mushrooms; Fireworks Rice (double recipe); Firecracker Cookies, ice cream.**

Notes: As a substitute for wild mushrooms, stem and quarter ¼ pound fresh shiitake mushrooms or 8 dried black Chinese mushrooms, soaked in hot water until soft. Or use ¼ pound fresh button mushrooms.

Crab and Asparagus Soup;
Stir-Fried Beef with Wild Mushrooms.

PORK AND SHRIMP IN TOMATO COCONUT SAUCE

½ pound boneless pork tenderloin or boned and trimmed loin chops

1 tablespoon dark soy sauce

1 tablespoon plus 1 teaspoon cornstarch

2 tablespoons plus 1 teaspoon peanut oil

½ pound raw shrimp

1 red bell pepper, stemmed and seeded

1 cup shelled fresh peas (about 1 pound unshelled)

1 cup thinly sliced small button mushrooms

3 cloves garlic, finely minced

1 tablespoon finely minced fresh ginger

dry sherry or water (optional)

Sauce

½ cup unsweetened coconut milk

3 tablespoons tomato sauce

2 tablespoons dry sherry

1 tablespoon oyster sauce

1 tablespoon curry powder

½ teaspoon Chinese chili sauce

¼ teaspoon crushed Sichuan peppercorns

It is quite common, especially at Chinese banquets, for an entrée to include both meat and seafood. Besides pork and shrimp, good combinations are filet mignon and scallops or chicken and fresh crab meat. One of my most creative students, David Black, devised this delicious combination of flavors and textures.

Advance Preparation

Trim fat from pork, then cut into very thin slices. Cut slices into pieces about 1 inch long and ½ inch across and place in a bowl. Add soy sauce, 1 teaspoon cornstarch, and 1 teaspoon oil. Mix thoroughly and set aside.

Shell and devein shrimp. Cut along top of shrimp, halving them. Rinse shrimp, then pat dry and set aside.

Cut pepper into thin slices. Cut across slices to make 1-inch pieces, then combine in a bowl with peas and mushrooms. Set aside.

In a small bowl, combine ingredients for sauce and set aside.

Last-Minute Cooking

Combine remaining tablespoon cornstarch with an equal amount of cold water; set aside.

Place wok over highest heat. When wok becomes very hot, add 1 tablespoon oil to center, then roll oil around sides of wok.

When oil just begins to smoke, add pork and shrimp. Stir-fry until pork loses raw outside color and shrimp turns white, about 2 minutes. Transfer to a work platter.

Immediately return wok to highest heat. Add remaining tablespoon oil to center, then put in garlic and ginger. Sauté a few seconds. Then add vegetables and stir-fry until they brighten, about 2 minutes. Add a splash of sherry or water to prevent peas from scorching, if necessary.

Return pork and shrimp to wok and pour in sauce. When sauce comes to a low boil, stir in a little of the cornstarch mixture so that sauce glazes the food. Taste and adjust seasonings, then pour out onto a heated platter or individual plates. Serve at once.

Serves: 2 as an entrée; 6 to 8 as part of an Oriental dinner.

Menu Ideas: A Thai dinner for 10 — Beef Satay (double recipe); Thai Papaya Shrimp Salad (substitute bay scallops for shrimp and double recipe); Pork and Shrimp in Tomato Coconut Sauce (double recipe, with 2 people stir-frying this simultaneously); Spicy Thai Noodles (double recipe); Flambéed Thai Bananas (double recipe).

LETTUCE-WRAPPED SPICY MEATBALLS

½ **pound ground beef**

½ **pound ground pork**

2 **green onions, minced**

2 **tablespoons minced fresh coriander (cilantro)**

2 **tablespoons light soy sauce**

1 **egg**

1 **teaspoon grated or finely minced orange peel**

¾ **teaspoon grated nutmeg**

½ **teaspoon Chinese chili sauce**

½ **teaspoon freshly ground black pepper**

4 **cloves garlic, finely minced**

1 **tablespoon finely minced fresh ginger**

½ **cup peanut oil**

1 **head bibb lettuce**

1 **bunch fresh coriander (cilantro)**

20 **mint leaves**

cornstarch, for dusting (pan-frying)

Spicy Lime Dipping Sauce (page 155)

Southeast Asians like to assemble lettuce-leaf packages containing meatballs, shrimp, or crisp spring rolls along with sprigs of mint and coriander leaves. They dip these packages into an aromatic sauce, and experience an exciting explosion of different textures and flavors. Arrange the greens and sauce on a platter in advance, then quickly broil or pan-fry the meatballs just before serving. Enjoy this dish as an appetizer, a light first course, or as a main dish, served with Scallop Thread Soup, warm crusty bread, and a dry white wine.

Advance Preparation

In a bowl, combine beef, pork, green onions, coriander, soy sauce, egg, orange peel, nutmeg, chili sauce, pepper, garlic, and ginger. Mix thoroughly, then rub a little oil on your hands and form 20 meatballs about 1 inch in diameter. Arrange on a lightly oiled plate and refrigerate until ready to cook.

Pull leaves from bibb lettuce and cut into 20 pieces about 3 inches square. On each lettuce square, place a sprig of coriander and 1 mint leaf. Arrange lettuce leaves on a serving platter and refrigerate until ready to serve.

Cooking

To broil meatballs, preheat oven to 550°F. Place meatballs on a small baking sheet. Turn oven up to Broil, place baking sheet about 4 inches from heat, and broil meatballs until no longer pink in center, about 3 to 4 minutes. (Leave oven door slightly ajar if using electric oven.)

To pan-fry meatballs, lightly dust them with cornstarch. Place a 12-inch skillet over medium-high heat. When frying pan is hot, add oil. When oil just begins to give off a wisp of smoke, add meatballs and pan-fry, turning them over in the oil, until golden brown and no longer pink in the center, about 4 minutes.

Place meatballs next to lettuce cups on the serving platter. Serve at once, accompanied by the dipping sauce. Each person wraps a lettuce cup around a meatball and dips one end of the package into the sauce.

Serves: 6 to 8 as an appetizer; 2 as an entrée.

Notes: The meatballs are most tender when made with only pork or with a combination of pork and beef (meatloaf mix). The fat in the pork keeps the meatballs moist. Ground lamb is also excellent, but ground chicken, turkey, and veal have far too little fat and make very dry meatballs.

ORIENTAL BRAISED VEAL SHANKS

12 dried black Chinese mushrooms

12 baby carrots

5 green onions

3 tablespoons peanut oil

6 1-inch-thick veal shanks (about 3 pounds total weight)

2 tablespoons cornstarch

Sauce

4 cloves garlic, finely minced

1 tablespoon finely minced fresh ginger

½ cup red wine

½ cup chicken stock

2 tablespoons oyster sauce

1 tablespoon Oriental sesame oil

1 teaspoon dark soy sauce

1 teaspoon sugar

½ teaspoon freshly ground black pepper

Osso buco fans: Here is an Oriental version seasoned with Chinese mushrooms, oyster sauce, and ginger. The tender meat and buttery marrow taste great along with a big green salad and hot sourdough rolls. Or make this dish one of several in a do-ahead Chinese meal.

Advance Preparation
Soak dried mushrooms in hot water until softened, about 20 minutes. Strain liquid through a fine-meshed sieve and reserve mushroom-flavored water. Discard stems and cut caps into halves or quarters. Set aside.

Trim and scrub carrots; set aside. Cut green onions on a diagonal into 1½-inch lengths; set aside until just before serving.

In a bowl, combine sauce ingredients; set aside until ready to cook.

Advance Cooking
Place wok or frying pan just big enough to hold the shanks over medium-high heat. Add peanut oil. When oil just begins to give off a wisp of smoke, add shanks and brown both sides until golden, about 8 minutes.

Pour off fat and add mushrooms and sauce. If liquid does not come two-thirds of the way up the shanks, add enough mushroom-flavored water to do so. Bring to a low boil, cover, reduce heat to low, and simmer shanks until tender, about 1½ hours. Turn shanks occasionally as they cook. When done, proceed with adding vegetables and completing the recipe, or cool to room temperature. If shanks are cooked more than 3 hours ahead of serving, transfer to a bowl and refrigerate until ready to serve.

Last-Minute Cooking
Combine cornstarch with an equal amount of cold water and set aside.

Bring veal shanks to a simmer over medium heat, then add carrots and simmer, covered, for 10 minutes.

With a slotted spoon, remove shanks from liquid and transfer to dinner plates. Add green onions to sauce and bring to a low boil over medium heat. Stir in a little cornstarch mixture to lightly thicken sauce, then pour sauce over shanks. Serve at once.

Serves: 3 as an entrée; 6 as part of an Oriental dinner.

Notes: You can easily double or triple this recipe to serve a larger number of people.

Another way to cook this dish is to use a deep baking dish that can double as the serving dish. After browning the shanks, transfer them to the baking dish, add the mushrooms and sauce, cover, and bake in a 325°F oven about 1½ hours. Add the carrots and green onions during the last 15 minutes, then when done remove dish from oven. Pour most of the sauce into a frying pan and bring to a low boil. Lightly thicken with the cornstarch mixture, then pour sauce back over shanks. Bring dish to table and serve.

Oriental Braised Veal Shanks.

CINNAMON-ORANGE MU SHU LAMB

1 cup dark soy sauce
½ cup light soy sauce
½ cup dry sherry
3 tablespoons sugar
2 cinnamon sticks
10 whole cloves
1 dried red chili (optional)
1 teaspoon Sichuan peppercorns
   peel from 1 orange
6 thin slices fresh ginger
4 lamb shanks (about 3 pounds total weight)
6 dried black Chinese mushrooms
2 cups slivered green cabbage
1 cup slivered carrots
2 green onions, slivered
3 eggs
2 tablespoons cornstarch
12 Peking pancakes (see Appendix)
2 tablespoons peanut oil
2 cloves garlic, finely minced
2 teaspoons finely minced fresh ginger
¾ cup hoisin sauce
   Sauce
2 tablespoons dry sherry
1 tablespoon light soy sauce
1 tablespoon Oriental sesame oil
½ teaspoon Chinese chili sauce
¼ teaspoon sugar
¼ teaspoon salt

Lamb shank meat, simmered in a rich sauce until tender, is later stir-fried with shredded cabbage, scrambled eggs, and mushrooms. When placed inside Peking pancakes, this mixture's contrasting textures and rich cinnamon flavor create a great taste sensation. The preliminary cooking of the lamb can be done a day in advance, but the meat tastes the most flavorful when simmered just hours before serving, then cut off the bone into bite-size pieces and left to cool in the sauce until you are ready to complete the last-minute stir-frying.

Advance Preparation

In a 2-quart saucepan, combine soy sauces, sherry, sugar, cinnamon, cloves, chili, peppercorns, orange peel, and sliced ginger. Add 4 cups water and place over low heat. Bring to a low simmer, cover, and simmer 1 hour.

Cut meat off bones in pieces as large as possible, then add to sauce and simmer until meat is tender, about 2 hours.

Remove meat from sauce and let cool. When cool enough to handle, cut into bite-size pieces. (If you are preparing this a day in advance, refrigerate meat at this point. Strain liquid through a sieve and store in refrigerator to have the next time you make this recipe.) If you are serving the dish in a few hours, return meat to liquid to cool completely and do not refrigerate.

Soak mushrooms in hot water until soft, about 20 minutes. Discard stems. Overlap caps and cut into shreds, then set aside. Combine with slivered vegetables and refrigerate until ready to finish cooking.

In a small bowl, combine 3 tablespoons of the cinnamon-soy liquid with the ingredients for the sauce. Set aside.

Into a small bowl, break eggs and beat well. Stir cornstarch with an equal amount of cold water and set aside.

Fold and reheat pancakes according to directions on page 152.

If meat has been left to cool in sauce, remove now from sauce. Strain and refrigerate or freeze the liquid to use when making this recipe again.

Place wok over highest heat. When wok is very hot, add 1 tablespoon peanut oil to center of wok and roll oil around sides of wok. When oil just begins to smoke, add eggs and stir-fry, scrambling them until they become firm, about 1 minute. Transfer eggs to a work platter.

Immediately return wok to highest heat and add remaining tablespoon peanut oil to center. Add garlic and ginger and sauté a few seconds. Add vegetables and stir-fry until cabbage turns a brighter color, about 2 minutes.

Add lamb and scrambled eggs to wok, then pour in sauce. When sauce comes to a low boil, stir in a little of the cornstarch mixture so that sauce glazes the food. Taste and adjust seasonings. Turn out onto a heated platter.

Serve lamb mixture with hot pancakes and a dish of hoisin sauce. Each person spreads a little hoisin sauce

across the center of a pancake, places about ½ cup of filling on top of the sauce, then rolls the pancake into a cylinder and folds one end upward to keep the filling from leaking out. The roll is eaten with the fingers.

Serves: 4 as an entrée; 6 to 8 as part of an Oriental dinner.

Menu Ideas: Oriental Christmas party for 10 — Spareribs with Secret Chinese Barbecue Sauce (make barbecue sauce a week in advance and refrigerate); Seafood Pot Stickers in Lemon Sauce (make sauce a day in advance; make dumpling filling in food processor on day of party); Shredded Chicken Salad (make dressing a day in advance; buy a barbecued chicken from market); Salmon Flower Soup (arrange soup bowls with flower design and refrigerate; chicken stock need only be reheated to finish soup); Cinnamon-Orange Mu Shu Lamb; Ginger Ice Cream (make 2 days in advance) accompanied with a chocolate sauce.

Notes: The best substitute for lamb shanks is country-style pork spareribs. Simmer in the cinnamon-soy liquid until tender, then proceed with recipe.

OVERLEAF: Veal Scaloppine with Shiitake Cream Sauce; Artichokes in Black-Bean Tomato Sauce.

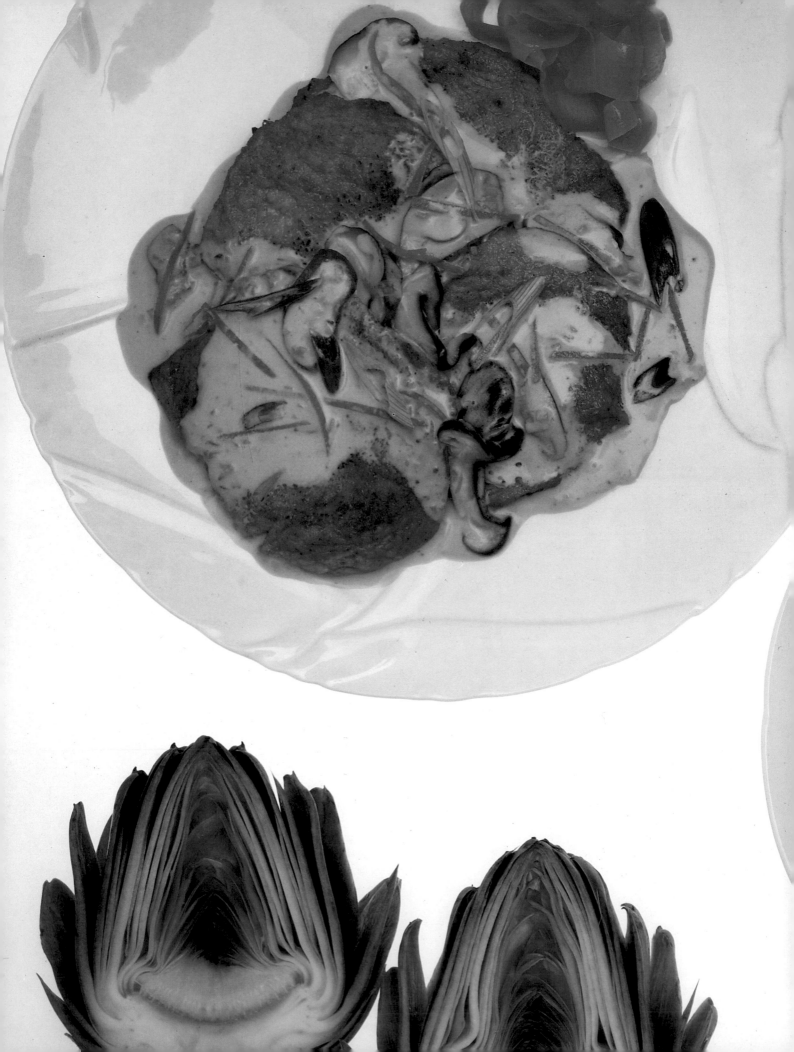

VEAL SCALOPPINE IN SHIITAKE CREAM SAUCE

- 4 ounces shiitake mushrooms
- 1 medium carrot
- 1 green onion
- freshly ground black pepper
- 4 veal scaloppine (½ pound total weight), pounded
- all-purpose flour, for dusting
- ¼ cup olive oil
- ¼ cup unsalted butter

Sauce
- ½ cup heavy (whipping) cream
- ¼ cup dry sherry
- 1 tablespoon light soy sauce
- 1 tablespoon Oriental sesame oil
- ½ teaspoon grated or finely minced orange peel
- ¼ teaspoon crushed Sichuan peppercorns
- ⅛ teaspoon Chinese chili sauce
- 1 tablespoon finely minced fresh ginger

The woody smell of fresh shiitake mushrooms infuses this cream sauce. For a variation, the sauce is superb on broiled sole, grilled chicken breasts, and homemade noodles or toss with won tons that you've just cooked in a big pot of boiling water.

Advance Preparation
Discard stems from mushrooms and cut caps into ⅛-inch-wide strips; set aside.

Cut carrot into paper-thin slices, then overlap slices and cut into shreds. Place shredded carrot in a sieve and pour 4 cups boiling water over it. Rinse in cold water and pat dry. Cut green onion into shreds, then set the onion and carrot aside to be used later as a garnish.

In a small bowl, combine sauce ingredients; set aside.

Cooking
Place dinner plates in a 140°F oven.

Sprinkle pepper on both sides of scaloppine. Lightly dust with flour, shaking off excess.

Place a 12-inch skillet over high heat. When pan is hot, add olive oil and butter. When butter begins to bubble, add 2 veal scaloppine. Cook about 20 seconds on each side — there should be no pink color or juice showing on surface — then transfer to heated plates in oven. Repeat cooking procedure with remaining veal.

Pour oil from frying pan and return pan to high heat. Add mushrooms and sauce, then bring to a furious boil. Boil, stirring, until sauce begins to turn light brown and thicken, about 4 minutes.

Spoon sauce over top of each veal scaloppine. Garnish with a little shredded carrot and green onion. Serve at once.

Serves: 4 as an entrée.

Menu Ideas: This is a very rich dish. Begin the evening with a dumpling appetizer, such as one of the recipes from Chapter 7. Follow with the veal and a fresh vegetable in a simple sauce, then a garden salad. Conclude the evening with a light lemon cake and good coffee.

Notes: You can make this dish successfully for 8 by using a 14-inch frying pan, which holds 4 veal scaloppine perfectly. Cook scaloppine in 2 batches.

COCONUT LAMB STEW

1½ pounds boneless lamb stew meat

1 large yam

2 tart cooking apples
juice from ½ lemon

½ cup shredded unsweetened coconut

3 tablespoons peanut oil

½ cup dark raisins

1 tablespoon cornstarch

Sauce

4 cloves garlic, finely minced

1 tablespoon finely minced fresh ginger

⅓ cup chopped fresh basil

2 teaspoons grated or finely minced orange peel

1 teaspoon grated nutmeg

1 cinnamon stick

1½ cups unsweetened coconut milk

2 tablespoons dry sherry

2 tablespoons curry powder

1 teaspoon Chinese chili sauce

½ teaspoon salt

Tender lamb, bright orange yams, crunchy apple slices, and plump raisins—all glazed in a coconut-curry sauce—makes a beautiful presentation served with Oriental Rice Pilaf and a tossed green salad.

Advance Preparation

Cut meat into bite-size pieces. Peel yam, then cut into ½-inch cubes; you should have about 1 cup. Place cubes in cold water. Core but do not peel apples. Cut apples into ½-inch cubes and toss with lemon juice. Set aside. (If preparing meat a day ahead, hold off preparing apples until last-minute cooking.)

Place coconut in a 10-inch skillet and set over medium-high heat. Toast coconut until light golden, about 2 minutes. Set aside

In a bowl, combine sauce ingredients; set aside.

Advance Cooking

Place a wok or heavy 12-inch frying pan over medium-high heat. When hot, add oil. When oil just begins to smoke, add meat and stir-fry until it loses its raw color, about 4 minutes. Add sauce to meat, bring to a low boil, cover, and reduce heat to lowest setting. Cook, stirring occasionally, until lamb is tender, about 1½ hours. (This can be completed a day in advance of serving.) If sauce appears oily, blot up oil using paper towels.

Last-Minute Cooking

Bring lamb back to a simmer, then stir in yams and raisins. Cover and simmer 15 minutes. If apples have not yet been prepared, then core and cut into ½-inch cubes. Add to stew, cover, and simmer another 5 minutes.

Remove cinnamon stick from sauce. Stir cornstarch with an equal amount of cold water, then stir into stew to lightly thicken over medium heat. Taste and adjust seasonings, then turn out onto a heated serving platter or individual plates. Sprinkle with toasted coconut and serve at once.

Serves: 4 as an entrée; 6 to 8 as part of an Oriental dinner.

Menu Ideas: a do-ahead Oriental dinner for 12 — New Wave Shrimp (triple recipe) with Oriental dipping sauces, Chinese Pickles (double recipe), Mahogany Chicken Wings (double recipe), Lemon Shrimp Salad (double recipe), Coconut Lamb Stew (triple recipe), Fireworks Rice (triple recipe), and Oriental Fruit Tart (double recipe). Plan this dinner at least a week ahead and complete the preparations with a friend — or give your staff the next day off!

SICHUAN LEMON VEAL CHOPS

1 tablespoon white sesame seeds
4 1-inch thick veal chops
 salt
 freshly ground black pepper
½ cup all-purpose flour
3 tablespoons peanut oil
4 tablespoons unsalted butter
1 tablespoon cornstarch
1 bunch chives, chopped
 Sauce
2 cloves garlic, finely minced
1 tablespoon finely minced fresh ginger
¼ cup dry vermouth
¼ cup chicken stock
1 tablespoon grated or finely minced lemon peel
2 tablespoons fresh lemon juice
2 tablespoons light soy sauce
1 tablespoon sugar
1 teaspoon dry mustard
½ teaspoon freshly ground black pepper
¼ teaspoon crushed Sichuan peppercorns

For busy executives, overworked mothers, and everyone behind schedule, here is an elegant dish for a quick dinner. Pan-fry these thick veal chops, transfer them to a preheated oven, and as they finish cooking make a lemon-pepper sauce in the skillet. The sweet butter swirled in at the last minute adds the perfect enrichment.

Advance Preparation
In a small ungreased skillet set over high heat, stir sesame seeds until light golden, about 2 minutes. Immediately pour out and set aside.

Prepare sauce. In a small bowl, combine garlic and ginger. In another small bowl combine remaining sauce ingredients; set aside.

Cooking
Preheat oven to 400°F.

Season chops with a sprinkling of salt and pepper. Dust lightly with flour, then shake off excess.

Place a 12-inch stainless-steel skillet (not cast-iron or aluminum) over medium-high heat. When hot, add oil and 3 tablespoons butter. When butter begins to bubble, add chops and cook on both sides until golden, about 6 to 8 minutes. Regulate heat so that oil is always sizzling but not smoking.

Transfer chops to a small baking pan and place in oven. Pour oil from skillet. Bake chops until they are still a little pink in center, about 15 minutes (Internal temperature should measure 160°F on a meat thermometer.)

Stir cornstarch with an equal amount of cold water and set aside.

When chops are nearly cooked, reheat pan over medium-high heat and add the garlic and ginger for the sauce. Sauté briefly, then add rest of sauce mixture. Bring to a boil and scrape up particles from surface of skillet. With sauce at a low boil, stir in a little of the cornstarch mixture to lightly thicken sauce. Remove from heat and stir in remaining tablespoon butter.

Transfer chops to heated dinner plates and spoon sauce over them. Garnish with chopped chives and toasted sesame seeds. Serve at once.

Serves: 4 as an entrée.
Menu Ideas: An easy dinner for 4 – Sichuan Lemon Veal Chops, a pasta salad, and apples and pears with various cheeses for dessert.
Notes: The veal chops also can be seasoned with salt and pepper, then grilled. When chops are nearly done, sauté garlic and ginger in a small skillet with 1 tablespoon butter. Add sauce mixture, bring to a boil, and thicken with a little cornstarch mixture. Stir remaining 1 tablespoon butter into sauce, baste the chops with some of the sauce, and serve, garnished with chives and toasted sesame seeds.

Paper-Wrapped Salmon; Sichuan Lemon Veal Chops.   171

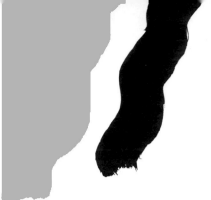

CHINESE CHILI WITH PEPPERS

¾   **pound ground lamb**

1   **tablespoon dark soy sauce**

1   **tablespoon dry sherry**

1   **tablespoon hoisin sauce**

1   **green bell pepper**

1   **red bell pepper**

1   **yellow bell pepper**

1   **small yellow onion**

2   **tablespoons cornstarch**

2   **tablespoons peanut oil**

1   **tablespoon finely minced fresh ginger**

4   **cloves garlic, finely minced**

    Sauce

½   **cup chicken stock**

2   **tablespoons dry sherry**

2   **tablespoons hoisin sauce**

2   **tablespoons oyster sauce**

1   **tablespoon bean sauce (see Appendix)**

1   **tablespoon Oriental sesame oil**

1   **tablespoon distilled white vinegar**

1½   **teaspoons Chinese chili sauce**

Stir-fried ground meat and diced vegetables in a spicy sauce produce an Oriental "chili" that can be mounded on steamed rice or buttered noodles to make a quick and satisfying dinner.

Advance Preparation

In a bowl, thoroughly combine lamb, soy sauce, sherry, and hoisin sauce. Set aside until ready to cook.

Seed and stem peppers, then cut into ½-inch cubes. Peel and coarsely chop onion. Set peppers and onion aside.

In a small bowl, combine sauce ingredients; set aside.

Last-Minute Cooking

Stir cornstarch with an equal amount of cold water, then set aside.

Place wok over highest heat. When wok becomes very hot, add 1 tablespoon peanut oil to center, then roll oil around sides of wok. When oil just begins to smoke, add lamb and stir-fry, pressing meat against the sides of the wok, until it loses its raw color and separates into small pieces, about 3 minutes. Transfer to a work platter.

Immediately return wok to highest heat and add remaining tablespoon peanut oil to center. Add ginger and garlic and sauté for a few seconds. Add vegeta-bles and stir-fry until peppers brighten and onion becomes transparent, about 2 minutes.

Return lamb to wok and pour in sauce. Bring sauce to a low boil, then stir in a little cornstarch mixture to lightly thicken. Reduce heat to low and simmer for 2 minutes. Turn out onto a heated platter or individual plates. Serve at once with steamed rice, noodles, or bread.

Serves: 2 as an entrée; 6 to 8 as part of an Oriental meal.

Menu Ideas: Easy dinner for 4 — Chinese Chili with Peppers (double recipe); Onion Bread (double recipe; cook before guests arrive, and reheat in oven); Steamed Corn with Chinese Herb Sauce; ice cream and coffee.

Notes: This dish is excellent made with ground pork, beef, or lamb, but not with ground veal, chicken, or turkey.

To simplify any stir-fry dish, substitute ¾ pound ground meat (pork, beef, or lamb) for the cubed or sliced meat or seafood. This shortens the preparation time but results in an equally good dish.

HOT-AND-PUNGENT LAMB WITH BROCCOLI

1 **pound boneless lamb cut from leg or loin, trimmed**
1 **tablespoon dark soy sauce**
1 **tablespoon dry sherry**
2 **teaspoons hoisin sauce**
2 **tablespoons plus 2 teaspoons cornstarch**
2 **tablespoons plus 2 teaspoons peanut oil**
1 **bunch broccoli**
3 **cloves garlic, finely minced**

Sauce

¼ **cup dry sherry**
2 **tablespoons light soy sauce**
1½ **tablespoons distilled white vinegar**
1 **tablespoon Oriental sesame oil**
1 **tablespoon honey**
1 **teaspoon Chinese chili sauce**
¼ **teaspoon salt**
2 **tablespoons minced fresh coriander (cilantro)**

This is one of my favorite recipes to teach in cooking classes. The rich flavor of the lamb perfectly matches the spicy sauce.

Advance Preparation

Cut lamb into very thin slices about ½ inch across and 1 inch long. Place in a bowl and add dark soy sauce, sherry, hoisin sauce, 2 teaspoons cornstarch, and 2 teaspoons peanut oil. Mix well.

Bring 8 cups water to a rapid boil. Next to your stove have a large bowl of ice water. Cut flowerettes off broccoli, then drop flowerettes into boiling water. When they turn bright green, in about 2 minutes, transfer them immediately with a slotted spoon to ice water. After 5 minutes, pat broccoli dry and refrigerate until ready to use.

In a small bowl combine ingredients for sauce. Set aside.

Last-Minute Cooking

Stir remaining 2 tablespoons cornstarch with an equal amount of cold water; set aside.

Place wok over highest heat. When wok is very hot, add 1 tablespoon peanut oil to center and roll oil around sides of wok. When oil just begins to smoke, add lamb and stir-fry, pressing meat against the sides of the wok, until it loses its raw outside color, about 2 minutes. Transfer to a work platter.

Immediately return wok to highest heat and add remaining tablespoon peanut oil to center. Add garlic and sauté a few seconds. Add broccoli and stir-fry until broccoli is heated through, about 1 minute.

Return lamb to wok and pour in sauce. Bring sauce to a low boil, then stir in a little of the cornstarch mixture to lightly thicken. Taste and adjust seasonings. Turn out onto a heated platter or individual plates. Serve at once.

Serves: 2 to 3 as an entrée; 6 to 8 as part of an Oriental meal.

Menu Ideas: Chinese dinner for 2 after the movies — Hot-and-Pungent Lamb with Broccoli, Marco Polo Noodles, and Grand Marnier Mocha Ice Cream.

OVERLEAF: Rack of Lamb in Hunan Barbecue Sauce; Brussels sprouts.

RACK OF LAMB IN HUNAN BARBECUE SAUCE

1 rack of lamb (about 2 pounds total weight)

Barbecue Sauce

5 tablespoons hoisin sauce

3 tablespoons honey

2 tablespoons dark soy sauce

2 tablespoons dry sherry

1 tablespoon Oriental sesame oil

1 tablespoon curry powder

1 teaspoon Chinese chili sauce

4 cloves garlic, finely minced

1 tablespoon grated or finely minced orange peel

1 tablespoon salted black beans, rinsed and chopped

¼ cup white sesame seeds

Nearly everyone associates Chinese cooking with hours of kitchen drudgery. Yet nothing is easier than rubbing a rack of lamb (or, for that matter, a veal loin or a New York strip steak) with a Chinese barbecue sauce and grilling or roasting the meat. The thick chops or steak, glazed with the rich sauce, would be delicious served with buttered parsley potatoes, a Caesar salad, and a fruit tart.

Advance Preparation

If the butcher has tied the rack of lamb to secure an outside layer of fat, untie the roast and remove and reserve the layer of fat.

In a bowl, combine all barbecue sauce ingredients except sesame seeds. In a small ungreased skillet set over high heat, stir sesame seeds until light golden, about 2 minutes. Immediately pour out and let cool momentarily, then add to sauce ingredients. Stir well.

Place meat in a stainless-steel or glass bowl and pour in sauce. Marinate for 2 hours, then drain and reserve marinade. Carefully re-tie fat onto the roast to prevent it from burning and drying out during cooking.

Cooking

Prepare a charcoal fire. When coals are ash-colored, grill meat, rotating occasionally and brushing on more barbecue sauce, until medium-rare in center, 30 to 40 minutes. Alternatively, roast in 400°F oven until meat thermometer registers 145°F.

Slice rack into chops. Place on individual heated plates, overlapping chops. Serve at once.

Serves: 2 as an entrée.

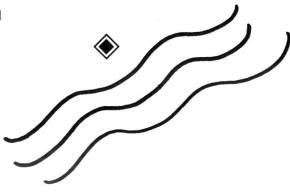

SWEETBREADS WITH CORIANDER-LIME SAUCE

1½ pounds sweetbreads

1 teaspoon salt

1 tablespoon fresh lemon juice

½ cup pine nuts (pignoli)

4 ounces fresh shiitake mushrooms

3 green onions

2 tablespoons cornstarch

3 tablespoons unsalted butter

3 cloves garlic, finely minced

2 limes, cut into wedges, for garnish

Sauce

¾ cup chicken stock

1 tablespoon Oriental sesame oil

2 teaspoons dark soy sauce

½ teaspoon Chinese chili sauce

½ teaspoon lightly crushed Sichuan peppercorns

½ teaspoon salt

3 tablespoons chopped fresh coriander (cilantro)

2 teaspoons grated or finely minced lime peel

Serving an ingredient unknown in traditional Chinese cooking, such as sweetbreads, lends a sense of drama to an Oriental dinner. The smooth texture and subtle flavor of sweetbreads combine nicely with a wide range of Oriental sauces.

Advance Preparation (7 to 9 Hours before Serving)
Place sweetbreads in a deep saucepan and cover with cold water.

Let soak for 1 hour, then drain and cover again with water. Add salt and lemon juice. Over medium-low heat, bring liquid to a low boil, reduce heat, and simmer for 10 minutes. Immediately rinse sweetbreads under cold water, then place in a shallow pan. Cover with waxed paper, then put a very large pot filled with cold water on top to weight down sweetbreads. Refrigerate for 6 to 8 hours. The weight gives the sweetbreads a better texture.

Pull away any thick pieces of outer membrane from the sweetbreads. Separate into bite-size nuggets and set aside until ready to cook.

Toast pine nuts in a 325°F oven until light golden, about 8 minutes. Set aside.

Stem mushrooms, then cut caps into quarters. Cut green onions on a diagonal into 1-inch lengths, then combine with mushrooms and set aside.

In a small bowl, combine sauce ingredients; set aside.

Cooking
Combine cornstarch with an equal amount of cold water and set aside.

Place a 12-inch skillet over medium-high heat. When hot, add 2 tablespoons butter. When butter begins to bubble, add garlic. Sauté for a few seconds, then add sweetbreads, mushrooms, and green onions. Sauté until mushrooms soften and green onions brighten, about 3 minutes.

Add sauce to skillet. When sauce comes to a low boil, stir in a little of the cornstarch mixture to lightly thicken, then add pine nuts. Taste and adjust seasonings. Remove from heat and stir in remaining tablespoon butter. Turn out onto a heated platter or individual plates. Serve at once, accompanied by lime wedges to squeeze over sweetbreads.

Serves: 4 as an entrée; 6 to 8 as part of an Oriental dinner.

Menu Ideas: New Wave Chinese dinner for 8 — California Won Ton Soup, Spicy Swordfish Salad, Sweetbreads with Coriander-Lime Sauce, Oriental Rice Pilaf, Chocolate-Chip Almond Cookies, and fresh fruit.

There are so many exciting ways to modify traditional Chinese dumpling, noodle, and rice dishes into new variations. For example, when Chinese steam, boil, pan-fry, or deep-fry dumplings, traditionally each person swishes the dumplings across various condiments such as vinegar, hot chili oil, and mustard for added flavor. This chapter offers a different approach. The dumplings — besides being filled with swordfish, salmon, and other ingredients not typical to Chinese cuisine — are cooked in a sauce or glazed with a dressing before being brought to the table. Speckled with coriander, ginger, and sesame seeds; pan-fried in a spicy orange sauce; or served with Chinese Salsa, the dumplings are accented by the flavor of each sauce. Any of the dumplings, which can be folded hours in advance of cooking, make an outstanding appetizer or light first course preceding a main dinner selection.

Standard noodle dishes offered by Chinese restaurants combine pan-fried or stir-fried noodles with meat or seafood. Requiring considerable preparation and last-minute cooking, most of these classic dishes are better tasted in restaurants than cooked at home.

Marco Polo Dumplings; Chicken Curry Dumplings.   179

We take a different approach, with five noodle recipes in this chapter that call for simply tossing boiled noodles with sauces rich in Oriental seasonings. Served as a first course Italian style, or as an accompaniment to any meat or seafood entrée, these are perfect quick dishes for impromptu meals. But if you want a more substantial noodle dish, Seafood on Pan-Fried Noodles makes a spectacular entrée for a small dinner party.

As for rice, why duplicate at home the ubiquitous bowl of plain steamed rice served by Chinese restaurants? Unless thoroughly washed, simmered in the precise amount of water, and kept warm during dinner, plain rice can become offensive rather than merely innocuous. This chapter suggests more palatable alternatives. In rice dishes offered here, Oriental seasonings and chicken stock are added to sautéed rice for a Pacific-style rice pilaf. Requiring only a few minutes of work and perfumed with flavors such as curry powder, saffron, tangerine peel, and chili, these dishes go perfectly alongside any entrée in this book.

Easy-to-prepare recipes in this chapter are Marco Polo Noodles, Tangy Citrus Noodles, Spicy Thai Noodles, Chinese Primavera, Noodles in Jade Sauce, Oriental Rice Pilaf, Fireworks Rice, and Curried Pineapple Rice.

MARCO POLO DUMPLINGS

- 4 dried black Chinese mushrooms
- 6 water chestnuts, preferably fresh
- 2 green onions
- 1 pound raw shrimp
- 1 egg white
- 1 tablespoon cornstarch
- 1 tablespoon light soy sauce
- 2 teaspoons dry sherry
- 1 teaspoon Oriental sesame oil
- ½ teaspoon Chinese chili sauce
- ¼ teaspoon salt
- 30 won ton skins
  cornstarch, for dusting

Dressing

- 2 tablespoons light soy sauce
- 2 tablespoons dry sherry
- ¼ cup red wine vinegar
- 2 tablespoons Oriental sesame oil
- 2 teaspoons hoisin sauce
- 2 teaspoons sugar
- 1 teaspoon Chinese chili sauce
- 2 cloves garlic, finely minced
- 1 tablespoon finely minced fresh ginger
- 1 tablespoon grated or finely minced tangerine or orange peel
- 3 tablespoons finely minced fresh coriander (cilantro)
- 4 tablespoons finely minced green onions
- 2 tablespoons white sesame seeds

One day, when I was in a hurry for something delicious, I dropped frozen dumplings into boiling water, cooked them until they floated to the surface, and then quickly tossed the dumplings with a little leftover Chinese salad dressing. The Chinese dumpling filling is authentic, but tossing the cooked dumplings with a sauce is more Italian than Chinese, thus the name here.

Advance Preparation
Prepare filling. Soak mushrooms in hot water until soft, about 20 minutes. Cut off and discard stems. Peel fresh water chestnuts, if using. Cut green onions into small pieces. Mince mushroom caps, water chestnuts, and green onions together by hand or in a food processor.

Shell and devein shrimp. Coarsely chop shrimp along with the egg white by hand or in a processor. Do not mince so finely that its texture is destroyed. Combine shrimp with mushroom mixture and add cornstarch, soy sauce, sherry, sesame oil, chili sauce, and salt. Mix thoroughly.

Within 5 hours of cooking, fold dumplings. Trim won tons into circles. Place 2 teaspoons of filling in the center of each won ton. Moisten the edges with water and fold dumplings in half over filling, being careful not to flatten filling. Press edges together. Dumplings will be half-moon shaped. Moisten each end of dumplings, then touch the moistened ends together. The dumplings should look like little caps. Place on a layer of waxed paper lightly dusted with cornstarch. Refrigerate, uncovered, until ready to cook.

Combine all dressing ingredients except sesame seeds. Purée in food processor, then transfer to a small dish. In a small ungreased skillet set over high heat, stir sesame seeds until light golden. Immediately pour out and set aside.

Last-Minute Cooking
Bring 4 quarts of water to a vigorous boil. Add the dumplings and give them a gentle stir. When the dumplings float to the surface (about 3 minutes), gently tip into a colander to drain.

Transfer dumplings to a mixing bowl. Add the dressing and toss. Transfer dumplings to a heated serving platter and sprinkle on sesame seeds. Serve at once.

Serves: 6 to 8 as an appetizer; 2 as an entrée.

SWORDFISH DUMPLINGS WITH CHINESE SALSA

- 4 dried black Chinese mushrooms
- 4 water chestnuts, preferably fresh
- 2 green onions
- 1 12-ounce bunch spinach, stemmed
- ¾ pound swordfish
- 1 egg white
- 1 tablespoon light soy sauce
- 1 tablespoon dry sherry
- ¼ teaspoon white pepper
- ¼ teaspoon salt
- 1 tablespoon finely minced fresh ginger
- 30 won ton skins
  cornstarch, for dusting
  Chinese Salsa (page 37)
  Dressing
- 2 tablespoons safflower oil
- 2 tablespoons rice vinegar
- 1 tablespoon light soy sauce
- ¼ teaspoon Chinese chili sauce
- ¼ teaspoon salt
- 2 tablespoons minced fresh coriander (cilantro)

The firm texture of swordfish wrapped in tender dumpling skins contrasts beautifully with pungent Chinese Salsa. Accompanied by Roast Citrus Chicken, Steamed Broccoli with Oriental Hollandaise Sauce, fresh fruit, and a dry white wine, this would be a lovely meal for six.

Advance Preparation
Prepare filling. Soak mushrooms in hot water until soft, about 20 minutes. Cut off and discard stems. Peel fresh water chestnuts, if using. Cut green onions into small pieces. Mince mushroom caps, water chestnuts, and green onions together by hand or in a food processor. Drop spinach leaves into 1 quart rapidly boiling water. When leaves wilt, in about 10 seconds, drain and rinse under cold water. Squeeze out all water, then mince spinach by hand. Stir into the mushroom mixture.

Coarsely chop the swordfish and combine with the egg white by hand or in a processor. Combine fish with the spinach mixture. Add soy sauce, sherry, white pepper, salt, and ginger. Mix thoroughly.

Within 5 hours of cooking, fold dumplings. Trim won tons into circles. Fold as described on page 181.

Combine ingredients for dressing. Set aside.

Last-Minute Cooking
Bring 4 quarts of water to a vigorous boil. Add the dumplings and give them a gentle stir. When the dumplings float to the surface (about 3 minutes), gently tip them into a colander to drain.

Transfer dumplings to a mixing bowl. Add dressing and toss. Transfer dumplings to a heated serving platter. Serve at once, accompanied by Chinese Salsa. Each person spoons the salsa over the dumplings.

Serves: 6 to 8 as an appetizer; 2 as an entrée.

Swordfish Dumplings with Chinese Salsa; Oriental Avocado Salad.

SALMON DUMPLINGS WITH CUCUMBER RELISH

Cucumber Relish
- ½ **hothouse cucumber**
- 1 **teaspoon salt**
- ½ **cup rice vinegar**
- ¼ **cup sugar**
- ¼ **teaspoon Chinese chili sauce**

Dumpling Filling
- 4 **dried black Chinese mushrooms**
- 1 **bunch chives**
- 1 **medium carrot**
- 1 **pound skinned and boned fresh salmon**
- 1 **egg white**
- 1 **tablespoon finely minced fresh ginger**
- 1 **tablespoon oyster sauce**
- 2 **teaspoons dry sherry**
- 1 **teaspoon Oriental sesame oil**
- ¼ **teaspoon sugar**
- ⅛ **teaspoon white pepper**
- 30 **won ton skins**
- **cornstarch, for dusting**
- 30 **small peas, for garnish**

My hands shook as I held the tray of dumplings. Julia Child had entered the kitchen. Yet within minutes Julia's natural manner and good humor made my thousand concerns evaporate. Salmon Dumplings was one of the dishes that evening. Use the finest quality fresh salmon, steam the dumplings briefly, and accompany them with a sweet-pungent relish to contrast with the delicate filling.

Advance Preparation
Prepare cucumber relish (can be made a day in advance). Cut cucumber in half and scoop out seeds. Cut crosswise into $1/16$-inch-wide pieces. Sprinkle evenly with salt and set aside for 1 hour. Meanwhile, in small saucepan combine vinegar, sugar, and chili sauce. Bring to a low boil, reduce heat to low, and simmer for 5 minutes. Cool to room temperature. Rinse cucumbers with cold water. Pat dry with paper towels and combine with pickling mixture. Let marinate for at least 1 hour.

Prepare filling. Soak mushrooms in hot water until soft, about 20 minutes. Cut off and discard stems. Mince mushroom caps and chives. Mince or sliver carrot. (If using a food processor, cut mushrooms, chives, and carrot into small pieces, then mince together in the processor.)

Cut salmon into small cubes and place in bowl. Add the egg white to the salmon and combine well (this can also be done in a food processor but avoid mincing salmon so finely that it loses all its texture). Add salmon mixture to mushroom mixture; then stir in the ginger, oyster sauce, sherry, sesame oil, sugar, and white pepper. Mix filling thoroughly.

Within 5 hours of cooking, fold dumplings. Trim won tons into circles. Add 1 tablespoon filling to the center of each won ton skin. Bring edges of skin up around filling. Place dumpling in the soft hollow of one hand between your thumb and index finger. Squeeze the "waist" gently with that same index finger while also pressing the top and bottom of the dumpling with your other index finger and thumb. The dumplings should look like round, thin cylinders with a flat top and bottom. Place dumplings on a layer of waxed paper lightly dusted with cornstarch. Put a pea in the center of each dumpling. Refrigerate, uncovered, until ready to cook.

Last-Minute Cooking
Drain cucumbers and place in decorative bowl.

Bring water to a vigorous boil in the bottom of a Chinese steamer. Place a layer of foil in the steamer tray, leaving 1 inch around the edge to allow steam to circulate. Rub foil with a little vegetable oil, then place dumplings on foil. Put tray over boiling water, cover, and steam until dumplings just become firm to the touch, about 5 minutes. Be sure not to overcook dumplings or salmon will be dry.

Remove steamer from heat. Lift out foil and slide dumplings onto a heated platter. Serve with pickled cucumbers.

Serves: 6 to 10 as an appetizer.
Notes: These dumplings are excellent pan-fried. Place a 12-inch nonstick frying pan over high heat. Add 2 tablespoons peanut oil, then add dumplings. Fry until bottoms brown, about 2 minutes. Add ½ cup water, then immediately cover. Cook dumplings until firm, about 2 minutes more. Remove cover and continue cooking dumplings until water boils away and dumpling bottoms become very dark. Tip out onto a platter and serve.

TANGY CITRUS NOODLES

salt
½ pound dried spaghetti-style noodles, preferably Chinese

Sauce

1 tablespoon finely minced garlic
2 tablespoons olive oil
3 tablespoons light soy sauce
2 tablespoons dry sherry
2 tablespoons rice vinegar
2 tablespoons Oriental sesame oil
1 tablespoon light brown sugar
½ teaspoon Chinese chili sauce
¼ teaspoon ground Sichuan peppercorns
1 teaspoon grated or finely minced orange peel
½ cup chopped green onions
¼ cup white sesame seeds

A few friends and I first tasted this dish at a Guilin road-side restaurant set among dramatic lime-stone peaks that climbed toward the sky. What began as a late-afternoon snack of dumplings became an early dinner of sautéed frogs legs in garlic sauce, fluffy omelets glazed with a sweet-pungent sauce, snake soup with fresh straw mushrooms, and these delicious citrus-flavored noodles. After that gastronomic adventure, we prepared for our formal banquet later that evening with a brisk walk along bicycle-lined streets.

Advance Preparation
Prepare sauce. Combine garlic with olive oil and set aside. In a small bowl, combine all sauce ingredients except sesame seeds. In a small ungreased skillet set over high heat, stir sesame seeds until light golden, about 2 minutes. Immediately tip out. Add to sauce.

Last-Minute Cooking
Bring at least 4 quarts of water to a vigorous boil. Lightly salt water, then add noodles. Cook noodles until they lose their raw taste but are still firm, about 5 minutes. Immediately drain in a colander. Shake out excess water, then transfer to a large bowl.

Meanwhile, in a small skillet set over medium-high heat, sauté garlic mixture. After 30 seconds, add remaining sauce ingredients and bring to a low boil. Remove from heat.

Add sauce to noodles, then toss well. Turn out onto a heated platter or individual plates. Serve at once.

Serves: 4 as a side dish with any entrée; 6 to 8 as part of an Oriental dinner.

Menu Ideas: Quick Oriental dinner for 6 – Spareribs with Secret Chinese Barbecue Sauce (2 sides of ribs), Scallop Thread Soup, Tangy Citrus Noodles (double recipe), and a lemon meringue pie.

Tangy Citrus Noodles.

SEAFOOD POT STICKERS IN LEMON SAUCE

4 water chestnuts, preferably fresh

2 green onions

1 12-ounce bunch spinach, stemmed

1 pound raw shrimp

1 egg white

1 tablespoon light soy sauce

¼ teaspoon Chinese chili sauce

1 tablespoon finely minced fresh ginger

2 teaspoons grated or finely minced lemon peel

30 won ton skins

  cornstarch, for dusting

2 tablespoons peanut oil

Sauce

1 teaspoon grated or finely minced lemon peel

¼ cup lemon juice

3 tablespoons sugar

2 tablespoons dry sherry

1 tablespoon light soy sauce

¼ teaspoon Chinese chili sauce

¼ teaspoon salt

1 tablespoon finely minced fresh ginger

Pot stickers, northern China's most famous dumplings, are steamed and then pan-fried until the bottoms are crisp. Traditionally, pot stickers are made with a homemade dough and require laborious pleating to create crescent shapes. However, if you buy won ton skins, fold the dumplings into cylinders, and steam them in an aromatic sauce rather than in water. As a word of caution, always use a nonstick skillet to guarantee easy removal of the dumplings from the pan. During the final minutes of cooking you can agitate the pan so that the dumplings turn over and are glazed with the delicious sauce.

Advance Preparation

Prepare filling. Peel fresh water chestnuts, if using. Cut green onions into small pieces. Then finely mince the water chestnuts and onions by hand or in a food processor. Drop spinach leaves into 1 quart of rapidly boiling water. When leaves wilt, in about 10 seconds, drain and rinse under cold water, then squeeze out water. Mince spinach by hand.

Shell and devein shrimp. Coarsely chop shrimp and combine with egg white by hand or in a processor. Combine shrimp with water chestnut mixture and add soy sauce, chili sauce, ginger, and lemon peel. Mix thoroughly.

Within 5 hours of cooking, fold dumplings. Trim won tons into circles. Fold as described on page 185.

Prepare sauce. In a small bowl combine ingredients and stir well. Set aside.

Last-Minute Cooking

Place a 12-inch non-stick skillet over high heat. Add oil and immediately add dumplings. Fry until bottoms become dark golden, about 2 minutes.

Pour in lemon sauce and immediately cover pan. Reduce heat to medium and steam dumplings until they are firm to the touch, about 2 minutes.

Remove cover. Over high heat, continue frying dumplings until the sauce reduces completely, about 1 minute. While frying, shake the pan so that the dumplings are glazed all over with the sauce. Tip out onto a heated serving platter and serve at once. Because of the lemon sauce, the dumplings should not be served with the traditional vinegar-chili oil accompaniment.

Serves: 6 to 10 as an appetizer.

Notes: Uncooked Pot Stickers can be frozen, although they are not quite as delicious as when fresh. To cook, pan-fry frozen dumplings over medium heat until dark golden, about 3 minutes. Because they take longer to cook, you may have to add a little water to the frying pan during the steaming stage.

SANTA BARBARA POT STICKERS

1 12-ounce bunch spinach, stemmed
2 green onions
⅔ pound ground pork
2 teaspoons finely minced fresh ginger
½ teaspoon grated or finely minced orange peel
1 egg
1 tablespoon light soy sauce
¼ teaspoon Chinese chili sauce
½ teaspoon salt
24 won ton skins
   cornstarch, for dusting
2 tablespoons peanut oil

Sauce
½ cup chicken stock
2 tablespoons dry sherry
2 teaspoons oyster sauce
1 teaspoon hoisin sauce
½ teaspoon Chinese chili sauce
¼ teaspoon sugar
2 teaspoons grated or finely minced orange peel

The following recipe, which I serve at my cooking school in Santa Barbara, uses the authentic pot-sticker filling but diverges from tradition by cooking the dumplings in a delicious spicy orange sauce rather than water.

Advance Preparation
Prepare filling. Drop spinach leaves into 1 quart rapidly boiling water. When leaves wilt, in about 10 seconds, drain and rinse under cold water. Squeeze out water, then mince spinach by hand. Mince green onions. Combine spinach, green onions, pork, ginger, orange peel, egg, soy sauce, chili sauce, and salt. Mix thoroughly.

Within 5 hours of cooking, fold dumplings. Trim won tons into circles. Fold as described on page 185.

Make sauce. In a small bowl combine ingredients and stir well. Set aside.

Last-Minute Cooking
Place a 12-inch nonstick skillet over high heat. Add oil and immediately add dumplings. Fry dumplings until bottoms become dark golden, about 2 minutes. Pour in orange sauce. Immediately cover pan, reduce heat to medium, and steam dumplings until they are firm to the touch, about 2 minutes.

Remove cover. Over high heat, continue frying dumplings until the sauce reduces completely, about 1 minute. While cooking, shake the pan so that the dumplings are glazed all over with the sauce. Tip out onto a heated serving platter. Serve at once.

Serves: 4 to 8 as an appetizer.

Notes: These dumplings can be frozen. See Notes, page 188.

CHINESE PRIMAVERA

salt
½ pound dried spaghetti-style noodles, preferably Chinese
1 tablespoon peanut oil
1 red bell pepper, stemmed and seeded
1 yellow bell pepper, stemmed and seeded
10 medium button mushrooms
3 green onions
2 tablespoons cornstarch

Sauce

3 cloves garlic, finely minced
1 tablespoon olive oil
¾ cup chicken stock
3 tablespoons dry sherry
2 tablespoons Oriental sesame oil
1 tablespoon light soy sauce
1 tablespoon oyster sauce
1 tablespoon distilled white vinegar
1 teaspoon Chinese chili sauce
½ teaspoon coarsely crushed Sichuan peppercorns
½ teaspoon sugar
½ teaspoon salt
1½ teaspoons grated or finely minced orange or tangerine peel

In a large skillet containing a richly flavored sauce, noodles are mixed with spring vegetables. After a brief cooking, Chinese Primavera is ready to be served. I love an easy technique like this for quick meals and also to minimize stress when giving a dinner party.

Advance Preparation

Bring at least 4 quarts of water to a vigorous boil. Lightly salt water and add noodles. Cook noodles until they lose raw taste but are still firm, about 5 minutes. Immediately drain in a colander. Rinse briefly under water. Shake out excess water, and transfer to a bowl. Stir in oil.

Cut peppers into matchstick-size pieces. Cut mushrooms into very thin slices. Shred green onions. Add vegetables to noodles and mix well. Set aside.

Prepare sauce. Combine garlic with olive oil and set aside. In a small bowl, combine remaining sauce ingredients.

Cooking

Mix cornstarch with an equal amount of cold water. Set aside.

Place a 12-inch skillet over high heat. In it sauté garlic mixture for a few seconds. Add remaining sauce ingredients and bring to a low boil. Add enough cornstarch mixture to lightly thicken.

Add noodles to sauce and stir over high heat until noodles are reheated and peppers turn a bright color, about 3 minutes. Taste and adjust seasoning. Turn out onto a heated platter or individual plates. Serve at once.

Serves: 4 as a side dish with a robust entrée; 6 to 8 as part of an Oriental dinner.

Menu Ideas: A quick family meal — broiled fish, Chinese Primavera, and a tossed green salad.

CHICKEN CURRY DUMPLINGS

1 12-ounce bunch spinach, stemmed

4 water chestnuts, preferably fresh

2 green onions

⅔ pound ground chicken

2 teaspoons finely minced fresh ginger

1 egg

1 tablespoon light soy sauce

¼ teaspoon Chinese chili sauce

24 won ton skins cornstarch, for dusting

2 tablespoons peanut oil

Sauce

¼ cup unsweetened coconut milk

¼ cup chicken stock

2 tablespoons dry sherry

2 teaspoons oyster sauce

1 tablespoon curry powder

½ teaspoon sugar

These pan-fried dumplings filled with freshly ground chicken and glazed with a coconut curry sauce make a perfect hors d'oeuvre. Set a few of these dumplings aside in the freezer so that they are available when a sudden urge for Chinese food strikes.

Advance Preparation

Prepare filling. Drop spinach leaves into 1 quart rapidly boiling water. When leaves wilt, in about 10 seconds, drain, rinse under cold water, and squeeze out water. Mince spinach by hand. Peel fresh water chestnuts, if using. Cut green onions into small pieces. Mince water chestnuts and green onions by hand or in a food processor. Combine spinach, water chestnuts, green onions, chicken, ginger, egg, soy sauce, and chili sauce. Mix thoroughly.

Within 5 hours of cooking, fold dumplings. Trim won tons into circles. Fold as described on page 185.

Prepare sauce. In a small bowl, combine ingredients and stir well. Set aside.

Cooking

Place a 12-inch non-stick skillet over high heat. Add oil and immediately add dumplings. Fry dumplings until bottoms become dark golden, about 2 minutes.

Pour in sauce. Immediately cover pan, reduce heat to medium, and steam dumplings until they are firm to the touch, about 2 minutes.

Remove cover. Over high heat, continue frying dumplings until sauce reduces completely, about 1 minute. While cooking, shake the pan so that the dumplings are glazed all over with the sauce. Tip out onto a heated serving platter. Serve at once.

Serves: 4 to 8 as an appetizer.

MARCO POLO NOODLES

salt

½ pound dried spaghetti-style noodles, preferably Chinese

Sauce

1 tablespoon finely minced garlic

1 tablespoon finely minced fresh ginger

2 tablespoons olive oil

¼ cup dry sherry

2 tablespoons oyster sauce

2 tablespoons rice vinegar

1 tablespoon Oriental sesame oil

1 teaspoon sugar

½ teaspoon Chinese pepper mix (see Appendix)

½ cup chopped green onions

Olive oil, herbs, and Italian cooking methods provide a perfect stimulus for creating Chinese-Italian dishes. In this recipe, boiled and drained noodles are tossed with a sauce of olive oil, ginger, oyster sauce, and rice vinegar to make a delicious and easy accompaniment to any entrée, whether Chinese, Italian, or American.

Advance Preparation
Prepare sauce. Combine garlic and ginger with olive oil and set aside. In a small bowl, combine remaining ingredients. Set aside.

Last Minute Cooking
Bring at least 4 quarts water to a vigorous boil. Lightly salt water, and add noodles. Cook noodles until they lose raw taste but are still firm, about 5 minutes. Immediately drain in a colander. Shake out excess water, then transfer noodles to a large bowl.

As noodles cook, set a small skillet over medium-high heat and sauté garlic and ginger mixture. After 30 seconds, add remaining sauce ingredients. Bring to low boil, then remove from heat.

Add sauce to noodles and toss well. Turn out onto a heated platter or individual dinner plates. Serve at once.

Serves: 4 as a side dish with any entrée; 6 to 8 as part of an Oriental dinner.

Menu Ideas: An Oriental dinner for 4 — Veal Scaloppine in Shiitake Cream Sauce, Marco Polo Noodles, and Garden Greens with Oriental Dressing.

FIREWORKS RICE

4 dried black Chinese mushrooms

1½ cups long-grain white rice (not instant or converted)

¼ cup pine nuts (pignoli)

2 cloves garlic, finely minced

1 tablespoon finely minced fresh ginger

3 tablespoons unsalted butter

½ cup dark raisins

⅓ cup minced green onions

Sauce

2¼ cups chicken stock

¼ cup tomato sauce

2 tablespoons dry sherry

1 tablespoon oyster sauce

2 teaspoons Oriental sesame oil

½ teaspoon sugar

½ teaspoon Chinese chili sauce

On the extremely practical Chinese method for eating rice, seventeenth-century Jesuit missionary Francesco Carletti observed: "Two slim sticks can pick up anything, no matter how tiny it is, very cleanly and without soiling their hands. For that reason they do not use tablecloths or napkins or even knives, as everything comes to the table minutely cut up. When they want to eat it, they bring the bowl it is in close to their mouth and then, with those two sticks, are able to fill their mouth with marvelous agility and swiftness."

Advance Preparation
Soak dried mushrooms in hot water until they soften, about 20 minutes. Discard stems and mince caps finely.

Place rice in a sieve. Wash under cold water, stirring with your fingers, until the water is no longer cloudy, about 2 minutes. Drain thoroughly.

Toast pine nuts in a 325°F oven until golden, about 10 minutes. Set aside.

Prepare sauce. In a small bowl, combine ingredients and set aside.

Cooking
Place a 3-quart saucepan over medium-high heat. Add the garlic, ginger, and butter. Sauté until butter sizzles, then add rice. Stir rice until coated with the butter and well heated, about 5 minutes.

Add the raisins, mushrooms, and sauce. Bring to a low boil, stirring, then cover, reduce heat to lowest setting, and simmer until all liquid is absorbed, about 18 to 24 minutes.

Remove cover. Stir in the green onions and pine nuts. Serve at once.

Serves: 4 to 6 as the side dish to any entrée; 6 to 8 as part of an Oriental dinner

Menu Ideas: An easy dinner for 4 — barbecued chicken, Fireworks Rice, avocado tomato salad, and baked apples

Notes: For suggestions on turning this into a main dish, see Notes on page 198.

Fireworks Rice.

SPICY THAI NOODLES

2 tablespoons minced roasted peanuts

⅓ cup minced red bell pepper

¼ cup minced green onions

¼ cup minced fresh coriander (cilantro)

2 cups bean sprouts

2 eggs

1 tablespoon peanut oil

salt

½ pound dried spaghetti-style noodles, preferably Chinese

Sauce

3 cloves garlic, finely minced

1 tablespoon peanut oil

3 tablespoons dry sherry

3 tablespoons light soy sauce

3 tablespoons tomato sauce

2 tablespoons lime juice, plus 2 limes

2 tablespoons light brown sugar

1 teaspoon Chinese chili sauce

1 teaspoon grated or finely minced lime peel

Thai cuisine is famous for its noodle dish seasoned with chopped peanuts, lime zest, minced coriander, and dried chilies. Needing only minutes of preparation and cooking, Spicy Thai Noodles go well with barbecued meats or as one of several dishes in an Oriental dinner.

Advance Preparation
In separate containers set aside peanuts, red pepper, green onions, coriander, and bean sprouts.

Beat eggs well. Place a 12-inch iron or nonstick skillet over medium-high heat. When hot, add 1 teaspoon oil and rub over surface with a paper towel. Add half the egg and roll it around the pan to form a thin pancake. When set, in about 30 seconds, flip over and cook for a few seconds on other side. Remove from pan. Lightly oil pan and make a second egg pancake. After pancakes cool, roll into cylinders and cut into shreds. Set aside.

Prepare sauce. Combine garlic with oil and set aside. In a small bowl, combine sherry, soy sauce, tomato sauce, lime juice, brown sugar, chili sauce, and lime peel. Set aside. Cut 2 limes into wedges and set aside.

Last-Minute Cooking
Bring at least 4 quarts water to a vigorous boil. Lightly salt water, then add noodles. Cook noodles until they lose raw taste but are still firm, about 5 minutes. Immediately drain in a colander. Shake out excess water, then transfer to a large bowl.

Meanwhile, in a small skillet set over medium-high heat, sauté garlic mixture. After 30 seconds, add remaining sauce ingredients. Bring to low boil, then remove from heat.

Add sauce to noodles. Add egg shreds and bean sprouts and toss well. Turn out onto a heated platter. Sprinkle with peanuts, red pepper, green onions, and coriander. Serve at once, accompanied by lime wedges.

Serves: 4 to 6 as a side dish with barbecued meats; 6 to 8 as part of an Oriental dinner.

Menu Ideas: An Oriental dinner for 4 — Jade Salad (omit scallops), Rack of Lamb in Hunan Barbecue Sauce, Spicy Thai Noodles, and Flambéed Thai Bananas.

NOODLES IN JADE SAUCE

salt

½ **pound dried spaghetti-style noodles, preferably Chinese**

1 **tablespoon peanut oil**

4 **ounces shiitake mushrooms**

2 **medium carrots, or 1 red bell pepper, stemmed and seeded**

½ **cup pine nuts (pignoli)**

1 **tablespoon cornstarch**

Sauce

2 **cloves garlic, finely minced**

1 **1-pound bunch spinach, stemmed**

2 **bunches chives**

16 **sprigs fresh coriander (cilantro)**

12 **basil leaves**

⅓ **cup chicken stock**

⅔ **cup heavy (whipping) cream**

½ **teaspoon salt**

¼ **teaspoon Chinese chili sauce**

The beautiful jade color comes from puréeing spinach, chives, coriander, and basil with cream. This is a terrific dish to accompany grilled chops or swordfish.

Advance Preparation

Bring at least 4 quarts of water to a vigorous boil. Lightly salt water and add noodles. Cook noodles until they lose raw taste but are still firm, about 5 minutes. Immediately drain in a colander. Rinse briefly under water. Shake out excess water and transfer to bowl. Stir in oil.

Discard stems from mushrooms. Stack mushroom caps and sliver. Cut carrots into very thin slices on sharp diagonal, then overlap slices and cut into shreds. Or cut pepper into shreds. Add vegetables to the noodles and mix well. Set aside.

Toast pine nuts in a 325°F oven until golden, about 10 minutes. Transfer to a small bowl and set aside.

Prepare sauce. In a food processor fitted with the metal chopping blade, chop garlic, spinach leaves, chives, coriander, and basil until finely puréed, then add stock, cream, salt, and chili sauce. Purée again. Transfer to a bowl and set aside. (This can be made up to a day in advance.)

Last-Minute Cooking

Mix cornstarch with an equal amount of cold water and set aside.

Place a 12-inch skillet over high heat. Add sauce and bring to a low boil. Add enough cornstarch mixture to lightly thicken.

Add the noodles to the sauce and stir over high heat until noodles are reheated and carrots or pepper turn a bright color, about 2 minutes. Turn onto a heated platter or individual plates. Sprinkle with pine nuts. Serve at once.

Serves: 4 as a side dish; 6 to 8 as part of an Oriental dinner.

ORIENTAL RICE PILAF

- 1½ cups long-grain white rice (not instant or converted)
- ¼ cup white sesame seeds
- 2 cloves garlic, finely minced
- 1 shallot, minced
- 3 tablespoons unsalted butter
- ½ cup dark raisins
- ½ cup minced green onions
- 3 tablespoons minced fresh coriander (cilantro)
- ½ cup minced red bell pepper
  Sauce
- 2½ cups chicken stock
- 2 tablespoons dry sherry
- 2 tablespoons light soy sauce
- 1 tablespoon Oriental sesame oil
- ½ teaspoon Chinese chili sauce
- ½ teaspoon salt
- 2 teaspoons grated or finely minced tangerine or orange peel

This rainbow-colored rice pilaf goes beautifully with a wide range of Oriental and American entrées. And it can be made in much larger quantities without affecting the quality. Perfumed with Oriental seasonings, every grain remains separate and distinct, even after reheating in the microwave days later. When we choose a rice dish for entertaining, Oriental Rice Pilaf is tops on our list.

Advance Preparation
Place rice in a sieve. Wash under cold water, stirring with your fingers, until water is no longer cloudy, about 2 minutes. Drain thoroughly

In a small ungreased skillet set over high heat, stir sesame seeds until light golden, about 2 minutes. Immediately tip out and set aside.

Prepare sauce. In a small bowl, combine ingredients and set aside.

Cooking
Place a 3-quart saucepan over medium-high heat. Add the garlic, shallot, and butter. Sauté until butter sizzles, then add rice. Stir rice until coated with the butter and well heated, about 5 minutes.

Add raisins and sauce. Bring to a low boil, stirring, then cover, reduce heat to lowest setting, and simmer until all liquid is absorbed, about 18 to 24 minutes.

Remove cover and stir in green onions, coriander, pepper, and sesame seeds. Serve at once.

Serves: 4 to 6 as the side dish to any entrée; 6 to 8 as part of an Oriental dinner.

Menu Ideas: A dinner for 4 — Sichuan Lemon Veal Chops, Oriental Rice Pilaf, Asparagus in Black-Bean Butter Sauce, and a fresh fruit sorbet.

Notes: This can be turned into a main dish by adding ¾ pound diced cooked meat, shrimp, crab, or scallops when stirring in sesame seeds at end of cooking process. Cover pot, then simmer rice 5 additional minutes to reheat meat or seafood.

Chinese Chili with Peppers; Oriental Rice Pilaf.

SEAFOOD ON PAN-FRIED NOODLES

salt

½ pound dried spaghetti-style noodles, preferably Chinese

½ pound raw medium shrimp

½ pound bay scallops

1 bunch thick asparagus

8 medium button mushrooms

1 red bell pepper, stemmed and seeded

2 green onions

2 tablespoons cornstarch

½ cup peanut oil

2 cloves garlic, finely minced

2 teaspoons finely minced fresh ginger

Sauce

⅔ cup chicken stock

2 tablespoons tomato sauce

2 tablespoons oyster sauce

2 tablespoons dry sherry

1 tablespoon light soy sauce

1 tablespoon Oriental sesame oil

½ teaspoon sugar

¼ teaspoon freshly ground black pepper

Pan-fried noodles, whose crunchy exterior hides a soft, tender center, are a marvelous foundation for stews, curries, or very saucy stir-fried dishes. The key technique is to boil the noodles hours in advance and let them dry on a plate unrefrigerated. Just before dinner, crisp the noodles using a heavy skillet that distributes the heat evenly.

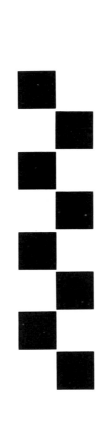

Cut the disk they form into wedges, transfer to a heated platter, and pour a stew or stir-fried dish across their golden surface. The exciting textural contrasts — soft interior noodles soaked in sauce, still crunchy exterior threads, and the savory topping — far outweigh the inconvenience of last-minute cooking.

Advance Preparation
Bring at least 4 quarts of water to a vigorous boil. Lightly salt the water, then add noodles. Cook noodles until they lose raw taste but are still firm, about 5 minutes. Immediately drain in a colander. Shake out excess water. Lightly oil the surface of a 12-inch round plate and spread noodles evenly across surface. Leave uncovered on a kitchen counter for at least 2 hours, turning noodle disk over once. (This can be done a day ahead and refrigerated, covered.)

Shell and devein shrimp, splitting them in half. Set shrimp and scallops aside.

Snap off and discard tough asparagus ends. Cut asparagus on a very sharp diagonal, rolling stalks one-quarter turn after each sharp diagonal cut. Set aside.

Thinly slice mushrooms. Cut pepper into ½-inch cubes. Cut green onions on a sharp diagonal into ½-inch lengths. Combine mushrooms, pepper, and onions. Set aside.

Prepare sauce. In a small bowl combine ingredients and set aside.

Cooking

Mix cornstarch with an equal amount of cold water and set aside. Preheat oven to 200°F.

Place a 12-inch iron skillet over medium heat for 5 minutes. Add ¼ cup peanut oil. When oil gives off a wisp of smoke, carefully transfer noodle disk to frying pan. Turn heat to medium-high and fry noodles until golden, about 6 minutes. Then turn noodles over, add 2 more tablespoons peanut oil around sides of pan, and fry until noodles are golden, about 6 minutes. Transfer noodles to a layer of paper towels placed on cutting board. Pat noodles to absorb oil, then with a long knife cut noodle disk into wedges. Transfer noodle wedges to a round serving plate and place in warm oven.

Place wok over highest heat. When wok becomes very hot, add 1 tablespoon peanut oil to center. Roll oil around sides of wok. When oil just begins to smoke, add shrimp and scallops. Stir-fry just until they turn white, about 2 minutes. Transfer shrimp and scallops to a work platter.

Immediately return wok to highest heat. Add remaining 1 tablespoon peanut oil to center. Add garlic and ginger and sauté a few seconds. Add asparagus and stir-fry, adding a few tablespoons of water to prevent scorching, until asparagus brightens, about 2 minutes. Add remaining vegetables and continue stir-frying until peppers brighten, about 1 minute.

Return shrimp and scallops to wok and add sauce. When sauce comes to a low boil, stir in a little of the cornstarch mixture so that sauce glazes the food. Taste and adjust seasonings. Pour mixture across surface of noodles. Serve at once.

Serves: 4 as an entrée; 6 to 8 as part of an Oriental dinner.

Menu Ideas: A family dinner for 6 — Chicken Velvet Soup with Mushrooms, Salmon Watercress Salad (omit salmon), Seafood on Pan-fried Noodles, Steamed Corn with Chinese Herb Sauce, and homemade lemon cake.

OVERLEAF: Curried Pineapple Rice.

CURRIED PINEAPPLE RICE

1 ½ cups long-grain white rice (not instant or converted)

⅓ cup slivered almonds

1 tablespoon finely minced fresh ginger

3 tablespoons unsalted butter

½ cup dark raisins

⅓ cup minced red bell pepper

½ cup minced green onions

1 to 1 ½ cups diced fresh pineapple

Sauce

2 ¼ cups chicken stock

¼ cup unsweetened coconut milk

2 tablespoons light soy sauce

2 tablespoons lime juice

1 tablespoon curry powder

½ teaspoon Chinese chili sauce

½ teaspoon salt

½ teaspoon grated or finely minced lime peel

Curry, lime, fresh pineapple, and toasted almonds add a Polynesian taste to this variation on rice pilaf. It goes well with barbecued meats, seafood entrées, and robust stews.

Advance Preparation

Place rice in a sieve. Wash under cold water, stirring with your fingers, until the water is no longer cloudy, about 2 minutes. Drain thoroughly.

Toast almonds in a 325°F oven until light golden. Set aside.

Prepare sauce. In a small bowl, combine ingredients and set aside.

Cooking

Place a 3-quart saucepan over medium-high heat. Add the ginger and butter. Sauté until butter sizzles, then add the rice. Stir rice until coated with the butter and well heated, about 5 minutes.

Add the raisins and sauce. Bring to a low boil, stirring, then cover, reduce heat to lowest setting, and simmer until all liquid is absorbed, about 18 to 24 minutes.

Remove cover and stir in almonds, pepper, green onions, and pineapple. Serve at once.

Serves: 4 to 6 as the side dish to any entrée; 6 to 8 as part of an Oriental dinner.

Menu ideas: A vegetarian dinner for 6 — Shredded Chicken Salad (omit chicken); Chinese Ratatouille; Onion Bread (to dip in ratatouille); Curried Pineapple Rice (soak 6 dried black Chinese mushrooms in hot water until mushrooms soften; substitute mushroom-flavored water for chicken stock and add diced mushroom caps along with mushroom water to the rice); Grand Marnier Mocha Ice Cream.

Notes: For suggestions on turning this into a main dish, see Notes on page 198.

CHINESE DUCK PIZZA

1 teaspoon active dry yeast

1 teaspoon sugar

¾ cup warm water (105°–115°F)

3 tablespoons Oriental sesame oil

1 teaspoon salt

2 cups bread flour

cornmeal, for dusting

Topping

½ Chinese roast duck, 2½ pounds

4 green onions

4 ounces fresh shiitake mushrooms

6 ounces part-skim mozzarella cheese

4 tablespoons minced fresh coriander (cilantro)

2 tablespoons white sesame seeds

3 tablespoons hoisin sauce

1 tablespoon finely minced fresh ginger

½ teaspoon Chinese chili sauce

One of the great aspects of Oriental cooking is the tremendous possibility for improvisation and culinary borrowings from other cuisines. Chinese Duck Pizza is such a dish.

Advance Preparation

Prepare dough. Sprinkle the yeast and sugar over the warm water. When bubbles appear on top (about 5 minutes), yeast has been activated. Stir in 2 tablespoons sesame oil and salt, then add yeast mixture to the bread flour and stir until a dough is formed.

Turn dough out onto a lightly floured surface. Lightly flour hands, then gather dough into a ball. Knead dough until smooth and elastic, working in a little more flour until dough is no longer sticky, about 8 minutes. Lightly oil a small bowl. Rotate dough in bowl, cover with a towel, and let rise about 30 minutes.

Knead dough briefly again. If making 1 large pizza, roll into ¼-inch-thick circle about 15 inches in diameter. If making individual pizzas, divide dough into 6 equal pieces and, using your hands, stretch dough into very thin circles about 5 inches in diameter. Place on a thin board or firm piece of cardboard that has been sprinkled generously with cornmeal. Brush top of dough with remaining sesame oil and let rise 30 minutes.

Meanwhile prepare topping. Remove meat from duck and shred. Mince or shred green onions. Discard mushroom stems; stack mushroom caps and shred. Grate cheese. Mince coriander. In small ungreased skillet set over high heat, stir sesame seeds until light golden, about 2 minutes. Immediately tip out and set aside.

Combine hoisin, ginger, and chili sauce. Rub across dough circle(s) to within ½ inch of the edge(s). Evenly sprinkle topping ingredients over sauce in this order: duck, green onions, mushrooms, coriander, a light sprinkling of cheese, and sesame seeds. Pizza(s) can be refrigerated at this point for several hours, but bring back to room temperature before baking.

Cooking

Preheat the oven to 550°F. (If using a pizza brick, preheat oven for 45 minutes; if using an iron baking sheet, preheat for 30 minutes.) Sprinkle pizza brick or pan with cornmeal. Slide pizza(s) onto preheated pizza brick or iron baking pan and bake until crust is golden, about 15 minutes. Remove pizza(s) from oven, sprinkle with minced coriander, and serve at once.

Serves: 2 to 3 as an entrée; 6 as a light first course when formed into individual pizzas.

Notes: As a substitute for the duck, try other barbecued meats, such as the Sichuan Barbecued Game Hens.

If you are just starting an adventure with Oriental cooking, this is the perfect chapter with which to begin your experiments. These brilliantly colored, crunchy vegetables capture the essence of how Chinese, Thai, and Vietnamese cooks treat vegetables. Using produce available at every supermarket, these recipes combine easy cooking techniques with quickly made sauces. The subtle blend of flavors and textures makes these recipes perfect accompaniments to any American or European entrée.

Each recipe steps beyond traditional Oriental seasonings and methods to make a new statement. A black bean sauce enriched with butter bathes steamed asparagus; baby carrots are sautéed until a citrus-anise essence turns them

Wild Mushroom Stir-Fry.

golden; layers of zucchini, mushrooms, and eggplant simmer in a rich bean sauce to produce an Oriental ratatouille, and white corn picked the day of cooking is rolled in melted butter alive with the taste of fresh ginger, Sichuan pepper, and lemon.

Easy-to-prepare recipes in this chapter are Steamed Corn with Chinese Butter Sauce, Steamed Broccoli with Oriental Hollandaise Sauce, Asparagus in Black-Bean Butter Sauce, Thai Coconut Peas, Wild Mushroom Stir-Fry, Grilled Oriental Eggplant, and Chinese Ratatouille.

WILD MUSHROOM STIR-FRY

- 6 dried black Chinese mushrooms
- ½ pound fresh wild mushrooms
- 3 tablespoons unsalted butter
- 2 cloves garlic, finely minced
- 1 shallot, finely minced
- 2 tablespoons chopped chives

Sauce

- 2 tablespoons chopped fresh basil
- ½ teaspoon grated or finely minced orange peel
- ½ cup heavy (whipping) cream
- ¼ cup dry sherry
- 1 tablespoon light soy sauce
- 1 tablespoon Oriental sesame oil
- ½ teaspoon Chinese pepper mix (see Appendix)

As interest in mushroom hunting expands, so does the variety of wild mushrooms sold at the best markets. Recently we have purchased fresh matsutake, shiitake, oyster, enoki, cèpes, and chanterelle mushrooms. Their musty, earthy smell is intensified by the flavor of the Oriental cream sauce, making this a great dish alongside barbecued meats or as a sauce to toss with fresh pasta.

Advance Preparation

Soak the dried mushrooms in hot water until softened, about 20 minutes. Cut off and discard stems. Cut caps into quarters.

With a damp towel, wipe fresh mushrooms. Cut off and discard stem ends. Cut large mushrooms in half or into quarters.

In a small bowl, combine ingredients for sauce.

Last-Minute Cooking

Place a 12-inch skillet over medium-high heat. Add the butter, garlic, and shallot. When butter melts and garlic begins to sizzle, add mushrooms. Sauté until mushrooms are glazed with the butter, about 1 minute.

Add sauce and bring to a low boil. Continue cooking at a low boil, stirring, until fresh mushrooms soften slightly and sauce thickens enough that a spoon leaves a path as you stir, about 4 minutes.

Transfer mushrooms to a heated serving dish or individual plates. Sprinkle with chopped chives and serve at once.

Serves: 4 as a small vegetable dish; 6 to 8 as part of an Oriental dinner.

Menu Ideas: Dinner for 4 — barbecued steaks, Wild Mushroom Stir-Fry, baked potatoes, garden salad, and Ginger Crème Brûlée.

Chinese Ratatouille.

Thai Coconut Peas.

CHINESE RATATOUILLE

3 medium zucchini

¾ pound button mushrooms

3 Oriental eggplants, or 1 very small globe eggplant

2 tablespoons olive oil

6 cloves garlic, finely minced

1 tablespoon finely minced fresh ginger

1 small yellow onion, minced

chopped parsley or fresh coriander (cilantro), for garnish

Sauce

¾ cup chicken stock

½ cup tomato sauce

¼ cup dry sherry

2 tablespoons bean sauce (see Appendix)

2 tablespoons hoisin sauce

2 tablespoons oyster sauce

1 tablespoon Oriental sesame oil

1 tablespoon red wine vinegar

½ teaspoon Chinese chili sauce

One of the exciting aspects of cooking Oriental food is its versatility. This is particularly true of sauces, many of which can be used interchangeably. For this recipe, the blend of fresh mushrooms, zucchini, and eggplant is simmered in a Beijing sauce traditionally put on top of noodles to create a wonderfully rich "meaty"-tasting dish. Chinese Ratatouille, good hot or cold, continues to improve in flavor for several days in the refrigerator. It is a delicious accompaniment to spicy garlic shrimp or a robust meat dish, and it makes a fine snack when reheated atop toasted whole wheat bread.

Preparation
Cut enough zucchini into ¼-inch-thick rounds to fill 2 cups. Slice enough mushrooms into ¼-inch-thick pieces to fill 2 cups. If using a globe eggplant, peel. Cut enough eggplant into rounds or cubes to fill 2 cups. Place zucchini, mushrooms, and eggplant in a large bowl and toss to combine evenly.

In a small bowl, combine sauce ingredients. Set aside.

Cooking
Place a 3-quart saucepan over medium-high heat. Add the olive oil, garlic, ginger, and onion. Sauté for 5 minutes, stirring occasionally.

Add the mixed vegetables. Pour in sauce and bring to a low boil. Reduce heat and cook at a low boil for about 1 hour, uncovered. Stir vegetables occasionally. Dish is ready when sauce thickens.

Serve hot, at room temperature, or cold, sprinkled with parsley or coriander.

Serves: 4 as the vegetable dish for an American dinner; 6 to 8 as part of an Oriental dinner.

Menu Ideas: Dinner for 4 — sautéed shrimp, Chinese Ratatouille, rice pilaf, green salad, and homemade cheesecake.

THAI COCONUT PEAS

2 tablespoons unsalted butter

3 cloves garlic, minced

3 cups shelled peas (3 to 4 pounds unshelled)

Sauce

2 tablespoons chopped fresh basil

2 tablespoons chopped fresh mint

2 tablespoons chopped green onions

1 cup unsweetened coconut milk

1 tablespoon dry sherry

¼ teaspoon salt

¼ teaspoon Chinese pepper mix (see Appendix)

¼ teaspoon Chinese chili sauce

juice from 1 lime

Sweet peas become starchy almost as quickly as corn. But, when you find small pods just picked from the vine and plenty of willing hands to pop out the peas, try combining them with this herb-scented coconut sauce. As an alternative to peas, use fresh asparagus tips, quartered fresh button mushrooms, or little rounds of zucchini.

Preparation and Cooking
In a small bowl, combine all ingredients for sauce except lime juice. Set aside.

Place a 12-inch skillet over medium-high heat and add the butter and garlic. When butter begins to bubble and garlic sizzles, add the peas and the sauce. Bring to a low boil, cover, reduce heat to low, and simmer until peas brighten and become tender, about 2 minutes.

Remove from heat and stir in lime juice. Turn out into a heated serving bowl or individual plates. Serve at once.

Serves: 4 as the vegetable course for an American dinner; 6 to 8 as part of an Oriental dinner.

Menu Ideas: Dinner for 4 — roast chicken with wild mushrooms, Thai Coconut Peas, couscous salad, and fresh fruit.

BABY VEGETABLES WITH CHINESE SEASONINGS

1 bunch baby carrots

¼ pound small button mushrooms

4 baby zucchini

16 very small snow peas

2 green onions

2 cloves garlic, finely minced

1 tablespoon peanut oil

2 tablespoons unsalted butter

1 tablespoon cornstarch

Sauce

¼ cup dry sherry

2 tablespoons oyster sauce

1 tablespoon Oriental sesame oil

½ teaspoon sugar

¼ teaspoon freshly ground black pepper

The combination of rich oyster sauce, nutty sesame oil, and butter has a magical effect on vegetables, whether just harvested from the garden or purchased at a supermarket. At the end of the recipe are listed some good vegetable combinations to try with this sauce.

Advance Preparation:
Scrub and trim carrots; cut in half lengthwise. Drop carrots into 1 quart of rapidly boiling water. When carrots brighten, transfer to ice water with a slotted spoon to chill, then drain and pat dry.

Thinly slice mushrooms. Cut zucchini into ½-inch-wide rounds. Snap ends off snow peas. Trim green onions and cut on diagonal into 1-inch pieces. Set carrots, mushrooms, zucchini, snow peas, and green onions aside.

Prepare sauce. In a small bowl, combine sauce ingredients. Set aside.

Last-Minute Cooking
Stir cornstarch with an equal amount of cold water. Set aside.

Place wok or 12-inch skillet over high heat. Add garlic, oil, and half the butter. When garlic sizzles, add the vegetables. Cook, uncovered, until vegetables brighten, about 2 minutes.

Add sauce, then lightly thicken with a little of the cornstarch mixture. Remove from heat and stir in remaining butter. Transfer to heated platter or individual plates. Serve at once.

Serves: 4 as the vegetable course for an American dinner; 6 to 8 as part of an Oriental dinner.

Menu Ideas: Dinner for 4 — pot roast, Baby Vegetables with Chinese Seasonings, hot rolls with unsalted butter, and apple pie.

Notes: Other combinations of vegetables are (1) ¼ pound fresh mushrooms, sliced; 2 medium zucchini, sliced; 1 red bell pepper, seeded and cubed; 2 green onions, cut into 1-inch pieces; (2) ½ bunch thin asparagus, cut diagonally into 1-inch pieces; 1 cup very thinly sliced medium carrots; 1 cup small snow peas, ends snapped off; 2 cups green cabbage, cut into ¼-inch slices; or (3) 1 each green, red, and yellow bell pepper, each seeded and cut into very thin strips; 8 dried black Chinese mushrooms, softened in hot water and caps shredded, or 4 ounces fresh shiitake mushrooms, caps shredded.

Baby Vegetables with Chinese Seasonings.

STEAMED BROCCOLI WITH ORIENTAL HOLLANDAISE SAUCE

1 bunch broccoli

7 tablespoons unsalted butter, melted

3 large egg yolks

2 tablespoons lemon juice

1 tablespoon unsalted butter, at room temperature

¼ teaspoon salt

¼ teaspoon ground Sichuan peppercorns

¼ teaspoon white pepper

1 teaspoon finely minced fresh ginger

1 teaspoon grated or finely minced lemon peel

Emerald green broccoli, glistening with a hollandaise sauce containing a hint of fresh ginger, Sichuan peppercorns, and grated lemon peel, is a visual and taste triumph. Sauce preparation can be completed far in advance, with the final assembly taking only two minutes. Try this sauce on any of the vegetables discussed in the Notes on page 223.

Advance Preparation

Trim ends off broccoli, then peel stems. Cut broccoli into small bunches of flowerettes with the stems still attached. Set aside.

Last-Minute Cooking

Bring water to a vigorous boil in the bottom of a Chinese steamer. Spread the broccoli evenly across a steaming tier, cover, and steam until bright green and tender, about 8 minutes.

Set a large saucepan of water over high heat and bring to a boil. Reduce heat to low and keep water at a simmer.

In a very small saucepan, beat the yolks and half the lemon juice. Add the tablespoon of room-temperature butter. Place the saucepan over the larger pan of simmering water and beat yolks with a whisk until sauce thickens to the consistency of heavy cream. Remove from heat and slowly beat in melted butter. Add salt, Sichuan peppercorns, white pepper, ginger, lemon peel, and remaining lemon juice. Keep the sauce warm for a few minutes by placing saucepan over warm (not simmering) water until broccoli is tender. Makes ¾ cup.

Transfer broccoli onto individual plates and nap with sauce. Serve at once.

Serves: 4 as a vegetable course for an American dinner; 6 to 8 as part of an Oriental dinner.

Menu Ideas: A light dinner for 4 — broiled sole, Steamed Broccoli with Oriental Hollandaise Sauce, and a basil-tomato salad.

Steamed Broccoli with Oriental Hollandaise Sauce.   219

ASPARAGUS IN BLACK-BEAN BUTTER SAUCE

2 pounds asparagus
1 tablespoon salted black beans
2 cloves garlic, finely minced
1 tablespoon white sesame seeds
1 tablespoon cornstarch
3 tablespoons unsalted butter

Sauce

½ cup chicken stock
2 tablespoons dry sherry
1 tablespoon light soy sauce
1 tablespoon Oriental sesame oil
½ teaspoon sugar
⅛ teaspoon white pepper

Stirring in a little butter just before drizzling the black bean sauce over tender asparagus spears adds a wonderful silky texture and rich taste. The sauce also is delicious on steamed salmon filets, sautéed shrimp, and fresh Dungeness crab.

Advance Preparation

Snap off and discard tough asparagus ends.

Place black beans in a small sieve and rinse under cold water. Press out excess water and chop coarsely. Combine garlic with black beans. Set aside.

In a small ungreased skillet set over high heat, stir sesame seeds until light golden, about 2 minutes. Immediately tip out of skillet and set aside.

In a small bowl, combine sauce ingredients. Set aside.

Last-Minute Cooking

Mix cornstarch with an equal amount of cold water. Set aside.

Bring water to a vigorous boil in the bottom of a Chinese steamer. Spread asparagus evenly across a steaming tier, cover, and steam until bright green and tender, about 4 to 6 minutes. Transfer asparagus to a heated platter or individual plates.

Meanwhile, place 2 tablespoons butter in a 10-inch skillet set over medium-high heat. When butter begins to sizzle, add black beans and garlic. Sauté until garlic sizzles, then add sauce. Bring to a low boil, then stir in enough cornstarch mixture to lightly thicken sauce. Remove from heat and stir in remaining tablespoon butter until absorbed by the sauce.

Spoon sauce over asparagus. Sprinkle with toasted sesame seeds and serve at once.

Serves: 4 as the vegetable course for an American dinner; 6 to 8 as part of an Oriental dinner.

Menu Ideas: Dinner for 6 — homemade ravioli, Asparagus in Black-Bean Butter Sauce, arugula and red pepper salad, and chocolate mousse.

BRUSSELS SPROUTS IN TANGERINE SAUCE

- 2 tablespoons slivered almonds
- 1½ pounds Brussels sprouts
- 1 tablespoon peanut oil
- 2 cloves garlic, finely minced
- 1 teaspoon grated or finely minced tangerine peel
- 2 tablespoons cornstarch
- 1 tablespoon unsalted butter

Sauce
- ½ cup tangerine juice
- 2 tablespoons dry sherry
- 1 tablespoon light soy sauce
- 1 tablespoon Oriental sesame oil
- ¼ teaspoon sugar
- ¼ teaspoon salt
- ¼ teaspoon Chinese chili sauce

I was amazed several years ago, when teaching in Oregon, to first see Brussels sprouts sold on the stalk, a long, cylindrical pincushion with little green balls popping out. Yet, even with Brussels sprouts of less freshness, the intense cabbage flavor perfectly matches this tangerine sauce and the toasted crushed almonds. This version is a nice change from standard vegetables when served with a leg of lamb, beef ribs, or a robust stew.

Advance Preparation

Toast almonds in a 325°F oven until light golden, about 12 minutes. Let cool to room temperature, then coarsely chop in a food processor.

Trim stems off Brussels sprouts and remove any tough outer leaves. Set aside.

Add peanut oil to garlic and tangerine peel and set aside.

In a small bowl, combine ingredients for sauce. Set aside.

Last-Minute Cooking

Combine cornstarch with an equal amount of cold water. Set aside.

Place Brussels sprouts evenly across tier of a Chinese steamer. Place over rapidly boiling water, cover, and steam until sprouts are bright green, about 10 to 12 minutes. They should be tender when prodded with a fork.

When sprouts are nearly cooked, place a wok over high heat. When hot, add garlic mixture. Sauté a few seconds, then add sauce. Bring sauce mixture to a low boil, add a little of the cornstarch mixture to lightly thicken. Add Brussels sprouts and stir with sauce to coat them well. Remove from heat and stir in butter. Transfer to a heated platter or individual plates. Sprinkle on almonds and serve at once.

Serves: 4 to 6 as the vegetable course for an American dinner; 6 to 8 as part of an Oriental dinner.

222

Pan-Fried Sichuan Chicken;
Steamed Corn with Chinese Herb Sauce.

STEAMED CORN WITH CHINESE HERB SAUCE

8 ears fresh corn, husked
½ cup unsalted butter
½ teaspoon crushed Sichuan peppercorns
½ teaspoon salt
¼ teaspoon white pepper
1 tablespoon finely minced fresh ginger
2 tablespoons finely minced chives
lemon wedges

One easy and satisfying way to cook vegetables is to briefly steam them and then drizzle on an Oriental-flavored butter sauce. This works well with corn, cooked the same day it's picked, as well as with asparagus, broccoli, Brussels sprouts, cauliflower, carrots, squash, and string beans. If you lay them in the tiers of a Chinese steamer, you can steam enough vegetables to serve ten people. The choice of vegetables, cooking times, and variations on the herb sauce are discussed at the end of the recipe.

Cooking

Lay corn in the rack of a Chinese steamer. Bring water in bottom of steamer to a boil.

Place a 12-inch skillet over medium heat. Add butter; when it melts, add the peppercorns, salt, white pepper, and ginger. Cook until ginger sizzles in butter, about 30 seconds. Remove from heat and stir in chives.

Place corn over rapidly boiling water. Cover and steam until tender. Corn picked that day will be cooked in 1 to 2 minutes.

Remove corn from steamer. Place corn, 1 ear at a time, in the seasoned butter mixture, roll quickly, and transfer to a heated serving platter or individual plates.

Serve at once with lemon wedges.

Serves: 4 to 6 as the vegetable course for an American dinner; 6 to 8 as part of an Oriental dinner.

Menu Ideas: Dinner for 4 (vegetarian) — homemade cream of tomato soup, Steamed Corn with Chinese Herb Sauce, and a tossed green salad.

Notes: There are many ways to vary the Chinese herb sauce. Taste and adjust the seasonings as you add 1 or more of these: a squeeze of lime juice, a few drops of sesame oil, 1 teaspoon of oyster sauce, and a little minced fresh coriander (cilantro) or garden herbs.

For other easy vegetable dishes, steam vegetables until bright-colored and tender, then drizzle on the herb sauce. Quantities and cooking times for 4 people: 2 bunches medium asparagus, tough stems snapped off — 4 minutes; 1 bunch broccoli, cut into small pieces and stems peeled — 8 minutes; 24 small Brussels sprouts — 12 minutes; 2 small cauliflower, broken into flowerettes — 12 minutes; 2 bunches medium carrots — 8 minutes; 1 pound squash, cut in half or quarters (zucchini, crookneck, pattypan) — 4 minutes; 1 pound thin string beans — 8 minutes.

BABY CARROTS IN ORANGE CARAMEL SAUCE

3 bunches baby carrots, or 1½ bunches medium carrots
1 tablespoon white sesame seeds

Sauce

2 cloves garlic, finely minced
2 teaspoons finely minced fresh ginger
½ teaspoon grated or finely minced orange peel
1 cup fresh orange juice
1 cup chicken stock
⅓ cup red wine vinegar
¼ cup sugar
2 tablespoons dry sherry
1½ teaspoons light soy sauce
¼ teaspoon salt
⅛ teaspoon ground Sichuan peppercorns
⅛ teaspoon white pepper
¼ star anise

This orange caramel sauce perfectly highlights the natural sweetness of baby carrots. You can make the sauce in advance, with only minutes needed for the final steaming and glazing of the carrots.

Advance Preparation

Scrub and trim carrots. If using medium carrots, cut in half lengthwise; place strips together and cut in half. Set aside.

In a small ungreased skillet set over high heat, stir sesame seeds until light golden, about 2 minutes. Immediately tip out of skillet and set aside.

Place garlic, ginger, and orange peel in a 12-inch skillet and add remaining sauce ingredients. Bring to a rapid boil over high heat and cook, uncovered, until sauce just begins to thicken, about 15 minutes. (Skillet can be covered and set aside at room temperature for several hours until you are ready to cook the carrots.)

Cooking

Bring water to a vigorous boil in the bottom of a Chinese steamer. Spread carrots evenly across steaming tier, cover, and steam until bright orange and tender, about 6 to 8 minutes.

Remove anise from sauce. Over high heat, bring sauce back to a rapid boil. Cook until it thickens and turns a caramel color; sauce is the right thickness when a spoon leaves a path in it. Transfer carrots to skillet and glaze with sauce. Turn onto a heated serving dish or individual plates. Sprinkle with sesame seeds and serve at once.

Serves: 4 as the vegetable course for an American dinner; 6 to 8 as part of an Oriental dinner.

Menu Ideas: Dinner for 4 — California Won Ton Soup, broiled fish, Baby Carrots in Orange Caramel Sauce, and Oriental Fruit Tart.

SEARED GREENS WITH GARLIC

- 1 **pound spinach, stemmed**
- 1 **bunch arugula**
- 1 **head bibb lettuce**
- 3 **cloves garlic, finely minced**
- 2 **teaspoons finely minced fresh ginger**
- 2 **tablespoons peanut oil**

Sauce

- 2 **tablespoons dry sherry**
- 1½ **teaspoons Oriental sesame oil**
- 1 **teaspoon grated or finely minced lemon peel**
- ½ **teaspoon salt**
- ¼ **teaspoon Chinese pepper mix (see Appendix)**
- ¼ **teaspoon sugar**

Mixed leafy greens such as spinach, arugula, and bibb lettuce are tossed with seasonings, then quickly seared in a blazing hot wok for this colorful Oriental "wilted salad." It contrasts nicely with grilled fish and roasted new potatoes.

Advance Preparation

Tear large spinach leaves in half. Discard arugula stems. Set aside bibb lettuce leaves, torn into smaller pieces, with spinach and arugula in a large mixing bowl.

Combine garlic and ginger with oil. In a small bowl, combine sauce ingredients. Set aside.

Last-Minute Cooking

Toss greens with sauce, evenly coating all the leaves.

Place wok over highest heat. When very hot, add garlic mixture, roll oil around sides of wok, then immediately add greens. Stir-fry greens, tossing evenly in the wok, until spinach just begins to wilt, about 1 minute. If spinach has begun to expel its moisture, you have cooked the greens too long. Immediately turn greens out onto a heated serving dish or individual plates. Serve at once.

Serves: 2 as the vegetable course for an American dinner; 4 to 6 as part of an Oriental dinner.

GRILLED ORIENTAL EGGPLANT

4 long Oriental eggplants
   juice from 1 lemon
1 tablespoon white
   sesame seeds
¼ cup light soy sauce
¼ cup dry sherry
2 tablespoons Oriental
   sesame oil
¼ teaspoon freshly ground
   black pepper
3 cloves garlic, finely
   minced
2 tablespoons unsalted
   butter

Slender purple or white Oriental eggplants are far superior to the globe variety for all recipes, Chinese, European and American. Oriental eggplants never need peeling, have no bitter taste, contain very few seeds, and do not absorb large amounts of oil when sautéed. Split in half, marinated with Chinese seasonings, and then grilled, Oriental eggplants are delicious as a side dish for hearty stews and barbecued meats.

Advance Preparation

Split eggplants in half lengthwise, leaving stems on. Rub with lemon juice and set aside.

In a small ungreased skillet set over high heat, stir sesame seeds until light golden. Immediately tip out of skillet and set aside.

In a bowl, combine soy sauce, sherry, sesame oil, and pepper.

Place a small skillet over medium heat. Add garlic and butter. When butter bubbles, add soy mixture. Stir to combine well; then pour into a shallow dish. Add eggplant to dish, cut side down, and marinate at least 30 minutes. (Eggplant can be left in dish all day, refrigerated.)

Cooking

Place eggplant on broiling pan, cut side up. Broil eggplant about 6 inches below heat until tender, about 5 minutes, brushing with marinade. Or, when grilling meat or chicken, place the eggplant on grill, cut side down. Grill about 3 minutes on each side, brushing eggplant with remaining marinade or a little melted butter.

Place eggplant on a heated platter or individual plates. Sprinkle with sesame seeds and serve at once.

Serves: 4 as the vegetable dish for an American dinner; 6 to 8 as part of an Oriental dinner.

Menu Ideas: Dinner for 4 — barbecued chicken, Oriental Grilled Eggplant, tomato-spinach salad, and peach cobbler.

Grilled Oriental Eggplant.   227

HOT GARLIC EGGPLANT

1 ½ pounds eggplant, preferably Oriental

¼ pound ground pork or lamb

2 teaspoons dark soy sauce

1 yellow onion

8 cloves garlic, finely minced

2 teaspoons finely minced fresh ginger

2 tablespoons peanut oil

Sauce

¼ cup dry sherry

3 tablespoons oyster sauce

1 tablespoon dark soy sauce

1 tablespoon Oriental sesame oil

½ tablespoon Chinese chili sauce

1 teaspoon sugar

Sichuan chefs excel at simmering eggplant with lots of garlic and chili in a rich sauce. Served as a side dish with barbecued meat, taken on picnics, or eaten cold from the refrigerator when Chinese-food passions strike, there is never enough of this eggplant.

Advance Preparation

If using a large globe eggplant, peel it. Cut eggplant into ½-inch cubes and set aside.

Combine meat with soy sauce. Mix well and set aside. Peel and coarsely chop onion. Set aside in a small bowl with the garlic and ginger.

In a small bowl, combine ingredients for sauce. Set aside.

Cooking

Place wok over high heat. When hot, add peanut oil. Roll oil around surface, then add meat. Stir-fry meat, pressing it against sides of wok, until it loses raw color and separates into individual grounds, about 3 minutes.

Pour excess fat from wok, then add garlic, ginger, onion, and eggplant. Stir-fry to combine evenly, then add sauce. Pour in a little more sherry or water so that sauce covers about half the eggplant. Cover and cook over high heat, until eggplant softens, about 5 minutes. Stir occasionally.

Remove cover and continue cooking eggplant until most of the sauce is reduced. Taste and adjust seasonings. Transfer to a heated platter or individual plates. Serve at once.

Serves: 4 as the vegetable dish for an American dinner; 6 to 8 as part of an Oriental dinner.

Menu Ideas: Dinner for 4 — braised beef ribs, Hot Garlic Eggplant, string bean salad, and homemade peach ice cream.

Notes: The ground meat adds a rich taste, but the dish is still good with the meat omitted.

SUZHOU FRIED POTATOES

3 large russet potatoes
½ red bell pepper, stemmed and seeded
6 tablespoons peanut oil
4 cloves garlic, finely minced
½ cup minced green onions
2 tablespoons minced fresh coriander (cilantro)

Sauce

¼ cup dry sherry
1 tablespoon Oriental sesame oil
1 tablespoon curry powder
½ teaspoon Chinese pepper mix (see Appendix)
½ teaspoon salt
¼ teaspoon Chinese chili sauce
¼ teaspoon sugar

Midway through a sustained eating spree in China, we found a plate of peppery French fries served at a lunch at the Nanlin Hotel in Suzhou. Completely incongruous — and welcome! These julienned potatoes are stir-fried in a spicy sauce and cooled to room temperature before undergoing a second frying. Served with a homemade soup and garden salad, this makes a nice vegetarian meal.

Advance Preparation

Wash, dry, but do not peel potatoes. Cut potatoes into ¼-inch-thick slices. Stack slices and cut enough into ¼-inch matchstick pieces to make 4 cups. Place in a large mixing bowl and wash with several changes of cold water until water no longer looks cloudy. Cover potatoes with cold water until ready to cook.

In a small bowl, combine sauce ingredients. Set aside. Cut red pepper into slivers and set aside.

Advance Cooking

Drain potatoes, then pat thoroughly dry with paper towels. Place wok over highest heat. When very hot, add 3 tablespoons peanut oil and the garlic. Sauté briefly and just before garlic browns add potatoes. Stir-fry potatoes over highest heat for 4 minutes.

Add sauce to wok and stir-fry another 2 minutes. Stir in green onions and coriander. Cook another 2 minutes, then turn out onto a plate. Let cool to room temperature. (Can be prepared to this point a day ahead and refrigerated.)

Last-Minute Cooking

Place wok over highest heat. When very hot, add remaining peanut oil. Roll oil around sides of wok, then add potatoes when oil begins to smoke. Every 30 seconds, briefly stir and toss potatoes, spreading them out against the hot sides of the wok to brown. When about half the potatoes are nicely browned, in about 8 minutes, stir in red pepper and cook another 2 minutes. Turn out onto a heated platter or individual plates. Serve at once.

Serves: 4 as a side dish for an American dinner; 6 to 8 as part of an Oriental dinner.

■ C H A P T E R   9

God created desserts first and, as an afterthought, added preliminary dishes. Those of us who realize this are willing to tolerate a succession of dishes in order to finally reach the meal's conclusion. Ideally these grand finales should be made with the necessities of daily life: thick whipping cream, sweet butter, flavorful Latin American coffee, Grand Marnier, and the richest, darkest European chocolate. As everyone who has traveled to China and Thailand can confirm, chefs there lack these "essentials," which explains their sad conclusions to otherwise exquisite meals. Because I believe that perfect desserts should end memorable dinners, this chapter offers a selection of desserts ranging from easy (and addictive) Chocolate Chip Almond Cookies to an elaborate fruit tart and rich ice creams. Whether serving a light dessert to conclude a substantial dinner or a decadent chocolate fantasy after one of the delicate entrées in this book, present an imaginative dessert with a little drama to surprise and delight your guests.

Easy-to-prepare recipes in this chapter are Chocolate Chip Almond Cookies, Firecracker Cookies, Almond Float Soup, Ginger Crème Brûlée, and Mango Sorbet.

Grand Marnier Mocha Ice Cream; Chinese Ginger Snaps.   231

GRAND MARNIER MOCHA ICE CREAM

¼ cup mocha java coffee beans, finely ground

10 ounces semisweet chocolate

6 large egg yolks

1 cup sugar

2 cups half-and-half

2 cups heavy (whipping) cream

½ cup Grand Marnier

I first made this ice cream years ago for a group of close friends who had gathered often in my kitchen for elaborate Chinese dinners, fine wines, and good conversation. Now a different type of feast draws to a close. Just as the recipe for Chinese spareribs, which began this book, welcomed you to our love of food and entertaining, so this delicious dessert serves as our farewell. Share it with special friends.

Advance Preparation
Place a coffee filter with ground coffee beans over a small bowl and slowly moisten grounds with 1 cup boiling water. Transfer filter over clean bowl and slowly pour brewed coffee through filter again to make an extra-strong cup of coffee. Combine 2 tablespoons of the coffee grounds and ½ cup coffee.

Cut chocolate into small pieces. Place in top of a double boiler along with coffee-ground mixture. Cook over low heat. When chocolate melts, in about 10 minutes, stir briefly with a whisk to combine evenly. Turn heat off and leave chocolate over the hot water.

Make the custard according to directions on page 234.

While custard is still hot, slowly pour in melted chocolate, stirring with a whisk to combine evenly. Chill at least 2 hours in the refrigerator.

Add heavy cream and Grand Marnier to mixture. Place in ice cream freezer and process according to manufacturer's instructions. Makes 2 quarts.

Serves: 10.

CHINESE GINGER SNAPS

- ½ **pound unsalted butter**
- 2 **cups sugar**
- 5 **tablespoons finely minced fresh ginger**
- 2 **eggs, beaten well**
- ½ **cup molasses**
- 1 **tablespoon white pepper**
- 2 **teaspoons distilled white vinegar**
- 1½ **teaspoons baking soda**
- ½ **teaspoon ground cinnamon**
- ¼ **teaspoon ground cloves**
- 4 **cups all-purpose flour**

Chef and cooking friend Grant Showley uses his grandmother's ginger snap recipe at his Newport Beach restaurant, Showley-Wrightson, but adds a generous amount of fresh ginger. This extra ginger and the astronomical amount of white pepper are what make this cookie outstanding. By rolling the dough into thin sheets, you can cut it into whimsical shapes before baking. Since leftover cookies freeze well, set aside a good supply in case the cookie monster strikes.

Advance Preparation

Place butter and sugar in a food processor fitted with cutting blade. Cream until very evenly combined, then remove lid and add the ginger, eggs, molasses, white pepper, and vinegar. Process to evenly combine, then add baking soda, cinnamon, and cloves. Process again to combine evenly.

Turn out into a mixing bowl. Work in flour, 1 cup at a time, until evenly mixed. Divide dough into 3 balls and wrap each in plastic wrap. Refrigerate at least 3 hours.

Baking

Preheat oven to 325°F. When dough is well chilled, roll out on a lightly floured board or pastry cloth into a sheet ¼ inch thick. Cut into desired shapes.

Line a baking sheet with cooking parchment. Place cookies ½ inch apart and bake until firm but not dried out, about 15 minutes. Serve at room temperature. (Cookies can be baked, then frozen indefinitely.)

Makes: 4 to 6 dozen cookies, depending on size.

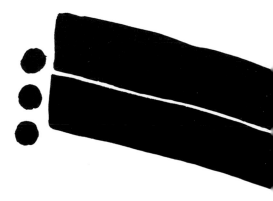

GINGER ICE CREAM IN PAPAYA SAUCE

¼ cup fresh ginger purée (see Notes)

6 large egg yolks

1 cup sugar

2 cups half-and-half

2 cups heavy (whipping) cream

10 fresh strawberries and 3 kiwis, for garnish (optional)

Papaya Sauce

1 papaya

2 tablespoons lime juice

2 tablespoons Curaçao

"Painted" Sauce

½ cup confectioners' sugar

⅓ of 1 egg white

⅛ teaspoon lemon juice

The flavor of grated fresh ginger adds an intense "clean" taste impossible to achieve using crystallized ginger or preserved ginger in syrup. At the end of the recipe are three techniques for producing a ginger purée completely free of any fibrous texture. The recipe gives two beautiful ways to embellish the ice cream: a "painted" sauce and a lovely presentation of strawberries and kiwis on the papaya sauce suggested to me by talented chef Osa Sommermeyer.

Advance Preparation

Prepare ginger purée; see Notes.

Make the custard. In a copper or stainless-steel mixing bowl, whisk egg yolks with sugar until mixture turns a pale yellow and sugar is completely absorbed, about 3 minutes.

Fill a large bowl or sink with cold water and a generous amount of ice. Put half-and-half in a 3-quart saucepan and heat until bubbles appear around edge. Pour slowly into the egg mixture, stirring with a whisk. Briefly beat mixture, then pour back into saucepan. Place empty mixing bowl in ice water.

Place egg mixture over high heat. Beat quickly with a whisk until the mixture becomes thick enough to lightly coat a spoon and nearly doubles in volume, about 3 minutes. Immediately pour custard into the chilled bowl and stir slowly with a whisk for 2 minutes.

Stir in ginger purée and chill for at least 2 hours.

Add heavy cream to custard and place mixture in ice cream freezer. Process according to manufacturer's instructions.

Assembling

Prepare papaya sauce. Peel papaya and scoop out seeds. Purée with lime juice and Curaçao in a food processor until completely smooth. Taste and adjust for seasonings, then chill until ready to use. Slice strawberries. Peel and slice kiwi. Refrigerate.

To make a painted decoration on the papaya sauce, combine confectioners' sugar, egg white, and lemon juice in a bowl. Stir until creamy, then transfer to a small pastry bag fitted with a ¼-inch metal tip.

Cover surface of 8 chilled dessert plates with a thin layer of papaya sauce. Put 1 large or 3 small scoops of ice cream in the center of each plate. If using the "painted" presentation, pipe a thin ribbon of white icing on the papaya sauce. With the tip of a skewer, cut back and forth across the thread of icing to make little swirls. If making the fruit presentation, on the papaya sauce alternate strawberry slices with kiwi slices.

Serve at once. Makes 2 quarts.

Serves: 10.

Notes: There are 3 techniques for making ginger purée, listed in order of preference. Begin with very fresh ginger, peeled. (1) Bring ¼ cup water and ¼ cup sugar to a boil. When sugar is dissolved, set aside. In an electric mini-chopper, place 2 tablespoons thinly sliced fresh ginger. Finely mince, then add 3 tablespoons syrup and purée. Pour out ginger purée and repeat procedure until you have ¼ cup ginger purée. (This very quick method yields fresh ginger purée with no traces of ginger fiber.) (2) Cut ginger into paper-thin slices. Stand a few ginger slices on edge inside the socket of a Susi garlic press (made by Zyliss) and force ginger through the holes. Scrape out fiber and repeat process until you have ¼ cup purée. (3) Some metal cheese graters have an intermediate-sized grater – not big holes or small bumpy grates. Rub ginger back and forth to yield 3 to 4 tablespoons.

As a substitute for fresh ginger, use twice as much finely minced preserved stem ginger plus some of the syrup to make a smooth purée.

Ginger Ice Cream in Papaya Sauce;
Chocolate Chip Almond Cookies.

CHOCOLATE CHIP ALMOND COOKIES

¾ cup slivered almonds (2½ ounces)
1 cup sugar
1 cup lard, cut into small pieces
2 eggs
1 tablespoon almond extract
1 teaspoon baking powder
½ cup semisweet miniature chocolate chips
2 cups all-purpose flour
48 whole blanched almonds

These crumbly cookies, speckled with chocolate chips and crushed toasted almonds, are far superior to Chinatown almond cookies. One of my students claims this recipe — which makes 48 cookies — is barely sufficient for two people!

Advance Preparation
Place slivered almonds on a cookie sheet and toast in a 325°F oven until golden, about 12 minutes. When cool, finely chop in a food processor and set aside.

In a food processor fitted with cutting blade, process sugar and lard until they are combined well. Remove lid and add 1 egg, almond extract, and the baking powder. Process briefly to combine evenly, then turn out into a mixing bowl. Stir in the chocolate chips and ground almonds. Work in flour until evenly mixed.

Divide dough in half, forming 2 soft balls. On a lightly floured surface, roll each ball into a cylinder about 1 inch thick and 12 inches long. Wrap in plastic and refrigerate at least 2 hours. (Dough can be refrigerated for up to 2 weeks or frozen indefinitely.)

Baking
Preheat oven to 375°F. If dough is frozen, remove from refrigerator 20 minutes before cutting into cookies.

Line a baking sheet with cooking parchment. With a sharp knife, cut dough into ½-inch wide rounds. Place 1 inch apart on cookie sheet. Lightly press a whole almond into the center of each cookie.

Beat remaining egg well. Using a pastry brush, brush a little egg across the top of each cookie. Bake cookies until golden, about 15 to 18 minutes. Let cool on baking sheet before removing to a rack. Cool to room temperature before serving. (Stored in an airtight container, cookies will stay crisp for 1 week.) Serve the cookies with fresh fruit or ice cream.

Makes: 4 dozen cookies.

Notes: Lard is what gives these cookies an incredible crumbliness. It is sold at the meat counter of practically every supermarket and lasts indefinitely in the refrigerator. If you're wondering about substitutions, vegetable shortening gives the cookies a disagreeable taste, and butter causes them to flatten into paper-thin wafers.

A nice variation is to roll the cylinders of dough in roasted, crushed almonds. When baked, each cookie will be coated around the edges with the almonds.

If you omit the chocolate chips, increase the flour by ½ cup.

FLAMBEED THAI BANANAS

- 1 tablespoon white sesame seeds
- 3 tablespoons shredded coconut
- 2 large firm underripe bananas
- 2 tablespoons unsalted butter
- 1 tablespoon finely minced fresh ginger
- 2 teaspoons grated or finely minced orange peel
- 2 tablespoons sugar juice of 1 lime
- 6 tablespoons Cognac
- 1 lime, cut into wedges, for garnish

Flaming bananas, sautéed for two minutes with orange peel, fresh ginger, lime, and toasted coconut, are an exceptionally easy dessert. Accompanied by chocolate truffles or scoops of Ginger Ice Cream, Thai Bananas are a perfect way to end a special evening.

Advance Preparation
Place a small ungreased skillet over high heat. Add sesame seeds and stir, toasting until light golden, about 2 minutes. Immediately tip out and set aside.

Return pan to high heat and add shredded coconut. Stir coconut until it turns a light golden, about 1 minute. Immediately remove and set aside.

Cooking
Peel bananas. Cut in half lengthwise.

Place a 12-inch skillet over medium-high heat. Add butter, ginger, and orange peel. When butter begins to bubble, add banana slices, cut side down. Sprinkle on the sugar. Add lime juice. Sauté bananas 1 minute. Carefully turn over and sauté until sauce begins to caramelize, about 1 minute. Transfer bananas to warm dessert plates. Sprinkle with sesame seeds and coconut.

Return frying pan to medium-high heat and add Cognac. As soon as Cognac is hot, ignite with a match. Immediately pour sauce over bananas. Serve at once with lime wedges.

Serves: 2 as a rich dessert; 4 when accompanied by ice cream.

Ginger Bavarian Cream.

238

Mango Sorbet; Firecracker Cookies.

GINGER BAVARIAN CREAM

2	tablespoons preserved stem ginger, plus syrup
1	tablespoon unflavored gelatin
2	cups milk
6	large eggs
⅔	cup sugar
1½	teaspoons vanilla extract
⅛	teaspoon cream of tartar
½	cup heavy (whipping) cream

Garnishes (choose 1)

½	cup heavy (whipping) cream and mint sprigs
	Raspberry Sauce (page 250)
½	pound semisweet dark chocolate, ½ cup heavy (whipping) cream, and 2 tablespoons Grand Marnier

Luscious Bavarian cream, served in wineglasses with rosettes of whipped cream and mint sprigs, makes a light ending to an Oriental dinner. As an alternative, chill the Bavarian cream in individual molds. Unmold onto dessert plates and surround with a raspberry or chocolate Grand Marnier sauce. The subtle ginger flavor in the cream comes from puréeing the amber nuggets of preserved stem ginger in an electric minichopper or blender. Grated fresh ginger would not be a good substitute, since its high acid content prevents the Bavarian cream from setting.

Advance Preparation

In an electric minichopper or electric blender, purée preserved stem ginger until no texture remains. If there is difficulty puréeing the ginger, add a few tablespoons of the syrup. Set aside.

Sprinkle gelatin over ½ cup cold milk, then stir to dissolve. Set aside.

Separate egg yolks from whites, placing yolks in a copper mixing bowl and whites in a 3-quart bowl. Add sugar to yolks and whisk until mixture turns a pale yellow and sugar is completely absorbed, about 3 minutes.

Place remaining milk in a 3-quart saucepan. Turn heat to high and cook until bubbles appear around edges, about 4 minutes. Pour all milk slowly into the egg yolk mixture, beating with a whisk. Briefly beat mixture to warm eggs and pour back into saucepan. Mean-

while, put empty mixing bowl in a larger bowl filled with ice water. Return saucepan to highest heat. Beat quickly with a whisk until the mixture is thick enough to lightly coat a spoon and nearly doubles in volume, about 4 minutes. (Be sure to stir vigorously and do not overcook the custard, or the yolks will curdle). Immediately tip custard into the chilled bowl. Stir in the milk-gelatin mixture, the puréed ginger, and the vanilla.

With an electric mixer, beat the egg whites. When doubled in size sprinkle in cream of tartar. Continue beating until stiff peaks form. Very gently fold them, one-fourth at a time, into the hot custard using a spatula. Let cool to room temperature.

When custard is about to set (the hot custard will cool to room temperature in 5 minutes if placed in copper mixing bowl over ice water), beat cream until stiff with an electric mixer. Gently stir into the Bavarian cream, then pour into 10 small decorative molds or 10 wineglasses. Refrigerate at least 4 hours or overnight.

If serving the dessert unmolded, prepare Raspberry Sauce or use the chocolate sauce. Cut chocolate into small pieces and place with cream in a small heavy saucepan. Put over lowest heat and stir until melted and evenly combined. Stir in Grand Marnier, then set aside in saucepan. (May be done hours ahead.)

Last-Minute Assembly

Prepare garnishes. If serving the Bavarian cream in wineglasses, use the first garnish. Just before dinner, beat cream until stiff peaks form, then place in a pastry bag. Make little rosettes of whipped cream on top of the Bavarian cream. Garnish with mint sprigs and serve with Chinese cookies or chocolates.

If using individual molds, fill a large container with hottest tap water. Dip each mold into water for 3 seconds, then invert onto a dessert plate. If using Raspberry Sauce, surround unmolded creams with cold sauce. If using chocolate sauce, reheat sauce over a larger pan of simmering water, then pour around Bavarian creams. Serve at once.

Serves: 10.

OVERLEAF: Chocolate Macadamia Nut Torte.

FIRECRACKER COOKIES

3 tablespoons white sesame seeds

⅔ cup shelled walnuts (2½ ounces)

⅔ cup slivered almonds (2½ ounces)

8 ounces pitted dates

1½ teaspoons grated or finely minced orange peel

1½ teaspoons grated or finely minced lemon peel

⅓ cup shredded coconut

36 square won ton skins

4 cups peanut oil

1 cup confectioners' sugar

These won tons are stuffed with a coconut-date filling, twisted like firecrackers, and sprinkled with confectioners' sugar.

Preparation

Stir sesame seeds in a small ungreased skillet over high heat until light golden, about 2 minutes. Immediately tip out of skillet and set aside.

Place walnuts and almonds in a food processor fitted with cutting blade. Turn processor on; as nuts are being chopped, feed dates down tube. Process until very finely chopped, about 30 seconds. Remove lid and add orange and lemon peels, coconut, and sesame seeds. Process again briefly to combine evenly.

Remove date mixture from processor. Using your hands, firmly press mixture into a ball. Place a won ton skin so that one of the corners is pointed toward you. Form 2 teaspoons of the filling into a cylinder and place across that corner. Lightly moisten opposite won ton tip with water. Holding the won ton tip closest to you, roll won ton into a cylinder around the filling. Lightly moisten inside each end of cylinder, then twist ends to resemble a firecracker. Repeat with remaining won ton skins.

Cooking

Place oil in a 12-inch skillet over medium-high heat. Heat oil until a strip of won ton skips across the surface. Adding about 12 won tons at a time, fry until cylinders turn a very light golden, about 1 minute.

Drain won tons on a wire rack, then sprinkle with confectioners' sugar. When cool, store in an airtight container. (Will remain crisp for about 3 days.) Serve on a pretty tray with dessert.

Makes: 3 dozen.

CHOCOLATE MACADAMIA NUT TORTE

1 cup unsalted macadamia nuts (see Notes)

2 tablespoons preserved stem ginger

5 ounces semisweet chocolate

10 tablespoons unsalted butter

1 cup sugar

4 eggs

⅓ cup fine unseasoned bread crumbs

1 tablespoon grated or finely minced orange peel

Sugar Syrup

3 tablespoons sugar

3 tablespoons Grand Marnier

Chocolate Glaze

2 ounces unsweetened chocolate

2 ounces semisweet chocolate

¼ cup unsalted butter

Decorations (choose 1)

½ cup confectioners' sugar, ⅓ egg white, and ⅛ teaspoon lemon juice

fresh raspberries and ½ cup heavy (whipping) cream

This very rich flourless cake is excellent after an Oriental meal, served in thin wedges with fresh fruit or homemade sorbet. The recipe, with a few modifications, comes from well-known San Diego cooking teacher Anne Otterson. It can be made a day in advance and left unrefrigerated.

Advance Preparation

Butter bottom and sides of a 9-inch round cake pan. Line bottom with cooking parchment, then rub top of paper with butter and lightly flour. Preheat oven to 375°F.

Place nuts in a food processor fitted with cutting blade. Mince until nuts resemble cornmeal. Set aside.

In an electric minichopper or blender, purée preserved stem ginger until no texture remains. Set aside 2 tablespoons.

Cut 5 ounces semisweet chocolate into small pieces. Melt in a small metal mixing bowl over simmering water.

Place butter and sugar in processor bowl and process until well combined. Add eggs and ginger purée; process until combined. Add melted chocolate to mixture and process briefly.

Turn out into a bowl. Stir in bread crumbs, ground nuts, and orange peel. Pour into pan and bake until a knife blade stuck in the center comes out clean, about 25 to 30 minutes.

Let torte cool 30 minutes. Place the bottom of a 9-inch springform pan on top of cake and invert cake to remove from pan. Cake is inverted onto this base so that it can be easily transferred after icing without the surface cracking. Carefully peel off parchment. Cool cake to room temperature.

Make sugar syrup. In a very small saucepan, bring 3 tablespoons water and sugar to a boil until sugar is dissolved. Turn out into a bowl. Cool to room temperature, then stir in Grand Marnier. Brush over surface of cake until absorbed.

In a small metal bowl, place ingredients for glaze. Melt over simmering water and stir to combine thoroughly. Cool over ice for about 1 minute, until chocolate just begins to thicken. Pour glaze onto center of cake. Quickly tip cake so glaze covers top surface with a little running down the sides. Using a spatula, coat sides of cake. (Can be made to this point a day ahead, and left unrefrigerated.)

Assembling

If making a painted decoration on cake, combine confectioners' sugar, egg white, and lemon juice in a small bowl. Stir until creamy, then transfer to a small pastry bag fitted with a ¼-inch metal tip. Make parallel lines of icing 1 inch apart across the cake. With a piece of string held tightly between your fingers or a long knife, make cuts across the white icing to create a feathered effect.

Or simply place a ring of raspberries around the edge of cake. Before serving, beat cream until stiff. Place in pastry bag and make small rosettes between each raspberry.

Serves: 10.

Notes: As a substitute for macadamia nuts, use hazelnuts or almonds. Toast them in a 325°F oven until light golden, about 15 minutes. Cool to room temperature before grinding.

You can freeze this torte unglazed. Defrost at room temperature, glaze, and decorate.

OVERLEAF: Almond Float Soup.

ALMOND FLOAT SOUP

1 package unflavored gelatin

¾ cup plus 2 teaspoons sugar

¾ cup milk

1 teaspoon almond extract

2 cups mixed fresh fruit (pineapple, strawberries, kiwi)

8 small fresh mint sprigs

Dessert soups, called "sweet water" by my Chinese guides, are rarely served by Chinese restaurants in this country. Made of puréed iced fruits or nuts, their slight sweetness, subtle flavor, and light body is a perfect conclusion to a lengthy banquet. Almond Float Soup, with little squares of almond jelly, fresh fruit and mint sprigs, is refreshing on a hot night, accompanied by Chinese cookies or chocolate mints and tall frosted glasses of iced tea.

Advance Preparation

In a 1-quart bowl, sprinkle gelatin over ¼ cup cold water to soften a few minutes. Stir to dissolve, then add 2 teaspoons sugar. Stir well and let rest 5 minutes.

Bring ¾ cup water to a boil. Pour over gelatin and stir until liquid is clear. Stir in milk and almond extract, then pour into a 6- by 8-inch pan and chill until set, about 2 hours. Cut into bite-size cubes.

In a small saucepan, place 3 cups water and remaining ¾ cup sugar. Bring to boil, dissolving sugar. Transfer to a bowl and let cool to room temperature. Add mint sprigs and chill at least 1 hour in the refrigerator.

Serving

Place syrup and mint leaves in a decorative glass serving bowl. Add the almond jelly and fresh fruit.

Serves: 4 as a light dessert, accompanied by Chinese Firecracker Cookies and a fine Chinese tea.

Notes: A good variation is to simmer 10 thin slices of fresh ginger in the syrup for 5 minutes. Leave ginger slices in syrup until just before serving.

GINGER CREME BRULEE

4   large egg yolks
5½   tablespoons sugar
2   cups heavy (whipping)
        cream
1¼   teaspoons vanilla
        extract
3   tablespoons very thinly
        sliced crystallized
        ginger
2   tablespoons raspberry
        jam

The silky richness of crème brûlée is a great conclusion to an Oriental feast. In this version, slices of crystallized ginger and tiny dots of raspberry jam hide at the bottom. While the recipe gives directions for caramelizing the sugar topping under the broiler, the only way to produce perfect results is to use an inexpensive propane blowtorch sold at most hardware stores. Your guests will be amazed by this technique!

Advance Cooking

Preheat oven to 350°F.

In a 2-quart bowl, beat yolks with 3½ tablespoons sugar until the mixture turns a pale yellow and the sugar is completely absorbed, about 3 minutes of vigorous beating with a whisk. Add cream and vanilla. Beat well.

Place a few slices of ginger in the bottom of four ¾-cup ramekins. Put a dot of raspberry jam in center of each ramekin. Carefully ladle in mixture and transfer ramekins to a small baking dish.

Add enough warm water to the baking dish to come halfway up ramekins. Place baking dish in oven and bake for 50 minutes. The top of the custards will become golden brown. Transfer ramekins to refrigerator and chill at least 3 hours. (This can be done a day ahead.)

Last-Minute Cooking

If using a broiler, preheat for 15 minutes.

Sprinkle about 1 tablespoon sugar on top of 1 ramekin. Roll sugar around surface to lightly coat, tipping excess sugar onto next ramekin. Continue with remaining ramekins. Place ramekins in a shallow pan, and surround with water and ice cubes. Place 2 inches from broiler and cook until sugar caramelizes, about 30 seconds.

Alternatively, light a propane torch. Turn flame to low and caramelize sugar tops. Serve at once.

Serves: 4 as a rich conclusion, accompanied by fruit and possibly Chinese cookies.

Notes: The caramel coating should be done at the last moment, since it does not stay crisp when done ahead and refrigerated.

COCONUT
ICE CREAM

1 cup shredded sweetened coconut

6 large egg yolks

1 cup sugar

2 cups half-and-half

1 teaspoon coconut extract

2 cups heavy (whipping) cream

mint sprigs, for garnish

Cookie Cups

1 cup blanched almonds (4 ounces)

¾ cup sugar

1 tablespoon grated or finely minced orange peel

2 tablespoons all-purpose flour

6 tablespoons unsalted butter, melted

2 tablespoons milk

Raspberry Sauce

12 ounces frozen raspberries, thawed to room temperature

2 tablespoons superfine sugar

3 tablespoons Cognac

This homemade ice cream, nestled in a lacy cookie cup and surrounded by a raspberry sauce, is a symphony of contrasting textures, tastes, and color. The cookie cups, based on a recipe by Jacques Pépin, can be made weeks in advance and frozen so that last-minute assembly of this elegant dessert takes only minutes.

Advance Preparation

In a 10-inch skillet set over medium-high heat, toast coconut until golden, about 2 minutes. Set aside.

Make the custard according to directions on page 234.

Add coconut extract, then chill for at least 2 hours.

Add heavy cream and half the shredded coconut to the mixture. Place in ice cream freezer and process according to manufacturer's instructions. Makes 2 quarts.

Prepare the cookie cups. Preheat oven to 325°F. Toast almonds until golden, about 15 minutes. Let cool completely.

Finely grind almonds in a food processor; there should be about 1 cup ground almonds. Pour into a 1-quart bowl and add sugar, orange peel, and flour. Stir in melted butter, then add milk.

Preheat oven to 375°F. Cut cooking parchment into twelve 6-inch square pieces. Place 1 square on a cookie sheet and add about 1½ tablespoons batter to center. Bake until golden, about 8 to 12 minutes. Cookie should spread out into a very thin circle, about 4 inches across.

Remove cookie from oven and wait about 45 seconds. While cookie is still hot, mold it into a cup by fitting it around the bottom of a small, inverted water glass or fluted mold. If cookie dough is too thin to handle, stir a little more flour into batter; if cookie does not spread out thinly enough to mold it, add a little more milk to batter. Bake 3 or 4 cookies at a time. (Store cookies for several days in a cookie jar, or indefinitely in the freezer.) Makes 12 cookies.

Make sauce. Purée raspberries in a food processor, then force through a fine sieve to strain out seeds. Stir in sugar and Cognac. Refrigerate. Makes 1 cup.

Assembling

Glaze the bottoms of 8 dessert plates with sauce. Place a cookie cup in center of each. Add 1 large scoop ice cream and sprinkle with toasted coconut. Garnish with a mint sprig. Serve at once.

Serves: 8.

Coconut Ice Cream.   251

ORIENTAL FRUIT TART

Pastry Dough

- 1¼ **cups all-purpose flour**
- ½ **teaspoon salt**
- ½ **cup unsalted butter, cut into small pieces**
- 2 **to 6 tablespoons ice water**

Pastry Cream

- 3 **egg yolks**
- ⅓ **cup sugar**
- ½ **teaspoon vanilla extract**
- 1 **tablespoon all-purpose flour**
- 1 **tablespoon cornstarch**
- 1 **cup milk**
- 1 **generous tablespoon puréed fresh ginger (see Notes, page 235)**

Caramel Syrup

- ½ **cup sugar**
- ¼ **cup water**

Fresh Fruit and Glaze

- **fresh fruit, to decorate top**
- ½ **cup apricot jam**
- 1 **tablespoon Cognac**

Each bite includes layers of fresh fruit, light ginger-flavored pastry cream, and crunchy caramelized sugar on flaky pastry. Assemble this dessert hours in advance and leave the tart out, unrefrigerated, so the pastry does not become soggy. A caramel coating on pastry is a technique Jacques Pépin uses on his wonderful tarts.

Advance Preparation

Prepare dough. Place flour, salt, and butter in the bowl of a food processor fitted with cutting blade. Place in freezer for 45 minutes. When very cold, process until mixture resembles cornmeal. Add a little cold water, processing again until dough holds together when pressed between your fingers. Turn out onto plastic wrap, press into a circle, wrap, and refrigerate for 1 hour.

Make pastry cream. Beat egg yolks and sugar until eggs turn a pale yellow. Beat in vanilla, flour, and cornstarch. In a saucepan, heat the milk until bubbles appear around edges, then stir hot milk into egg mixture. Pour back into saucepan and place over medium-high heat. Beat with a whisk until mixture becomes very thick, about 2 minutes. Turn out into a bowl and stir in half the ginger purée. Refrigerate at least 1 hour.

Preheat oven to 375°F. On a lightly floured board or chilled pastry cloth, roll dough out into a narrow rectangle about 6 by 18 inches until ¼ inch thick. If you place the rolling pin on top of 2 long, narrow ¼-inch-thick strips of wood, the pastry will roll out more easily and be of uniform thickness.

Transfer pastry to a baking sheet with no sides that has been lined with cooking parchment. Trim and discard ragged edges from pastry. Cut a ½-inch-wide strip of pastry from each side. Moisten edges with water, and lay the strips, trimmed to fit, on top of the moistened edges, pressing with your fingers to make the strips adhere. The thicker edges around the pastry hold in the pastry cream. Prick bottom with fork. Cover pastry with foil and place a layer of pastry weights or beans on top. Bake until edges become light golden, about 15 minutes. Remove foil and bake until a deep golden color, about 15 minutes more.

When pasty has cooled to room temperature, prepare syrup. Place sugar and water in a small saucepan over medium-high heat. Bring to a boil and continue boiling until sugar turns dark golden, about 5 minutes. Immediately pour over pastry, spreading the caramel with an oiled spatula into a thin layer. When cool, transfer pastry to a flat serving plate or board.

Assembling
Spread pastry cream evenly across inside surface of pastry. Decorate with fresh fruit. Heat apricot jam to a low boil, then force through a strainer. Add Cognac and remaining ginger purée. Brush generously over fruit. (Dessert can be assembled in the morning, but do not refrigerate or the pastry will become soggy.)

Serves: 8.

MANGO SORBET

1   **cup sugar**
3   **ripe mangoes**
¼   **cup lemon juice**
1   **tablespoon Grand Marnier**

The luscious trio of Mango Sorbet, Chinese cookies, and cappuccino is a perfect conclusion to any dinner. For an elegant presentation, serve the sorbet in cookie cups centered on a light custard sauce.

Advance Preparation
In a small saucepan, bring 2 cups water and sugar to a low boil over medium-high heat. Stir and boil until sugar is dissolved. Transfer to a bowl and chill at least 2 hours.

Peel mangoes. Cut off mango flesh and purée in a food processor. To 2 cups of purée, add lemon juice and Grand Marnier. Refrigerate.

When sugar syrup is thoroughly chilled, stir in mango purée. Place in an ice cream freezer and process according to manufacturer's instructions. Makes 6 cups.

Serves: 8 as a refreshing dessert, accompanied by little cookies or chocolates.

APPENDICES

CHINESE EQUIPMENT AND COOKING TECHNIQUES

STEAMERS AND STEAMING PROCEDURES

There are few cooking techniques as easy as steaming. The food is placed on a plate and the plate is put on a metal or bamboo steamer tier set over rapidly boiling water. The boiling water creates steam, which swirls around the food to cook it. When layering several tiers, remember that the food in the top tier cooks at the same rate as the food in the bottom tier, provided the steam can circulate easily around the food.

Inexpensive aluminum and bamboo steamers are available at all Chinese markets. Aluminum steamers range in diameter from ten to thirty inches and consist of a pot to hold the boiling water, two tiers with perforated holes, and a lid. We recommend aluminum because it is easy to clean.

Bamboo steamers are beautiful; however, their disadvantages outweigh their aesthetic appeal. They are difficult to clean and allow flavors to carry over from one dish to another. You also need a separate container to hold the boiling water. We use ours only when serving dumplings at the table.

For limited use, a steamer can be improvised from equipment you probably already have. Select a large pot such as a deep roasting pan, electric frying pan, or wok and add a few inches of water. Bring water to a boil. Meanwhile, put food on a heatproof glass plate. Position an inverted heatproof bowl or perforated can in the boiling water to create a stand for the plate so water cannot touch the food. Cover with a pot lid or aluminum foil and steam according to recipe instructions.

WOKS

A wok is the practical, multipurpose, concave Chinese cooking utensil used to create a vast range of delicious dishes. Spring rolls slide down the sides to deep-fry in hot oil without a splash. Fish steams to perfection on an elevated rack set above rapidly boiling water and covered by the domed lid. Stews bubble gently over low heat. The sloping sides of a wok require less oil than Western frying pans. When given a swish, stir-fried ingredients automatically fall to the bottom, hottest part of the wok for quick, even cooking. Because of the pan's shape, Chinese food — particularly all stir-fry dishes — *tastes better* than the same recipe made in another utensil.

Woks range from the inexpensive, traditional heavy steel type sold by Oriental markets to the deluxe, modern stainless-steel and copper woks available at gourmet shops. I prefer heavy steel woks because they distribute the heat evenly. After frequent use, they acquire a beautiful black luster; it is this black "seasoning" that gives them a nonstick surface and contributes a special "wok flavor" to stir-fried dishes. However, steel woks need to be specially seasoned, used frequently, and carefully cleaned. If this does not appeal to you, purchase a stainless-steel, nonstick, or copper wok. But avoid the electric wok. Even at its highest setting, an electric wok never becomes hot enough for stir-frying, so the food boils in its own juices.

Buy a fourteen- or sixteen-inch wok with a long wooden handle. For stir-frying on a gas stove, get a wok with a round bottom. Remove the grill from the burner and place the round-bottom wok directly on the jets so the flames leap up around the sides of the wok. (Stir-fried dishes cook quickly and taste much more succulent than if the wok is placed on the grating or elevated above the burner by the useless "wok ring.") For electric stoves, buy a flat-bottom wok. The flat bottom rests on the largest electric coil, so the high heat is conducted directly from the coil to the surface of the utensil. Using a flat-bottom wok on an electric stove produces just as delicious food as a round-bottom wok on a gas stove.

The heavy steel woks sold by Oriental markets require special care. These come coated with a thin layer of oil. Scrub the wok thoroughly inside and out with hot soapy water, using a scouring pad. The wok is clean when the gray coating no longer comes off on your hands. Dry the wok, then place it over high heat. When the wok becomes hot to the touch, "season" it by adding ¼ cup peanut oil to the center. With a paper towel and spoon, coat the inside surface with oil; as the oil begins to smoke slightly, remove the wok from the heat. Let cool completely, then wipe the oil from the wok. With repeated use, the wok "seasoning" gradually turns black, creating a nonstick surface. Provided no one scrubs the seasoning off or boils water in the wok for steaming, which removes the seasoning, the wok never needs to be seasoned again.

Clean your steel wok as you would a good omelet pan. Place it in a sink and fill with hot water. After a few minutes, or after dinner, use hot water and a sponge to rub off all food particles sticking to the sides. Never use soap or an abrasive pad, since these remove the seasoning. Dry the wok over medium heat, then

store for future use. Do not add oil to the inside surface before storage, since this eventually turns into a sticky, rancid layer that must be scrubbed off.

PRINCIPLES FOR STIR-FRYING

If stir-frying is new to you, review these principles to ensure success:

1. Cut food into smaller pieces than you think necessary. The smaller the food is cut, the more quickly it will cook and the better it will taste.

2. Cut all ingredients for a recipe to the same shape and size. This ensures even cooking and a more attractive dish.

3. Never stir-fry more than 1 pound of meat or seafood at once. If you double a recipe, have a friend stir-fry the second portion in another wok, following the same procedure.

4. Do all stir-frying over highest heat, with the temperature never reduced. This is true even if you have a commercial stove.

5. Place the ingredients next to the wok in the order in which they will be cooked.

6. Whenever an ingredient changes color, proceed to the next step. For example, when the stir-fried meat loses its raw color, remove it from the wok. As soon as the ginger and garlic turn white, add the vegetables. When the stir-fried vegetables brighten, pour in the sauce.

7. Undercook everything. If you find yourself saying, "I'll just cook this a little longer," it has probably already been overcooked.

8. When the sauce comes to a boil, stir in a *little* of the cornstarch mixture. Add only enough thickener so the sauce lightly glazes the food.

9. Serve the finished dish *immediately*.

255

ORIENTAL INGREDIENTS

The recipes in this book use a small number of Oriental herbs, spices, and condiments. Since most Chinese supplies sold in supermarkets are mediocre products, it is worth the effort to acquire the same brands Chinese chefs use. Check your telephone Yellow Pages for local Oriental markets selling these brands or use the mail-order sources listed here.

If you are beginning an adventure with Oriental cooking, start with the following items, which are the basis for nearly all the recipes in this book. They cost only a few dollars and last indefinitely.

Chinese chili sauce
unsweetened
  coconut milk
hoisin sauce
light and dark soy
  sauce

oyster sauce
plum sauce
red sweet ginger
rice sticks
salted black beans
Oriental sesame oil

The following Oriental stores provide mail-order service:

Wing Chong Lung Company
922 South Pan Pedro Street
Los Angeles, California 90015

Oriental Food Market
2801 West Howard Street
Chicago, Illinois 60645

Star Market
3349 North Clark Street
Chicago, Illinois 60657

Dragon Trading Company
943 Dopler Street
Akron, Ohio 44303

Oriental Market
502 Pampas Street
Austin, Texas 78752

Ming's Market
85—91 Essex Street
Boston, Massachusetts 02111

Arugula: Also known by its French name *roquette*, arugula is a small, nutty green used in salads. Sold in three-inch-long bunches, it adds a marvelous flavor to Oriental salads, or to soups, when stirred in just before serving. During the warm summer months, arugula can be grown easily from seeds available at most nurseries; look for packets labeled "Rocket." *Storage*: Store as you would salad greens. *Substitute*: When not available, substitute watercress leaves.

Bean sauce: Bean sauce, sometimes called "brown bean sauce," is a pungent condiment made from yellow beans, flour, salt, and water. It is used as an ingredient for sauces, such as in Barbecued Sea Bass in Beijing Meat Sauce. While this condiment is sold in a puréed form labeled "ground bean sauce," purchase only bean sauce containing parts of the beans, since this guarantees that top-quality beans have been used. The sauce's unusual taste is not immediately appealing to all, and preparations containing it always include a little sugar to counter the slight salty taste. *Storage*: Sold both canned and in glass jars. If canned, transfer to a jar and seal tightly. Will keep indefinitely when refrigerated. *Substitute*: None. *Best brands*: Koon Chun Bean Sauce and Yuet Heung Yuen Bean Sauce.

Bean sprouts: Called "vegetables for the teeth" by the Chinese, these are three-day-old mung bean sprouts. They are highly perishable; if they do not look pearly white, do not buy them. Very fresh bean sprouts add a marvelous crunchy taste to salads or to stir-fried dishes when added at the very end of the cooking process. *Storage*: Will keep for two days if refrigerated in a plastic bag lined with paper towels. *Substitute*: Matchstick-cut hothouse cucumber or jicama.

Bean threads: Also known as "cellophane noodles," "glass noodles," "transparent noodles," and "Chinese vermicelli," these are thin, nearly translucent, dried noodles made from ground mung beans. Wrapped tightly in small bundles, they are first soaked in hot water, then cut into shorter lengths and added to soups or spring roll fillings. Bean threads put directly from the package into hot oil will puff up dramatically in size as do rice sticks. (However, since bean threads acquire a stale taste unless eaten immediately, rice sticks are a better choice when you need masses of light, deep-fried noodles to mix into Oriental salads.) Bean threads are increasingly stocked in the gourmet section of most supermarkets. *Storage*: Keep indefinitely at room temperature. *Substitute*: Rice sticks. *Best brand*: No preference.

Black bean hot sauce: Made from chilies, salted black beans, soy sauce, garlic, and orange rind, this ingredient adds a spicy, complex, rich taste when added to sauces. But use it judiciously, in ½-teaspoon amounts, for it can quickly overwhelm all other flavors. *Storage*: Sold in glass jars. Keeps indefinitely when refrigerated. *Substitute*: You can improvise a "house blend" by combining rinsed and chopped black beans, garlic, grated orange peel, Chinese chili sauce, and peanut oil. *Best brand*: Mai Ling China, Inc.

Black beans, salted: Also called "fermented black beans," these are small, wrinkled, salted black beans that add a fragrant flavor to sauces. They are always rinsed, coarsely chopped, and then combined with ginger and garlic for stir-fried dishes or rubbed across the surface of fish filets. *Storage*: Keep indefinitely at room temperature. *Substitute*: None. *Best brand*: Purchase salted black beans sold in a yellow cardboard canister. These are the kind that chefs in Hong Kong use, and they are far superior to the salted black beans sold in plastic bags. Ask for Yang Jiang Preserved Beans with Ginger, Pearl River Bridge brand.

Bok choy: Known as "Chinese cabbage" or "Chinese chard," bok choy is called "white vegetable" by the Chinese. Its tender, long white stalks and bright green leaves add a subtle flavor to soups and stir-fried dishes. This is one of the Chinese vegetables increasingly stocked by supermarkets across the country. *Storage*: Will keep for one week in the refrigerator. *Substitute*: Chard, tender celery ends, or other quick-cooking vegetables.

Cabbage, napa: Called "white teeth of the dragon" by the Chinese, napa or "celery" cabbage is increasingly stocked by supermarkets. It has firm, tightly packed light green leaves and a slight celery taste. *Storage*: Napa cabbage keeps for nearly two weeks if wrapped in plastic and refrigerated. Discard any wilted outside leaves. *Substitute*: Leafy celery stalks, bok choy leaves, and tender green cabbage.

Chicken stock: While recipes in this book taste best with unsalted homemade stock, when necessary canned stock can be substituted. *Best canned brand*: Swanson Chicken Broth.

Chili sauce, Chinese: Used in Sichuan, Hunan, Singapore, and Thailand, this very spicy condiment is made with chilies, garlic, salt, and oil. Half a teaspoon is sufficient to transform a dish from mild spiciness to fiery intensity. The dozen imported brands are variously labeled "chili paste with garlic," "chili sauce," and simply "chili paste or sauce." They are superior in flavor to the spicy Chinese condiment made from soybeans called "hot bean sauce." *Storage*: Keeps indefinitely in the refrigerator. *Substitute*: None. *Best brands*: Cock Brand Delicious Hot Chili Garlic Sauce and Szechuan Chili Sauce, sold in a 6-ounce black-labeled can.

Chinese pepper mix: The recipes in this book often call for this blend of peppers. To make, place an equal amount of whole black, white, and Sichuan peppercorns in a small ungreased skillet. Turn heat to high and stir until peppercorns smoke lightly. (Roasting the peppercorns heightens their flavor.) Immediately tip out and cool. Transfer to a pepper grinder, ready for use. This is the pepper mix to use on freshly cooked pasta, scrambled eggs, or any dish in which you want a more complex aromatic flavor. Placed in small Lucite pepper grinders, this mix makes a nice gift for cooking friends. *Storage*: Lasts indefinitely. *Substitute*: None.

Cloud ears: Called "cloud ears" or "tree ears" by the Chinese and packaged in this country with the name "black fungus" or "dried vegetable," these are small, black, cornflake-size mushrooms that require soaking in warm water to regain their original size. While having no taste, black fungus is prized by the Chinese for its crunchy texture and medicinal qualities. There is another much larger variety called "wood ears" that you should not purchase, since it has a tough, coarse texture. To use cloud ears, soak in hot water for twenty minutes until soft. Rinse thoroughly and discard soaking water.

Cloud ears can be added to stir-fried dishes, soups, and salads. *Storage*: In dried form, keeps indefinitely at room temperature. *Substitute*: None. *Best brands*: Buy small cloud ears in 1-ounce bags.

Coconut, shredded: Recipes in this book using this ingredient refer to the sweetened shredded coconut sold in every supermarket.

Coconut milk: Excellent canned unsweetened coconut milk is sold by every Oriental market. Purchase a Thai brand whose ingredients are just coconut, water, and a preservative. Occasionally, the coconut milk is so thick it needs to be diluted with a little water. *Storage*: Once opened, it keeps for a week in the refrigerator. *Substitute*: Fresh coconut milk. *Best brands*: Since there is some variation in flavor among brands, purchase different ones, then open, taste, and make a note about the one you prefer. I like the coconut milk produced by A.C. Products, sold in a 5.6-ounce blue can.

Coriander, fresh: Called accurately by the Chinese "fragrant greens," this leafy, small, parsleylike plant has a distinct pungent flavor, and it takes some people several tries before they really appreciate its delicious taste. Fresh coriander is sold in Italian, Spanish, and Mexican groceries, as well as increasingly in supermarkets across the country. It may be called "fresh coriander," "Chinese parsley," or "cilantro," and it is available year round. *Storage*: Fresh coriander is highly perishable. Do not wash until ready to use. Wrap roots in a dampened paper towel before refrigerating in a plastic bag. Will last for about five days. *Substitute*: Fresh coriander has a completely different taste from ground coriander seeds. When unavailable, or for those who do not care for the taste, fresh mint is a good substitute.

Cornstarch: Many of these recipes use a mixture of cornstarch dissolved with cold water to thicken sauces. This ensures that the sauce glazes the ingredients and prevents any watery liquid from collecting on the bottom of the serving platter. If you stir a few drops of peanut oil into the cornstarch mixture, it will help prevent the cornstarch from giving the sauce a starchy taste or causing the sauce to lump. Never add all the cornstarch mixture to thicken a sauce. Just add a very small amount and let the sauce come to a low boil; if the sauce does not thicken enough to lightly coat a spoon, then stir in a little more of the mixture. *Substitutes*: Any other starch such as tapioca, rice, or potato starch.

Curry paste: A blend of many different seasonings mixed with oil, curry paste has numerous advantages over curry powder, including a much more complex taste and a longer shelf life. *Storage*: Once opened, keeps indefinitely at room temperature. *Substitute*: The flavor will not be as complex, but an adequate substitute is to use curry powder and double the amount. *Best brands*: Koon Yick Wah Kee Factory Best Curry, made in Hong Kong, and any good Indian curry paste sold in supermarkets.

Curry powder: Trying to achieve a special taste from curry powder is about the same as using store-bought ground pepper. *Storage*: Keep away from heat and on a dark shelf to retard gradual loss of flavor. *Best brands*: In general, curry powders sold by cookware stores and gourmet shops have a superior flavor to brands sold in supermarkets.

Dry sherry: Chinese chefs in China use a dry rice wine similar in taste to dry sherry. I always use a moderately priced domestic dry sherry. Use whichever you prefer.

Eggplant, Oriental: This slender purple vegetable, about four to eight inches long, tastes far superior to the large globe European eggplant. Its tender skin makes peeling unnecessary; the virtually seedless interior has no bitter taste; and, when sautéed, the eggplant does not absorb large amounts of oil. They are available from spring through fall in all Oriental markets. Choose small, firm eggplants with shiny skins. *Storage*: Last for two weeks when refrigerated. *Substitute*: Improve all European eggplant recipes by substituting Oriental eggplant. In Oriental recipes, substitute small globe eggplant only as a last resort.

Fish sauce: Fish sauce is used in Thai and Vietnamese cooking the way the Chinese use soy sauce. Made by layering fresh anchovies or squid with salt in wooden barrels, it is fermented for several months to produce a watery but very flavorful liquid. Always buy fish sauce produced in Vietnam or Thailand, which is superior to those from other countries. Purchase the light amber-colored sauces rather than the darker products, which will quickly overpower a dish. *Storage*: Once opened, lasts indefinitely at room temperature. *Substitute*: None. *Best brand*: Squid Brand Fish Sauce.

Five-spice powder: A powdered blend of various spices including anise, fennel, cinnamon, Sichuan pepper, and cloves, this is a great favorite of the Cantonese for marinades, poultry, and fish. Five-spice powder is sold in 1-ounce bags in Oriental markets and by some supermarkets in the spice section. *Storage*: Keeps indefinitely at room temperature if tightly sealed in a jar. *Substitute*: None. *Best brand*: The powder sold by Oriental markets is best.

Ginger, crystallized: These are slices of fresh ginger that are candied and coated in sugar. Their sweet, sharp ginger flavor makes them excellent chopped and sprinkled over ice cream or as a candy served with fresh fruit. They are available in most supermarkets and all Oriental stores. *Storage*: Keeps indefinitely at room temperature sealed in a jar. *Substitute*: None.

Ginger, fresh: Absolutely indispensable for Oriental cooking, these pungent and spicy knobby brown rhizomes are sold by supermarkets in the produce section. Buy firm ginger with smooth skin. To use, never peel ginger. Cut off and discard the exposed end. Cut very thin slices, then finely mince by hand or in an electric minichopper. *Storage*: Store ginger in a dark cupboard, where it will stay fresh for up to a month. This is better than placing ginger in the refrigerator, where moisture quickly causes it to spoil, or freezing ginger, which affects the flavor. When the skin begins to wrinkle and the rhizome softens, discard ginger. If fresh ginger is not always available, mail-order a large quantity, then place ginger in a jar, cover with dry sherry, and refrigerate. While fresh ginger lasts indefinitely covered in sherry, it slowly loses its pungent flavor. *Substitute*: There are no substitutes, since dry powdered ginger has a different taste, and preserved and crystallized ginger are too sweet.

Ginger, preserved stem: These are small amber knobs of ginger preserved in heavy syrup. Their mild flavor and delicious accompanying syrup are a great addition to homemade ice creams, cakes, mousses, and salad dressings. *Storage*: Once opened, keeps indefinitely at room temperature provided the syrup covers the ginger nuggets. *Substitute*: Red sweet ginger. *Best brand*: Originally sold only in green pottery containers by Oriental markets, preserved stem ginger is now sold in glass jars in many supermarkets.

Ginger, red sweet: Sold in glass jars at most Chinese markets, these are pieces of bright red ginger in a heavy syrup and are not to be confused with Japanese red pickled ginger. *Storage*: Once opened, will keep indefinitely at room temperature provided the syrup covers the ginger pieces. *Substitute*: Preserved stem ginger. *Best brands*: Mee Chun Preserved Red Ginger Slices in Syrup and Koon Chun Red Ginger in Syrup.

Hoisin sauce: Hoisin sauce — a thick and sweet, spicy, dark brownish red condiment — is customarily spread across pancakes for mu shu pork and Peking duck; it flavors many stir-fried dishes; and it is the base for delicious Chinese barbecue sauces. Made with soy bean flour, chilies, garlic, ginger, and sugar, hoisin sauce is one of the Chinese condiments most loved by Americans. It is sold by Oriental markets both in glass jars and canned. *Storage*: Once opened, keeps indefinitely at room temperature. If canned, open and transfer to a glass container. *Substitute*: None. *Best brand*: No Oriental condiment varies so much in quality from brand to brand. Buy only Koon Chun Hoisin Sauce.

Jicama: Jicama, a brown-skinned Mexican root vegetable, has a sweet white interior with a crunchy texture It makes a great addition to salads. Ranging in size from that of an orange to a cantaloupe, jicama is sold by many supermarkets. Peel with a small knife before using. *Storage*: Jicama will last for two weeks in the refrigerator if you cover the cut surface with plastic wrap. *Substitute*: Fresh water chestnuts are a good substitute for jicama in salads, but jicama is not a good substitute for fresh water chestnuts in cooked dishes, since jicama does not maintain its crunchy texture during cooking.

Monosodium glutamate (MSG): A white crystalline powder sold under various brands such as Accent and Ajimoto, MSG is used by chefs of little skill to rejuvenate food of poor quality. Also sold in large plastic bags in Oriental markets, sadly MSG has become a staple seasoning in many Chinese restaurants and can cause throbbing headaches. Chinese cooks who take pride in their cuisine agree that monosodium glutamate is a crutch. It is neither recommended nor used in this book.

Mushrooms, dried black Chinese: Chinese markets sell a wide variety of dried mushrooms. When softened in hot water, they add a wonderful meaty flavor to soups, stir-fried dishes, and stews. The thicker the cap, the higher quality and more expensive the mushroom. To use, soak mushrooms in a generous amount of hot water. When they soften, cut off and discard the stems. Strain the mushroom-flavored water through a fine-meshed sieve and use it as a substitute for chicken stock. A similar Japanese variety called "dried forest mushrooms" is sold in many supermarkets, but since dried Chinese black mushrooms sold by Chinese markets are far less costly, it is a good idea to get them by mail order. Indicate the number of ounces you wish to buy. *Storage*: Sealed in jars, they last indefinitely unrefrigerated. *Substitute*: For stir-fried dishes, soups, and stews, substitute fresh mushrooms although the flavor will not be as intense. For spring rolls and dumpling fillings, fresh mushrooms are not a good substitute since they do not have the density of the dried variety.

Mushrooms, enoki: These are little clumps of mushrooms on long threadlike stems joined together at the base. Their wonderful sweet smell and delicate appearance make them a great addition to salads or as a garnish. To use, cut off the base and separate the mushroom threads. Do not wash. *Storage*: Sold in small plastic bags at top supermarkets, they will stay fresh for about four days, refrigerated. *Substitute*: None.

Mushrooms, shiitake: Fresh Japanese forest mushrooms, which are never sold at Oriental markets because of their expense, are appearing increasingly in fine general food markets. Shiitake mushrooms possess an incredible fragrance and are delicious sautéed in butter as an accompaniment for grilled meats, part of stir-fried dishes, simmered in cream sauces, and thinly sliced for salads. They are, however, not good chopped and used in dumpling fillings since they do not have the intense flavor and density of dried mushrooms. Shiitake mushrooms are completely clean and should never be washed. Just discard the tough stem before using the cap. *Storage*:

Kept in a paper bag, they will last up to two weeks in the refrigerator. *Substitute*: Dried Chinese mushrooms, although the flavor is not quite the same.

Noodles, Chinese dried spaghetti-style: Thin, dried spaghetti-type noodles are sold in 1- to 5-pound boxes at all Oriental markets. They are inexpensive, cook quickly, and have a nice firm texture. *Storage*: Indefinitely at room temperature. *Substitute*: Any dried thin spaghetti-style noodle.

Oyster sauce: Also called "Oyster flavored sauce," this oyster "ketchup" gives dishes a marvelous rich taste without a hint of its seafood origins. A pinch of sugar is usually added to dishes using oyster sauce to counteract the slightly salty taste. *Storage*: Keeps indefinitely in the refrigerator. *Substitute*: None. *Best brand*: Lee Kum Kee Oyster Flavored Sauce, Old Brand.

Peanut oil: The subtle flavor of peanut oil and its ability to be heated to a high temperature without smoking are the reasons to choose this oil for sautéing, stir-frying, and deep-frying. *Storage*: Lasts for at least a year at room temperature without turning rancid. *Substitutes*: Corn oil, safflower oil, grape seed oil, and soybean oil.

Peking pancakes: Peking pancakes, northern China's version of flour tortillas, are used as a wrapping for stir-fry dishes, barbecued meats, and Oriental salads. Peking pancakes are sold frozen in Chinese markets and can also be purchased freshly made from some Chinese restaurants. *Substitutes*: Flour tortillas. *Best brand*: Homemade Peking pancakes taste the best. *To make*: Stir 14 tablespoons boiling water into 2 cups unbleached white flour. Knead until smooth, then set aside for 15 minutes. Roll out on floured surface until dough is ¼ inch thick. Cut into 3-inch circles. Clean all flour from board. Lightly coat board with Oriental sesame oil. Place two pieces of dough on top of each other, separated by ½ teaspoon Oriental sesame oil. On the oiled board, roll the two pieces of dough into a very thin 6-inch circle. Roll from the center out and do not turn the dough over. Fry in an ungreased skillet over medium-high heat 45 seconds on one side, then 15 seconds on the other side. Pull pancakes apart while hot. Oil board and repeat with remaining dough. Stack pancakes, wrap with plastic wrap, and refrigerate 5 days or freeze indefinitely. Makes 12 to 16 Peking pancakes. *To reheat*: Just before reheating, fold each pancake in quarters. Cook 2 minutes in a Chinese steamer. Use at once.

Plum sauce: This chutneylike condiment is made with plums, apricots, garlic, red chilies, sugar, vinegar, salt, and water. It is different from a condiment found only on the East Coast called "Duck Sauce," which is made with plums, apples, and spices. The thick consistency and sweet, spicy flavor of plum sauce makes it an ideal addition to barbecue sauces and as a dip for crisp, deep-fried won tons or chilled shrimp. It is available in tins and glass jars at all Oriental markets and in many supermarkets. *Storage*: If canned, once opened, transfer to a glass jar and seal. Keeps indefinitely unrefrigerated. *Substitute*: None. *Best brand*: Koon Chun Plum Sauce.

Radicchio: Radicchio is a small, tightly bunched head of red-leafed chicory. Torn or slivered in salads or sautéed, its bittersweet flavor and bright color have made this a favorite of chefs at top restaurants. It is available at many supermarkets in their produce section. *Storage*: Stored in a plastic bag in the refrigerator, it will last for ten days. *Substitute*: While the unusual taste and color of radicchio cannot be duplicated, you can substitute another green such as endive.

Radish, long white: Sold in most supermarkets across the country, these are 6- to 12-inch-long slender white radishes often called "icicle radish" or "daikon." Their mild, sweet flavor adds a wonderful taste to stir-fried dishes; when cut into cubes they can be added to stews, and when in julienne pieces to salads. *Storage*: Wrapped in a plastic bag, this radish will last up to two weeks refrigerated. *Substitute*: You could substitute the much sharper red radish or use another fresh vegetable.

Rice, white long-grain: The Chinese eat white long-grain rice, while the Japanese prefer the stickier short-grain variety. This rice should not be confused with the inferior "converted" or "minute" brands, which are precooked and dried at the factory before packaging. White rice is available at all Oriental markets and all supermarkets, sold in small clear plastic bags. *Storage*: Keeps indefinitely at room temperature. *Substitute*: None.

Rice paper: Rice paper is a very brittle, tissue-thin dried sheet made from rice and water. Oriental markets sell stacks of these, tightly wrapped in plastic, either in circles or cut into smaller wedges. Before use, the rice paper must be softened by dipping each sheet in hot water or in beer or by brushing the surface with beaten egg. About one or two minutes later, the sheet softens and is ready to be wrapped around ground meat or seafood mixtures for deep-frying. *Storage*: Keeps indefinitely at room temperature. *Substitute*: None.

Rice sticks: Rice sticks are long, thin, dried rice-flour vermicelli. Rice sticks put directly from the package into hot oil instantly puff up into a huge white mass many times their original size. They are the essential ingredient in many Chinese salads and are used as a bed upon which to place stir-fried dishes. For cooking instructions, see page 69. Rice sticks are available at all Oriental markets. *Storage*: Keep indefinitely at room temperature. *Substitute*: None. *Best brand*: Sailing Boat Brand Rice Sticks.

Rice vinegar: Clear Japanese rice vinegar with its mild flavor is particularly good for pickling, for salad dressings, and in seafood sauces. Avoid inferior rice vinegars labeled "seasoned" or "gourmet," which indicate that sugar and often monosodium glutamate have been added. Nor should Japanese rice vinegar be confused with Chinese rice vinegar, which has too mild a taste for these recipes. Rice vinegar is available at all Oriental markets and in most supermarkets. *Storage*: Keeps indefinitely at room temperature. *Substitute*: Possibly Champagne vinegar, although this has a sharper taste. *Best brand*: Marukan Rice Vinegar.

Sesame oil, Oriental: Sold in small bottles, sesame oil is a nutty golden brown oil made from toasted crushed sesame seeds. It is used to season food and never as cooking oil, since its low smoking temperature causes it to ignite. This is an ingredient, similar to hoisin sauce, that varies greatly in quality. Unfortunately, most Oriental sesame oil sold by supermarkets has a harsh taste, so look for sesame oil in Oriental markets. *Storage*: At room temperature, will last for at least a year before turning rancid, and will last indefinitely in the refrigerator. *Substitute*: None. *Best brand*: Sona Sesame Oil. Kadoya Sesame Oil is another good brand, but since it has a very pronounced flavor use it in much smaller quantities. Avoid Dynasty Sesame Oil.

Sesame seeds, white: White sesame seeds are sold in the spice section of every supermarket but are far less expensive when purchased at Oriental markets. They are used in many recipes when toasted until a light golden in an ungreased skillet. *Storage*: Since white and toasted sesame seeds turn rancid quickly, keep them in the freezer.

Sichuan peppercorns: Labeled "Szechuan pepper," "wild pepper," "fagara," and "fa tsiu," these are small reddish brown seeds from the prickly ash tree. They have a beautiful aromatic flavor without the spice of black or white peppercorns. They are available at cookware stores, gourmet shops, and at all Oriental markets, sold in 2-ounce plastic bags. To use, place Sichuan peppercorns in an ungreased skillet and toast until the pepper smokes slightly. Transfer to a coffee or spice grinder and pulverize. Tip into a sieve with a medium mesh and shake. The light brown shells remaining in the sieve have no taste and should be discarded. *Storage*: Store ground Sichuan pepper in a small glass spice jar. The aromatic flavor will last for about six months. *Substitute*: None. *Best brand*: No preference.

Snow peas: These flat, light green pods are sold year round by many supermarkets. If snow peas are soft when purchased, soaking them in cold water for thirty minutes will restore their texture. To use, snap off and draw the stem end down the ridge to remove the string. Whether stir-fried, blanched for salads, or added to soups, snow peas are cooked only until they turn bright green. *Storage*: Keep for at least a week in a plastic bag in the refrigerator. *Substitute*: Sugar snap peas or another quick-cooking vegetable.

Soy sauce, dark: Sold in bottles of varying sizes, dark soy sauce, also called "heavy" or "black" soy, is light soy sauce with the addition of molasses or caramel. Chefs use it to add a richer flavor and color to sauces. Never confuse this with "thick" soy sauce sold in jars, which is a syrup-like molasses that will ruin the taste of any recipe in this book. One way to tell the difference between dark and light soy sauce is to shake the bottle. Dark soy sauce will coat the sides of the bottle whereas the more watery light soy sauce will not. *Storage*: Once opened, keeps indefinitely at room temperature. *Substitute*: None. *Best brands*: Mushroom Soy Sauce.

Soy sauce, light: Light or "thin" soy sauce is the most common soy sauce used in Chinese cooking. Made from soy beans, roasted wheat, yeast, and salt, good light soy sauce is available at all Oriental markets and in most supermarkets. It is used as a table condiment, in stir-fried dishes, and for soups where a light color and delicate taste are desired. If you are concerned about sodium, it is better to reduce the quantity of soy sauce in a recipe, rather than the more expensive low-sodium brands which have little taste. *Storage*: Once opened, keeps indefinitely at room temperature. *Substitute*: None. *Best brands*: Superior Soy Sauce, Pearl River Bridge Brand, and Kikkoman Soy Sauce. When buying Superior Soy Sauce, look carefully at the label, for the manufacturer bottles another soy called "Soy Superior," which is dark soy sauce.

Star anise: Eight-pointed brown "stars" of anise add a distinct taste to any dish. They should be used judiciously, or all other flavors will be overpowered. They are available at all Oriental markets, sold in small plastic bags. *Storage*: Always store star anise in a tightly sealed glass jar, or its flavor will creep into every packaged item in the pantry. *Substitute*: Fennel seed, although the flavor is not quite as intense.

Water chestnuts: Water chestnuts, the size of an English walnut, are botanically no relation to chestnuts. They are a black-skinned water bulb grown in southern and eastern China. Called "horses' hooves" by the Chinese, water chestnuts are often covered with a thin layer of mud to prevent them from drying out. Their very sweet taste and crunchy texture are as different from those of their canned cousins as fresh asparagus is from canned. On the West Coast, fresh water chestnuts come from Hong Kong, while along the East Coast they are grown in Florida. Fresh water chestnuts are available only in a few large Chinatown communities but are sold throughout the year. When buying fresh water chestnuts, squeeze each one and discard any that are soft; these are rotten in the center. Under cold running water, peel off the skin using a small knife. They can now be used raw in salads or added to soups or stir-fried dishes, minced for dumpling fillings, and dipped in chocolate. Their wonderful taste and texture remain unchanged despite lengthy cooking. *Storage*: Unpeeled water chestnuts last for two weeks wrapped in plastic and refrigerated. *Substitutes*: If you are not fond of canned vegetables, do not use canned water chestnuts! In dumpling fillings, substitute minced carrot. For stir-fried dishes, substitute another fresh vegetable. In Oriental salads, substitute jicama.

Won ton skins: Won ton skins, measuring about three inches square, are thin egg-noodle wrappers. They are sold by every Oriental market and in many supermarkets. Purchase the thinnest ones, preferably fresh and not frozen. The latter, which dry and become brittle in the freezer, tend to tear when folded for dumplings. *Storage*: Keeps for two weeks in the refrigerator if tightly sealed. *Substitute*: None.

INDEX

Page numbers in **boldface** contain illustrations.

Designed by Rita Marshall
Composed in ITC Symbol Book and Futura Extra Bold
by Trufont Typographers, Inc., Hicksville, N.Y.
Printed and bound by Arti Grafiche Motta S.p.A,
Arese (Milan), Italy